I0824811

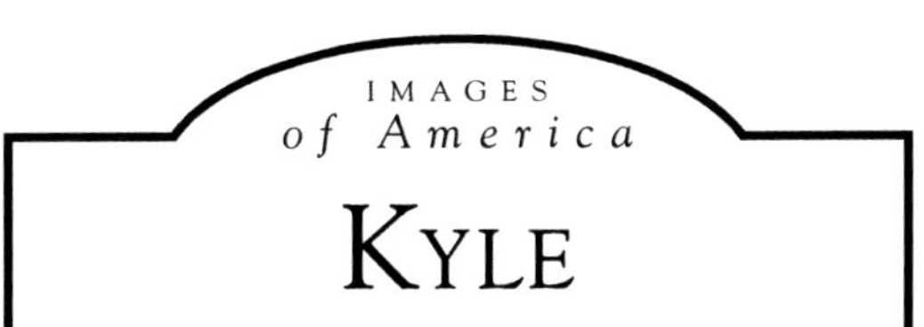
IMAGES
of America
KYLE

On the Cover: This sign in Kyle, posted in 1940, reflects the opposing perceptions of the town over the years. Whether Kyle is "city" or "country" often depends on the observer's perspective. (Courtesy of the Neal Douglass Collection, Austin History Center, Austin Public Library.)

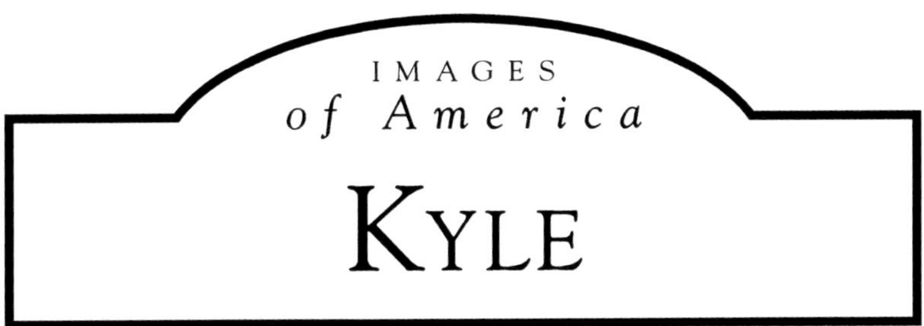

Betty Harrison and the
Hays County Historical Commission

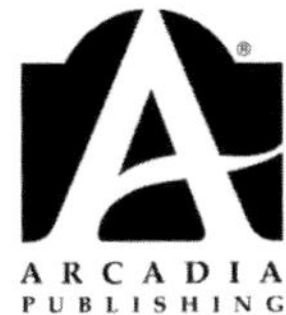

ISBN 978-1-4671-3491-0

Published by Arcadia Publishing
Charleston, South Carolina

Printed in the United States of America

Library of Congress Control Number: 2015945757

For all general information, please contact Arcadia Publishing:
Telephone 843-853-2070
Fax 843-853-0044
E-mail sales@arcadiapublishing.com
For customer service and orders:
Toll-Free 1-888-313-2665

Visit us on the Internet at www.arcadiapublishing.com

To Bob Barton and Moe and Gene Johnson, all of whom experienced and helped preserve important events in the history of Kyle.

Contents

ACKNOWLEDGMENTS

Without the encouragement and support of friends from the Kyle community, this book would not have been possible. Special thanks go to Linda Schmeltekopf and Jane Word Kirkham for sharing their family's pictures and asking others to do the same. Members of the Immanuel Baptist Church (IBC) shared photographs from their church history. Friends at the *Hays Free Press* (HFP), especially David White and Cyndi Slovak-Barton, provided valuable assistance locating and scanning photographs from their files. Hays County Historical Commission members Jim Cullen and Robert Frizzell shared items from their memorabilia collections to be included in the book. Photographs from the Hays County Courthouse Museum (HCCM), most of which were provided by Cindy McCoy from her work on the *Clear Springs and Limestone Ledges* book, were important additions to this book. Betty Harrison, member of the Hays County Historical Commission since 2007 and retired Hays CISD teacher and administrator, collected the photographs and wrote the text of the book. Her doctoral dissertation (University of Texas at Austin, 2005), a history of the Kyle schools, provided background information for the book.

Without the diligent work of earlier historians—Ann Miller Strom (*Kyle: The Prairie City*) and Frances Stovall, Dorothy Wimberley Kerbow, Maxine Storm, Louise Simon, Dorothy Woods Schwartz, and Gene Johnson (*Clear Springs and Limestone Ledges*)—details of events and places in Kyle would not have been preserved and accessible to be included in this book. Knowing that their work was done before the days of computers and digital photography makes their achievements even more impressive. Special editions of both the *Kyle News* and the *Hays Free Press* have also captured faces, places, and events that would have been lost to time.

Thanks to editors Lily Watkins and Jeff Ruetsche for their patience and encouragement throughout the production of the book.

INTRODUCTION

The town of Kyle traces its origins to July 24, 1880, when two families deeded 200 acres of land to the International–Great Northern Railroad as the site for a town on their new rail line between Austin and San Antonio. Residents for the newly created town came primarily from two existing nearby settlements—Mountain City, three miles to the west, and the Blanco community, four miles southwest on the Blanco River.

The land where present-day Kyle is located was originally public land of the Republic of Texas, granted to Zachariah Hinton in 1844. This 2,390-acre tract extended from the Blanco River to Plum Creek. After Hays County was formed in 1848, county tax assessor and collector Eli T. Merriman sold 2,380 acres of the Hinton tract for $7.50 at auction for taxes due to Claiborne Kyle, a Tennessean who had migrated to Texas. However, Hinton paid the taxes and redeemed the land. He later sold parcels of the land to William Vaughn in 1854 and to David E. Moore in 1858. In 1871, Moore sold two pieces of the land to his daughter Annie Kyle, wife of Capt. Fergus Kyle, Claiborne Kyle's son. This tract, south of Plum Creek, was part of the land deeded to the railroad in 1880 to create the town of Kyle.

In the late 1870s, the International–Great Northern Railroad planned a rail line between Austin and San Antonio. When the railroad officials discovered that the rail line missed existing communities, they proposed creating a new town. The railroad selected the Moore-Kyle land from several proposed by landowners in northeast Hays and southwest Travis Counties. Mary Kyle Hartson, daughter of Fergus Kyle, recalled her father's meeting with railroad magnate Jay Gould in his private railcar, which resulted in Gould choosing her family's site for the town. The Moore and Kyle families received "$1 and the enhanced value to be given and which is contemplated to arise to our lands and which property by the location and speedy construction of the International–Great Northern Railroad and for further consideration of the depot thereon." On September 1, 1880, the International–Great Northern Railroad deeded the land to the Texas Land Company, a corporation owned by railroad stockholders, for $2,000 but retained land for the depot and right-of-way. The Texas Land Company employed Martin Groos to survey the town, and on September 7, 1880, Groos filed a town map with the county clerk that identified the town as Kyle, named for Capt. Fergus Kyle.

The railroad began laying tracks and scheduled an auction under a live oak tree that still stands on Sledge Street to sell lots in the new town of Kyle. Earlier histories name October 14 as the day of the auction, but more recent research indicates that it possibly was held on September 25. The railroad invited the entire community to the auction and offered free rides to encourage people to attend. All of the business lots and most of the residential lots were sold that day. In 1875, Col. R.J. Sledge purchased land east of what is now Kyle for a plantation like those he knew in the Brazos Valley of Texas. The next year, he moved his family from Chappell Hill in Washington County, Texas, to the Pecan Springs plantation, where he built a house, a gin, and assorted outbuildings near Plum Creek. Sledge owned 5,000 acres, with plans to produce cotton and food crops in the valley, use the prairie for hay and grazing, and raise sheep on the hillsides. He raised mules and horses for power to cultivate the fields and had a fondness for race horses. Like a typical Southern plantation owner, Sledge always rode a beautiful horse.

By 1880, the year that the town of Kyle was created, Sledge realized that he had more land than he could develop and that the available laborers could not help fulfill his expectations for the plantation. He proposed to colonize the Pecan Springs area with German immigrants, as had been done in Washington County and in nearby New Braunfels. Beginning in 1881, Sledge sold small plots of land in Plum Creek valley to several families from New Braunfels.

Sledge and his wife, Nancy Jackson, both had ties not only to Washington County, but also to the Baptist Church and to Baylor University, then located at Independence. Sledge combined his religious interest with his economic goals and colonized his Pecan Springs land with German Baptist immigrants. Sledge partnered with German-born Frank Kiefer, who had converted from Catholicism when enrolled in Baylor in 1850. Kiefer was charged with recruiting 20 German families to immigrate to Kyle and develop small farms on the Pecan Springs plantation, with a special request for sheep herders. In 1882, Kiefer found two men—shepherd Carl Wiegand and friend Christian Siebenhausen—who were both born Lutheran but had converted to German Baptist, that were interested in Sledge's offer. The two families—two men, two women, and nine children—traveled from Germany to Amsterdam by rail and then sailed to New York. They arrived by train in Kyle on March 15, 1883, eager to claim their chance to become landowners in a democratic country rather than peasants in a monarchy. Since they spoke only German, connecting with Sledge, who did not know exactly when they were to arrive, was difficult. However, he eventually sent his son to pick them up from the depot where they had spent the night.

By 1885, two more families, who were relatives of the first two men, joined the German immigrants in Kyle. Sledge also recruited German Baptist families from Alabama after a chance meeting with Andrew Heidenreich resulted in two more German families moving to Pecan Springs instead of to Kansas as they had planned. More families from Germany as well as several from other German Baptist communities in Texas joined them over the next few years. In 1886, the Kyle German Baptist Church was organized with 16 charter members. Children of the German families attended the Hemphill School until it consolidated with Kyle in the 1940s.

Prior to 1911, children in Kyle attended school in a variety of locations, including Summit and Blanco Chapel (later consolidated as Independence Hall); the Kyle Seminary, affiliated with the Baptist church; and Willie Andrews's Science Hall school, which was briefly housed in Kyle. The Independence Hall school was located northwest of Kyle on FM 150 West. During a scandal involving the Kyle Seminary, the Kyle Public School Board purchased the property at which the present Kyle Elementary School is located and moved Independence Hall into town. A subscription school was held on that site during the final year of the seminary's operation (1889–1890). In 1890, trustees of the Kyle Graded Free School Community No. 2 were authorized to sell the old Independence Hall property and apply the proceeds to the improvement of school property in Kyle. Dropping the name Independence Hall, the Kyle Public Free School began functioning in September 1890. The building was constructed in 1890 on the current Kyle school property and used until 1910, when it was demolished, and a larger and more modern school structure was built. On April 1, 1913, a special act of the 33rd legislature made Kyle an independent school district. Children of all ages attended school in the new two-story building constructed in 1911 and learned traditional subjects as well as lessons that went far beyond their textbooks. One such lesson occurred in October 1911. Cal Rogers made a transcontinental airplane flight from Brooklyn, New York, to Pasadena, California, with the route of his 49-day flight taking him across central Texas. Rogers was advertising a soft drink (called Vin Fiz) and followed a route that paralleled railroad lines, where a train decorated with banners accompanied him on his journey. Kyle's school superintendent Sam Eaton informed students that he would watch for the plane on October 19, 1911, and when he sighted it, he would sound a gong to signal students to march in an orderly fashion outside to see the plane fly over—a sight none had viewed before. Hours passed without a sign of the plane, but the excitement of the students prevented much learning from occurring. Finally, someone spotted the plane, and everyone realized at once that the plane was not flying over Kyle but was descending. The planned organized march out of the building turned into a riot, as children slid down stairs, jumped out of windows, and ran through doors to see the aviator and his plane. Mechanical failure had caused the plane to land, but Rogers was unharmed. Rogers and his plane remained in Kyle until Sunday morning, marking the first time an airplane touched Hays County soil. Unfortunately, not long after he reached California in his Curtiss-Burgess biplane, Cal Rogers died when his plane crashed. The young people in Kyle, however, had glimpsed the future that Friday afternoon in 1911.

The World War I years were difficult for all Americans but particularly for those of German descent. The Kyle German Baptist Church, which in 1917 had dual affiliations with the North American German Baptist Conference and the Southern Baptist Convention, held services in German until the Texas Legislature passed the Texas Disloyalty Act in 1918 in response to increasing anti-German sentiment in the state, forbidding the use of German. In response, Rev. Robert Vasel had the sermon translated into broken English and read it to the congregation, few of whom understood much of what was said. Ironically, eight young men from the congregation served in the war, and one did not return.

Constructed in 1911, the two-story school building served primarily white students in Kyle until 1938. Until 1960, Kyle schools were segregated by race and ethnicity. Separate schools for black and Mexican children were common in Texas until the middle of the 20th century, and Kyle schools were no exception. The years between 1931 and 1945 were times of dramatic change—economically, socially, and politically—in the United States. Even small rural communities like Kyle felt the impact of those changes. By 1931, public notices stating that businesses would no long accept credit were common in the *Kyle News*. The depth of the economic depression was symbolized by the closing of the Kyle State Bank later that year. The dry goods store was liquidated by creditors but reopened under new ownership. After financial reorganization (and the pledging of $25,000 in stock), the bank reopened as Citizens State Bank in March 1932, but better days for Kyle were still far in the future.

In 1933, local citizens held a meeting to discuss how Kyle could pursue government rehabilitation programs to put unemployed laborers to work. The possibility of constructing a new school building emerged from this meeting, and an application was submitted to federal government authorities. Over the next few years, as cotton was plowed under and cattle purchased by the government in efforts to improve agriculture prices, several relief programs came to Kyle, and a relief office opened in city hall. A sewing room employed 10 women, and a tannery employed 30 men. Federal relief funds supported an adult Mexican school, as well as a Works Progress Administration (WPA) adult school for African Americans. By far, the most significant impact of the relief efforts on the schools was the construction of new school buildings using WPA funds. At a cost to the district of $5,000, the trustees proposed to undertake the $21,000 project to build a gymnasium-auditorium and home economics cottage, as well as to make general improvements to the school grounds and athletic fields. The project began in January 1936 and employed 29 men. Later that year, trustees asked the voters of the Kyle school district for additional bond funds to complete the project. In 1938, the Kyle school district once again used WPA funds, along with bonds, to replace the classroom building. The building constructed at that time, now the Kyle Elementary School, still serves students in Kyle.

During the 1930s, some vocal Kyle residents opposed America's involvement in the world crises that ultimately resulted in war. When war actually came, however, Kyle residents (including students) responded with support for the effort. The Depression and World War II changed the culture of Kyle in many ways. WPA-sponsored adult education programs for both Mexican American and African American residents expanded educational opportunities beyond the traditional school years. Service in the military sent young men and a few young women out of Hays County to places they had never seen.

Social changes in postwar Kyle attributed to expanded life experiences, including discussions and actions that resulted in full integration of the schools and ultimate consolidation of the district with two surrounding districts. A highlight of the 1950s was the success of the high school basketball team, led by coach William M. "Moe" Johnson. Hired in 1954, Johnson saw the Kyle Panthers football program move from six-man to eight-man (1958–1959) to 11-man (1960). While his football teams were successful, his basketball teams posted phenomenal records. His team was the district champion every year and won regional every year from 1956 to 1960, advancing to the state tournament each year. Although his team never won a state championship, they were semifinalists three times and finalists in 1959. Overall, Johnson's basketball teams won 172 games and lost 34, for a winning percentage of 83.5 percent. During his tenure as coach, his teams lost only one home game and no district games at home in the rock gym built with WPA funds two decades earlier. Having established himself as a successful coach, Johnson was the school board's choice to replace the retiring superintendent of the Kyle schools in 1960.

Increased student enrollment, expansion of school facilities, and integration of both Mexican American and African American students characterize the changing nature of the era. During this time, federal government funding brought special programs and additional teachers to assist with a growing and increasingly diverse student population. Voters made the decision for Kyle schools to consolidate with Buda and Wimberley in 1967, the culmination of several years of work by local citizens favoring the benefits a larger school district could offer its students. Moe Johnson was the logical choice as the new superintendent, since he had grown up in Buda and both taught and coached in Kyle. He was tasked with bringing two former rivals together. While consolidation represented improved opportunities for all students and increased efficiency, it also marked the end of the unity that an exclusively Kyle school promoted.

One

Founding and Early Years

Following the auction under the oak tree in the fall of 1880, the new town created by the International–Great Northern Railroad grew quickly. In November 1880, just two months after the filing of the town map, Tom Martin opened Kyle's first business—a combination saloon and meat market—in a frame building at the southwest corner of the public square. Martin was also a Deputy US Marshal. Soon after, three other saloons opened in competition. In its first year of existence, Kyle added a livery stable (operated by W.C. Weatherford), a dry goods store (owned by Otto Groos from New Braunfels), a grocery store (owned by D.A. Young), a general merchandise store (run by W.E. Roach, who also served as postmaster), a hotel called Hays House (owned by the Houstons), a gin (owned by Ezekiel Nance) and a lumberyard (run by H.C. Wallace). Within two years, the population of Kyle was estimated at 500. After 1883, however, development was slower than before. Nicholas Schlemmer of New Braunfels, who had declined the opportunity to be the first postmaster in Kyle in 1880, returned in 1884 and opened a general mercantile store, eventually constructing a stone building in 1890. Kyle remained unincorporated until 1895, when voters approved incorporation as a village, only to vote to reverse the decision in 1897. In 1906, another vote for incorporation passed.

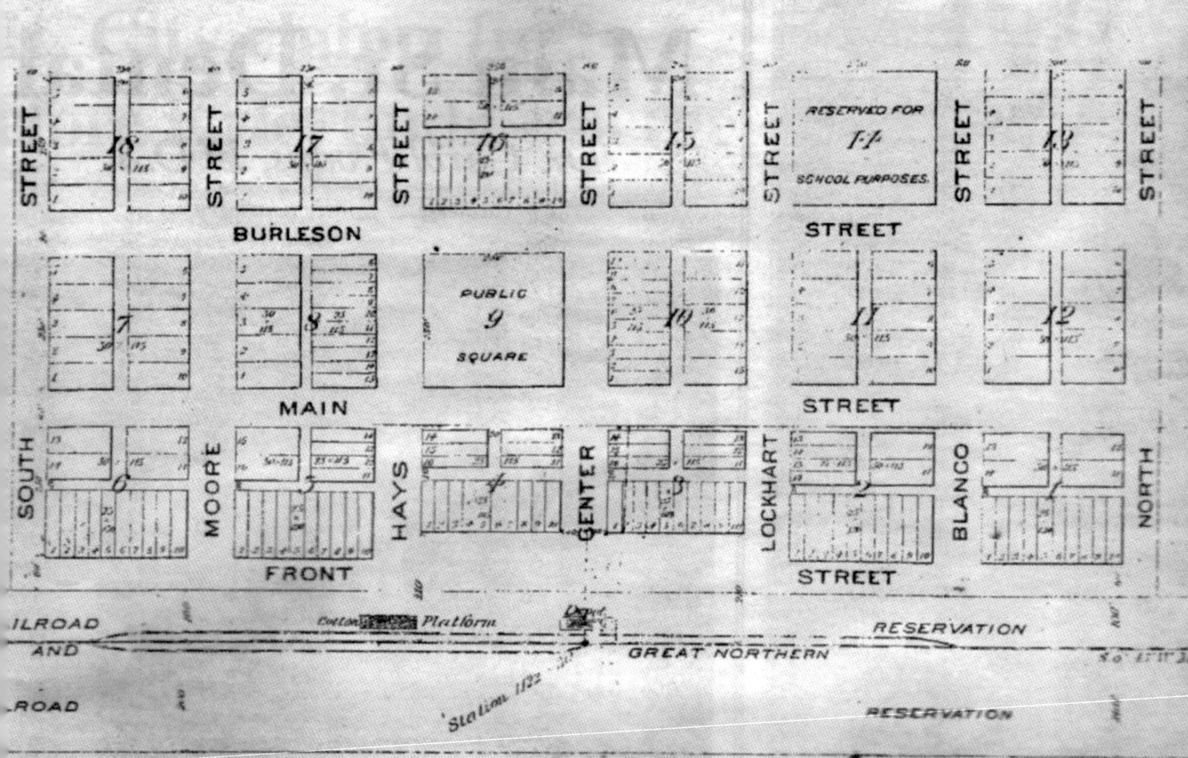

Surveyor Martin Groos filed this town map in the office of the county clerk of Hays County on September 7, 1880, identifying lots in 18 blocks along the railroad right-of-way. The Texas Land Company deeded the land the town needed for streets and alleys. By the time the map was filed, the town was named Kyle in honor of Capt. Fergus Kyle. (Courtesy HFP.)

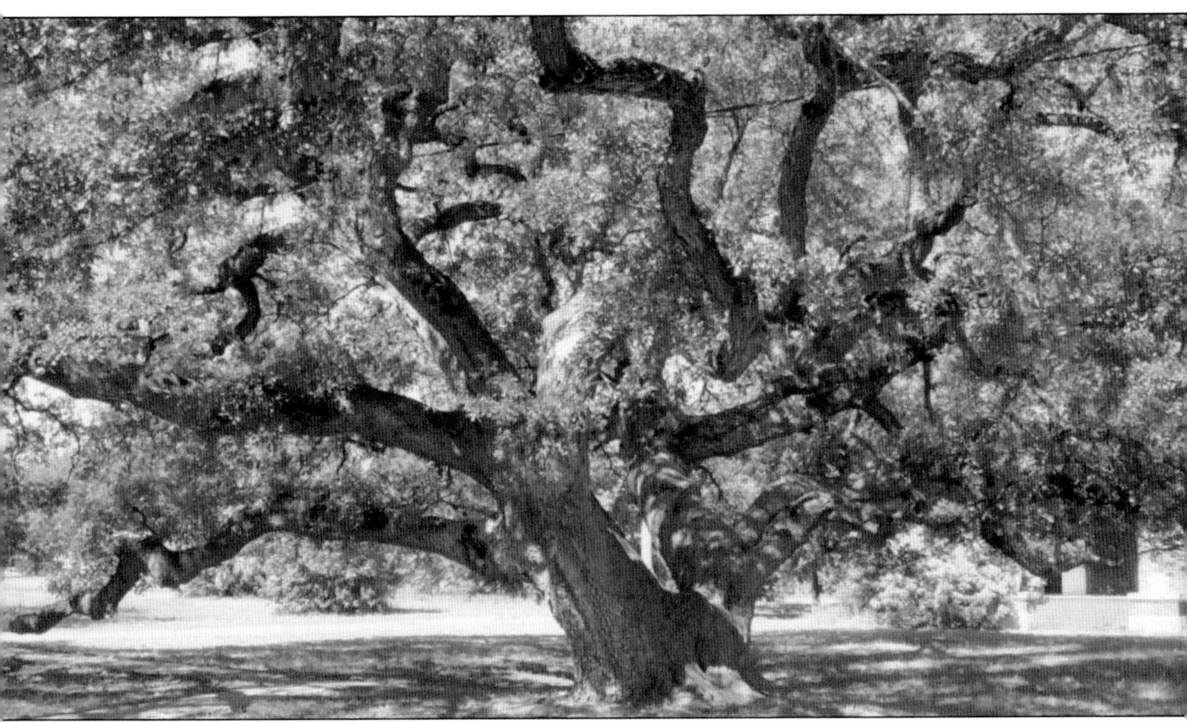

Under the branches of this live oak tree, residential and business lots for the new town of Kyle were sold at auction in the fall of 1880. The lots were sold by the Texas Land Company, a subsidiary of the International–Great Northern Railroad, to create a town on the new rail line between Austin and San Antonio. This tree still stands in Kyle in front of a private residence on Sledge Street. (Courtesy of Jill Lear.)

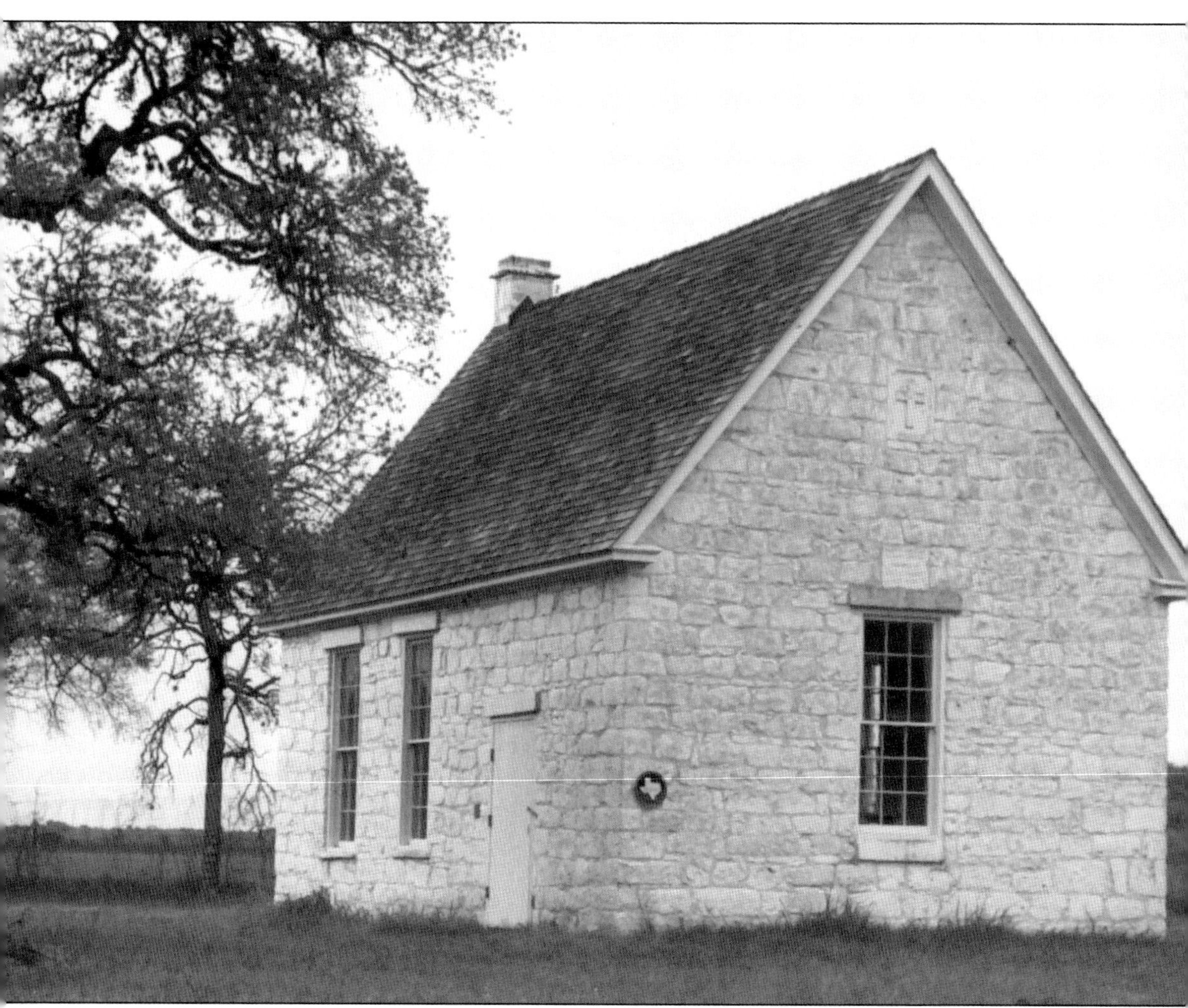

Built of limestone and cypress hand-split by Ezekiel Nance on his property near the Blanco River in 1865, the Blanco Chapel served as a school and church until 1881. The building was later used by the Mexican Presbyterian Church, and in 1885, the pews were given to the Kyle Seminary. Today, the chapel is on private property (McCoy Ranch) and is not open to the public. The Blanco Chapel was among the first buildings in Hays County to receive a recorded Texas Historical Landmark designation. (Courtesy HCCM.)

David A. Young, a Tennessee native and Civil War veteran, moved his mercantile business from Mountain City to Kyle when the lots were sold for the town. Young died of abdominal pain not long after the building was completed, leaving his widow with seven young children. (Courtesy of the Word family.)

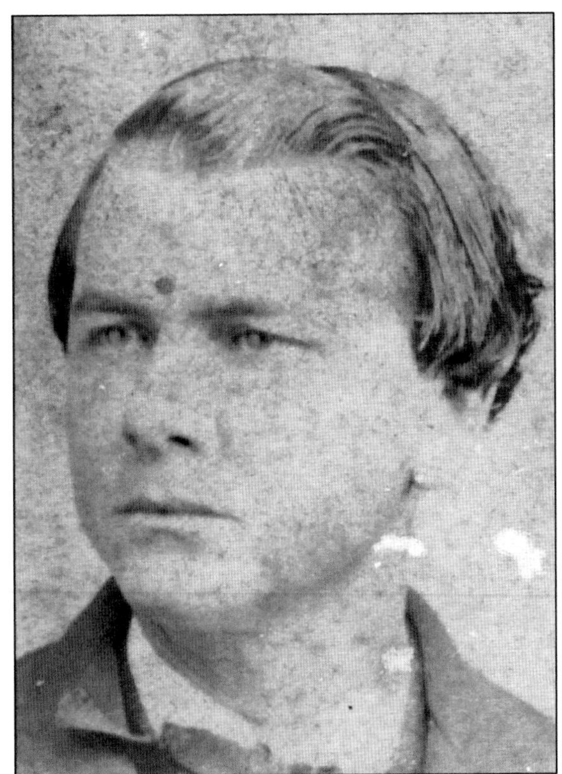

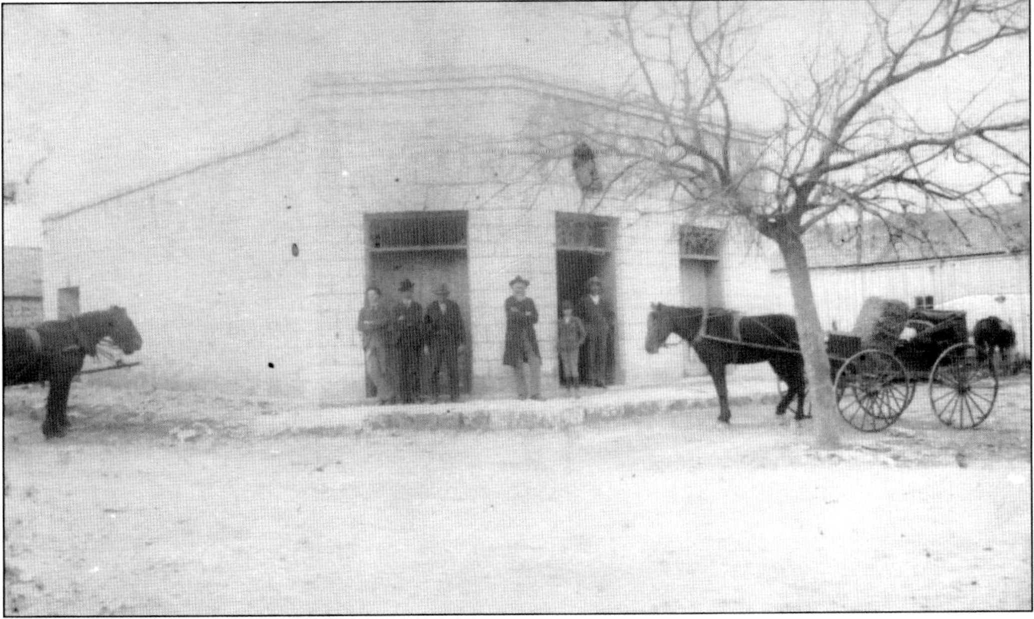

This rock building was the first permanent structure in Kyle. It was constructed by owner David A. Young to house his mercantile store in 1881. The building, on the northwest corner of the town square, later served as a firehouse for the Kyle Volunteer Fire Department. The building was later acquired by Kyle rancher M.G. Michaelis Sr., who gave it to the town on May 13, 1936, in appreciation of the firemen's efforts to fight a fire on his ranch. (Courtesy of the Word family.)

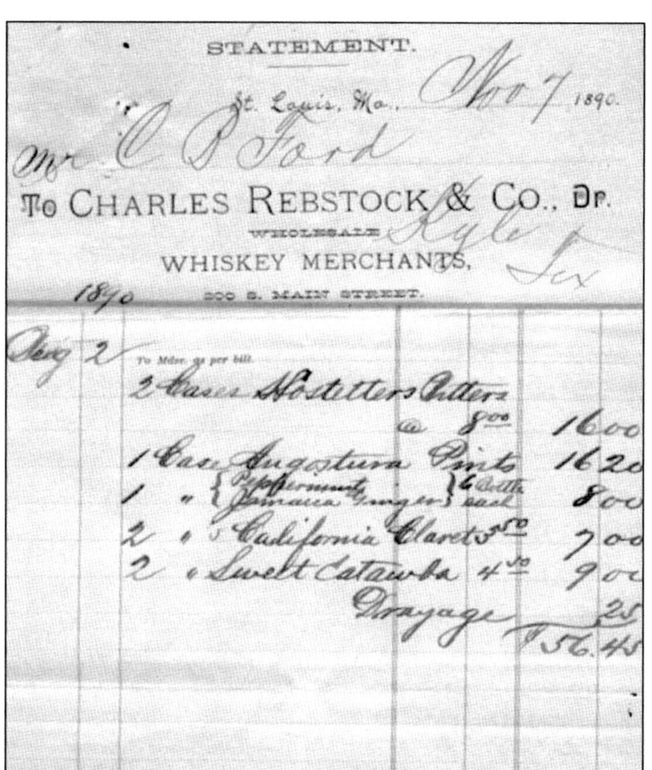
STATEMENT.

St. Louis, Mo., Nov 7 1890.

Mr C P Ford Kyle Tex

To CHARLES REBSTOCK & CO., Dr.

WHOLESALE

WHISKEY MERCHANTS,

200 S. MAIN STREET.

1890		
Aug 2	To Mdse. as per bill.	
	2 Cases Hostetters Bitters @ 8.00	16.00
	1 Case Augostura Pints	16.20
	1 " {Peppermint / Jamaica Ginger} 6 bottle each	8.00
	2 " California Claret 3.50	7.00
	2 " Sweet Catawba 4.50	9.00
	Drayage	25
		$56.45

This invoice is from one of the saloons in Kyle, operated by C.B. Ford. Reports describe Kyle as a "wild and wooly" town, with saloons, horse racing, and gambling. Stories of men cutting each other with knives and shooting each other with six-shooters and Winchesters were common. The wild atmosphere did not last long, however, since saloons were voted out in 1898. (Courtesy of Jim Cullen.)

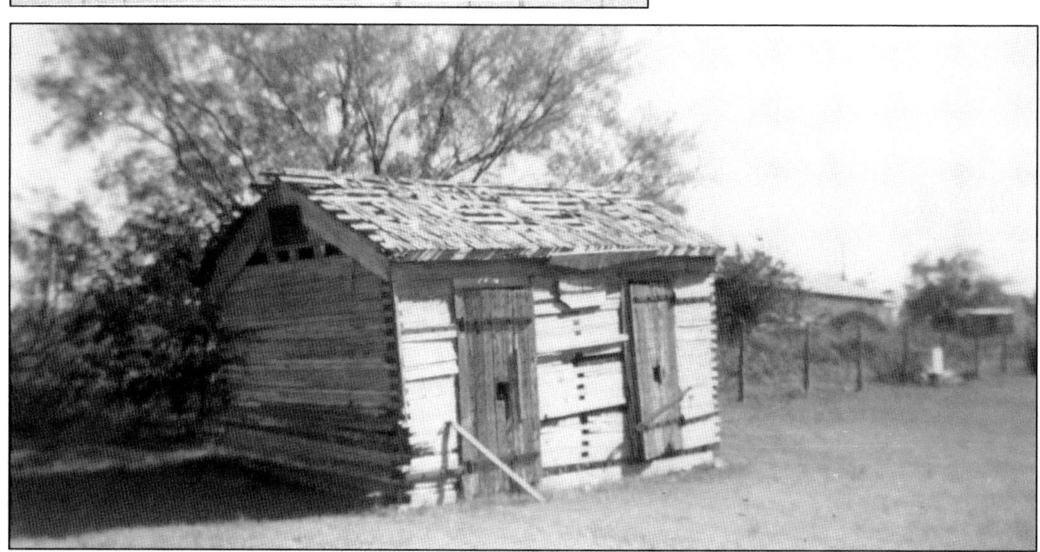

In 1884, possibly in response to the "wild" atmosphere in Kyle, the Hays County Commissioner's Court appropriated $100 and gave Kyle one of the old cells from the county jail, which was moved to Kyle and located at the intersection of Center and Front Streets, near the present CVS store. Once Kyle became a quieter place, the unused jail was sold and moved in the 1960s to the Texana Village at San Marcos tourist attraction Aquarena Springs. In 1950, however, the citizens who opposed selling alcohol in Kyle used the jail as part of their campaign in a local election by attaching a sign to the jail that read "Kyle Jail in 1896, Not Used Since Kyle Voted Dry!" (Courtesy HFP.)

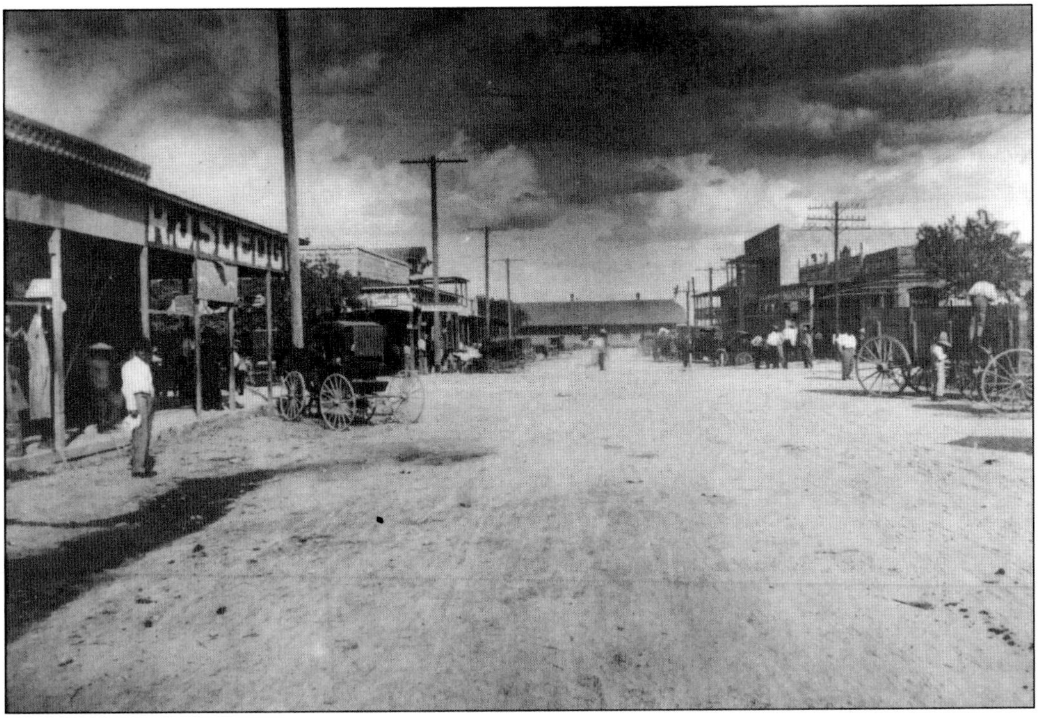

Kyle grew quickly during its first few years of existence. This view of Center Street shows the many businesses that were built by 1900, as well as the depot at the end of the street (Courtesy HFP.)

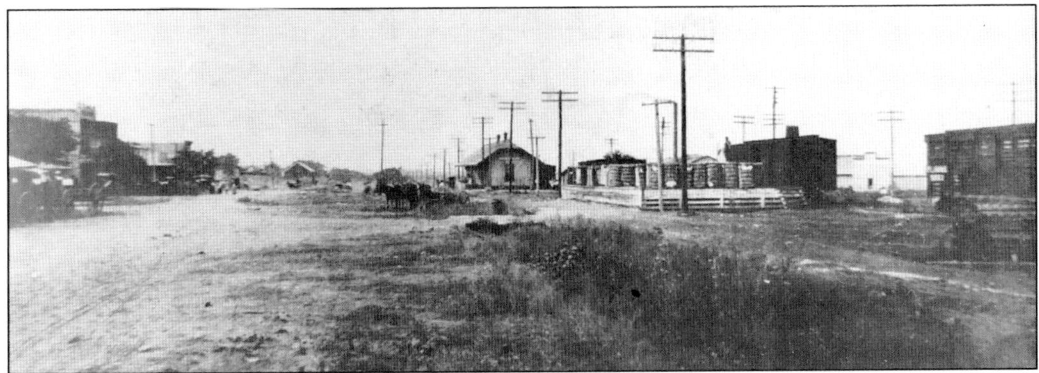

The depot was built by the International–Great Northern Railroad not long after the railroad created the town of Kyle, replacing the tent where it first conducted business. The wooden depot was destroyed by fire in 1916. (Courtesy HFP.)

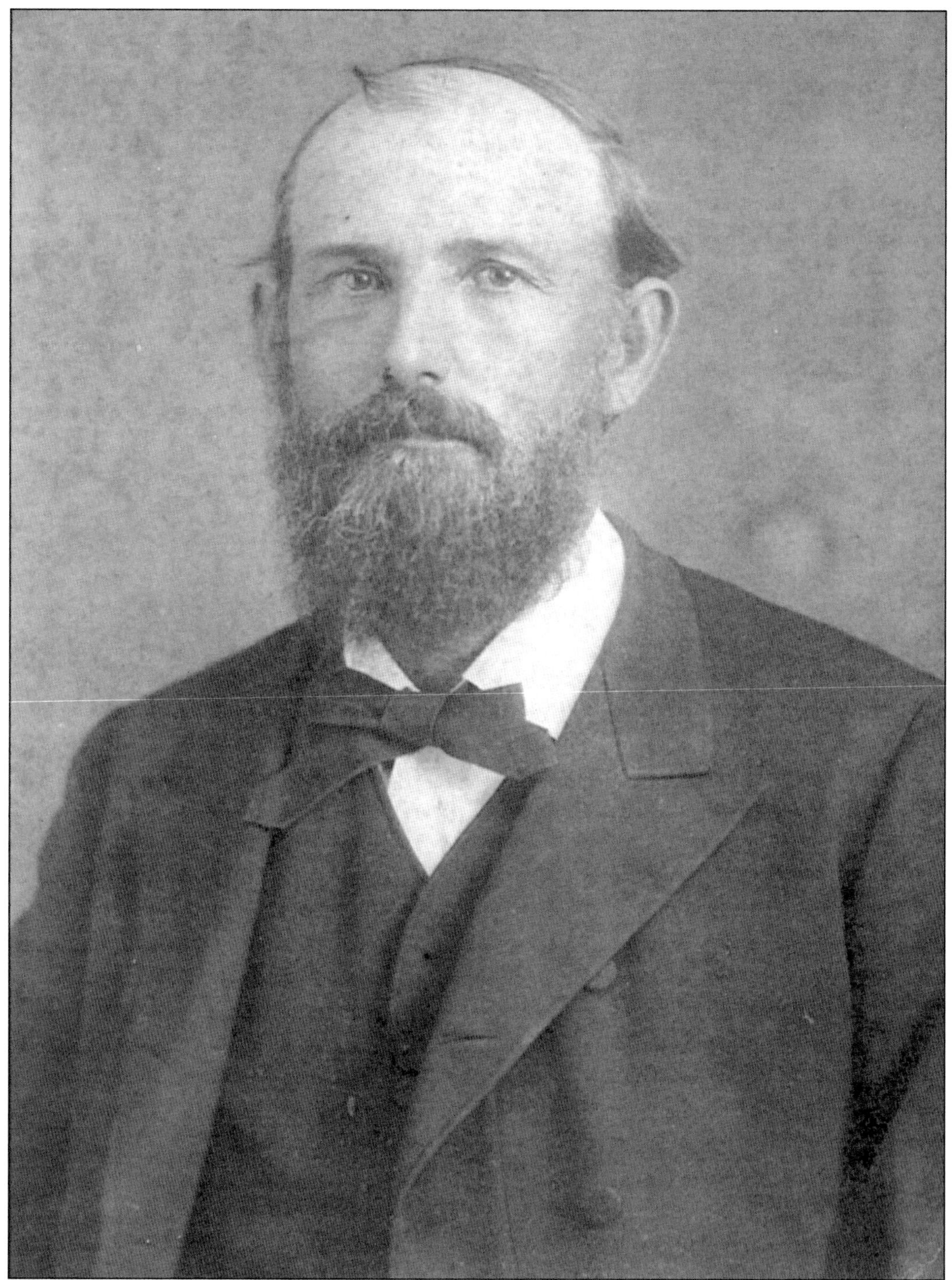

Col. Robert John Sledge was the most prominent landowner east of the site selected for Kyle. He built the Pecan Springs plantation and later brought German immigrants to colonize the area. He donated property in town for a church for African American residents, and the church still bears his name today (Sledge Chapel). Sledge died in 1900. (Courtesy of the Word family.)

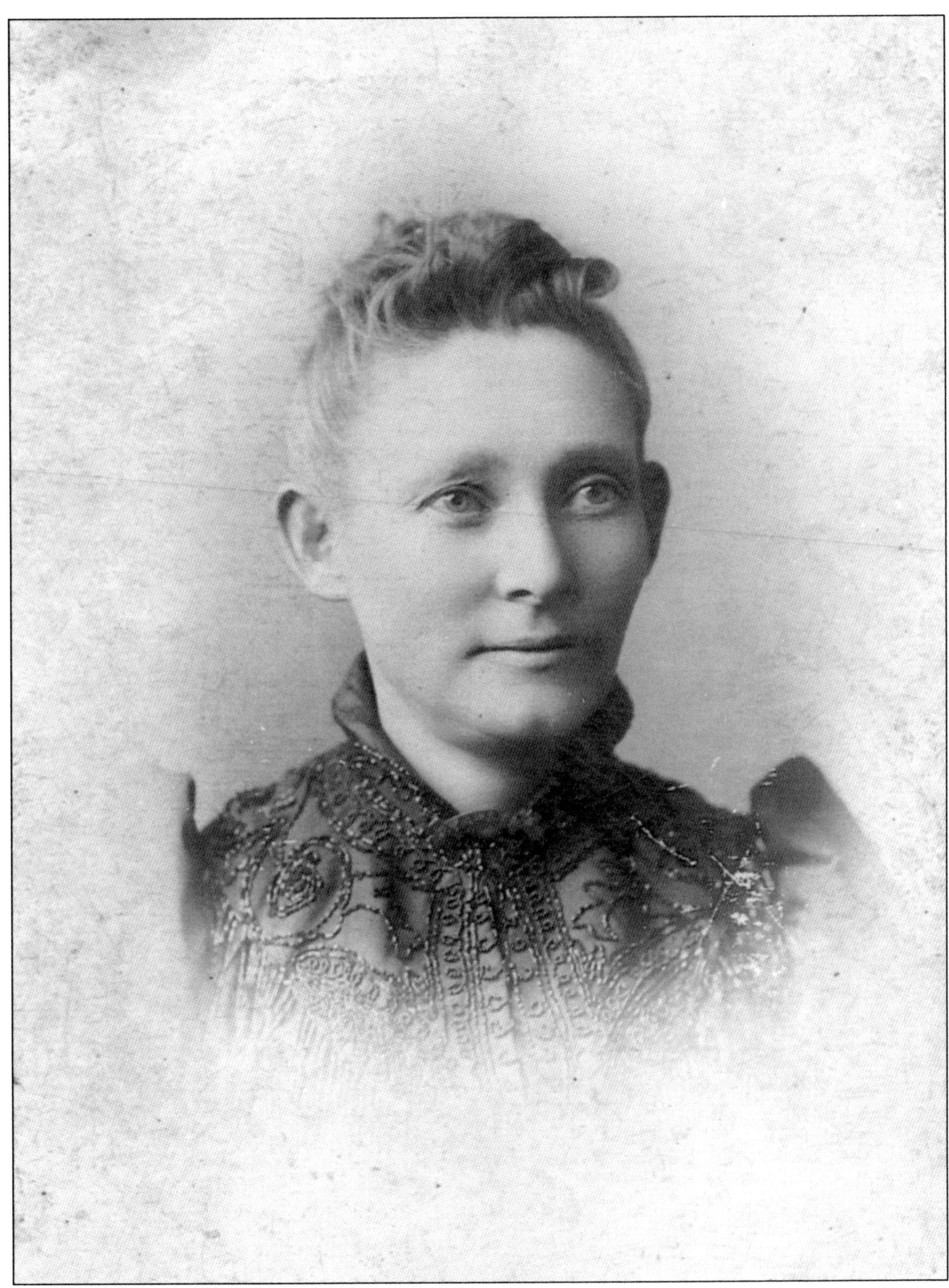

Nancy Jackson married Col. Robert Sledge in 1867. The daughter of a wealthy planter in Washington County, she moved with Sledge to the Pecan Springs plantation in 1876. About the time Kyle was founded, Sledge realized that his land was too much to manage with the workers available, which prompted him to solicit German Baptist families to colonize the area. The Germans first worked as laborers, then as renters, and ultimately became landowners. (Courtesy of the Word family.)

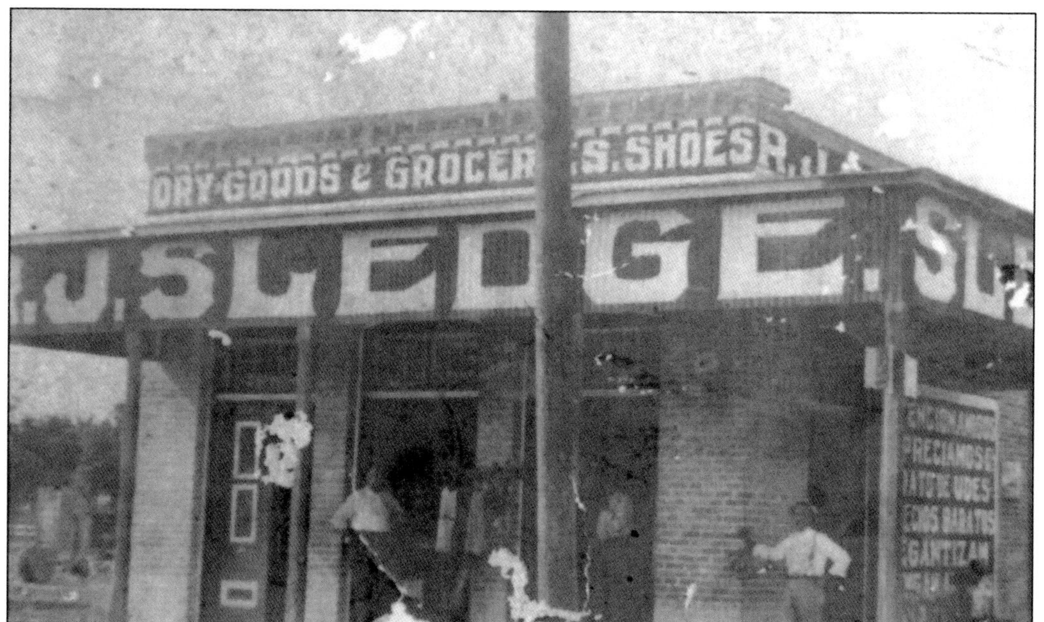

In addition to his land ownership, Sledge owned and operated a dry goods store on Center Street, one of the first businesses in Kyle. The sign on the side of the building is written in Spanish. (Courtesy HCCM.)

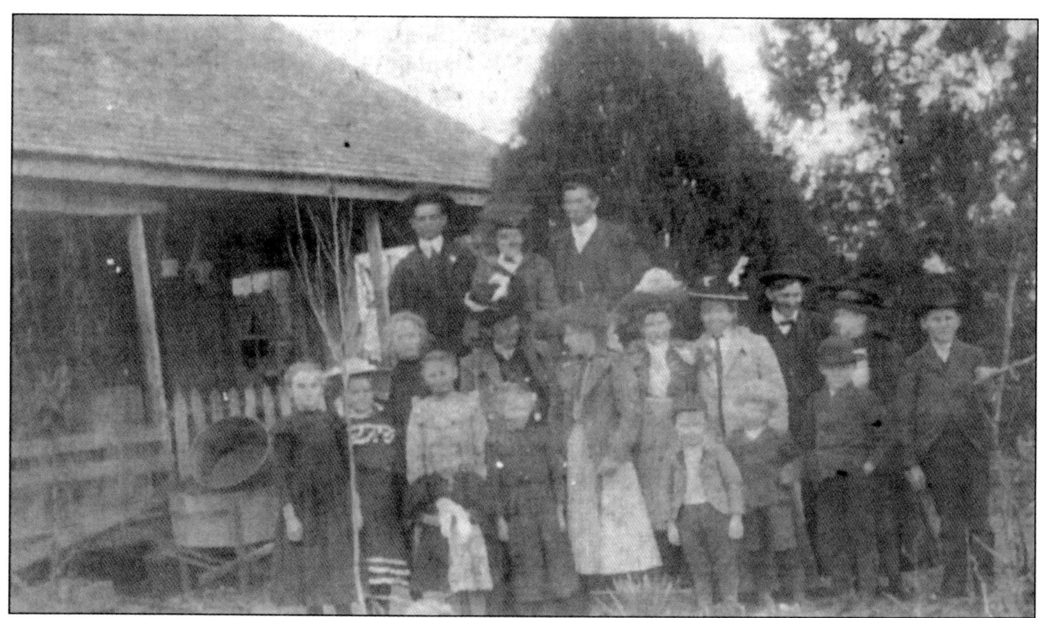

Soon after they arrived at Pecan Springs, the German immigrant families formed a church called the Kyle German Baptist Church on February 16, 1886, at the home of George Wiegand. The group, initially 16 members, met in homes until they were able to construct a church building. (Courtesy IBC.)

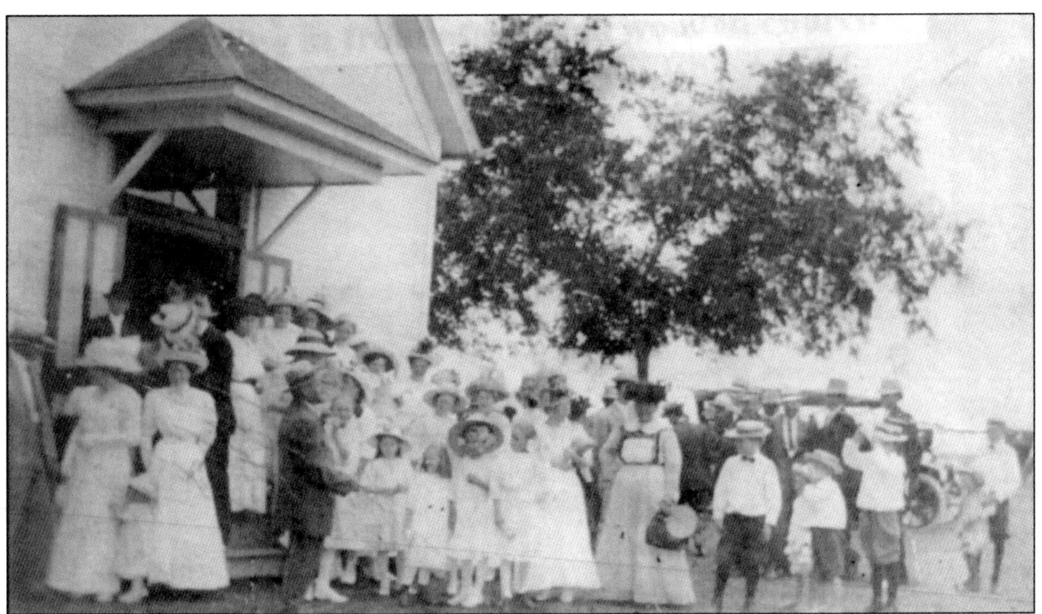

Within a few years, the Kyle German Baptist congregation grew in numbers and prosperity. This gathering outside the new church building reflects that growth. (Courtesy IBC.)

Land for the new church building was donated by Franz Marstaller, but donations of funding and labor for the construction came from all members. When the church was completed in 1893, it was debt-free. This building was used by the Kyle German Baptist congregation until it burned in 1939, when sparks from nearby burning trash ignited the building. (Courtesy IBC.)

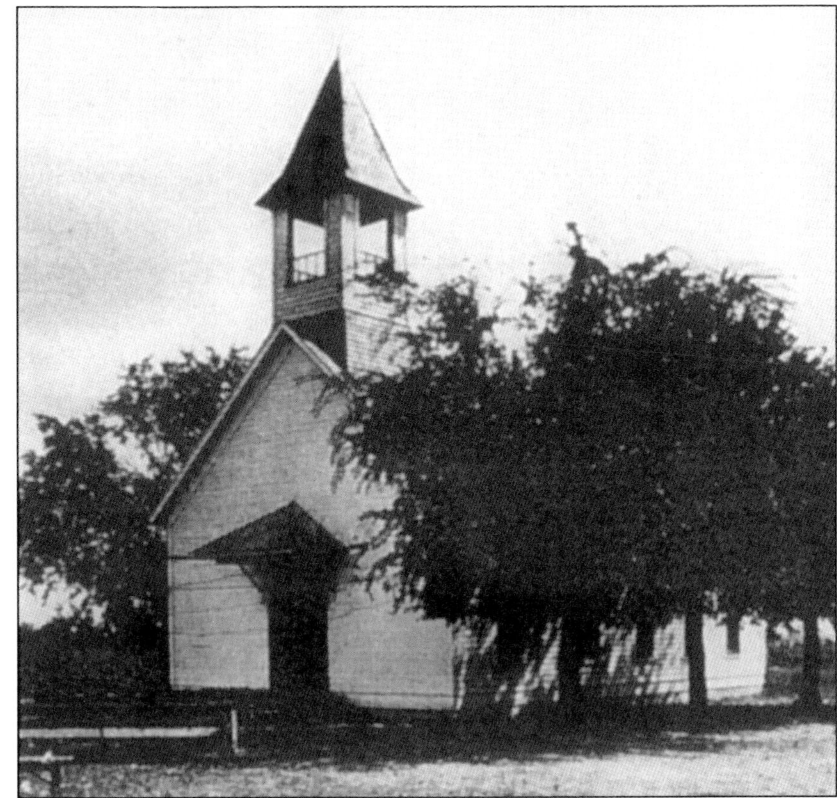

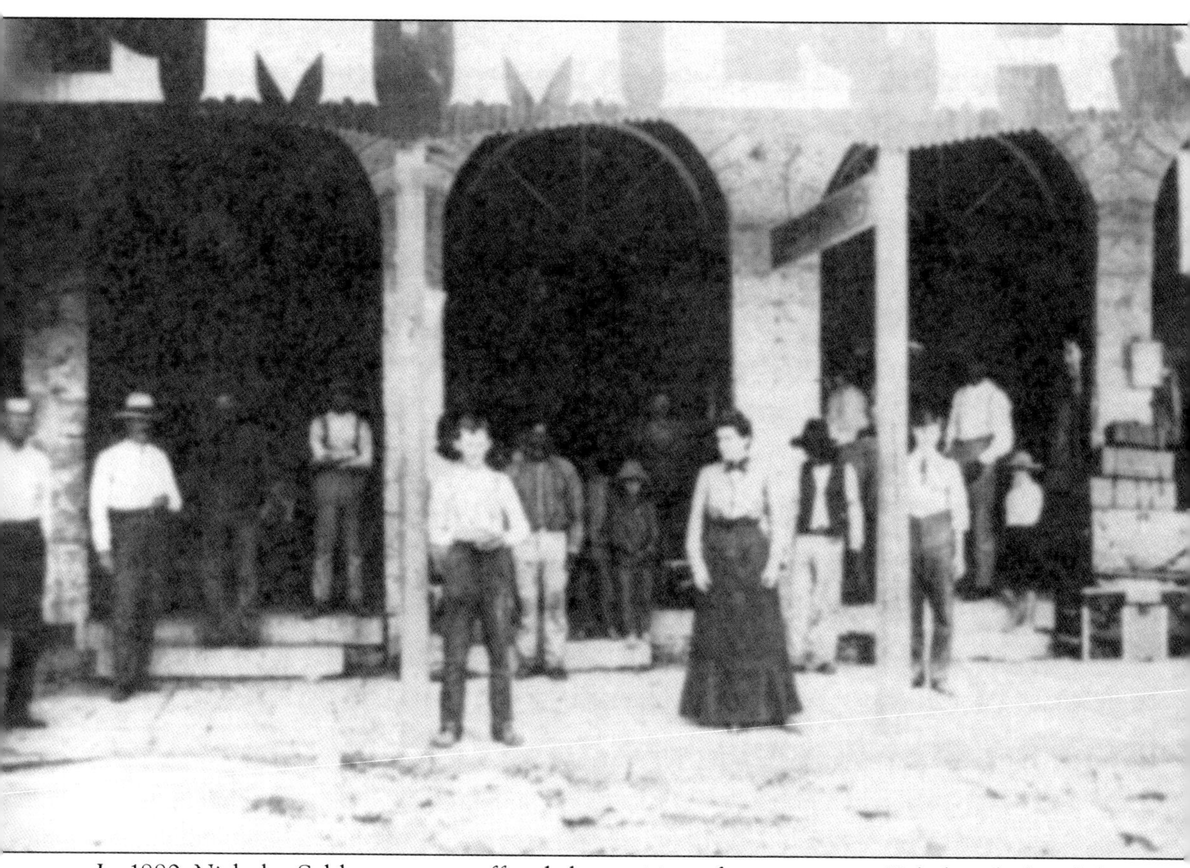

In 1880, Nicholas Schlemmer was offered the position of postmaster in Kyle but declined the appointment and later took a leave of absence from the International–Great Northern Railroad when they assigned him to the Kyle Station. Destined to live in Kyle, Schlemmer was hired to run the Texas Express Company office in Kyle and eventually added an Express office store in the same building in 1884. In 1890, he constructed a large rock building on Center Street and called his store Schlemmer Mercantile Company. (Courtesy HFP.)

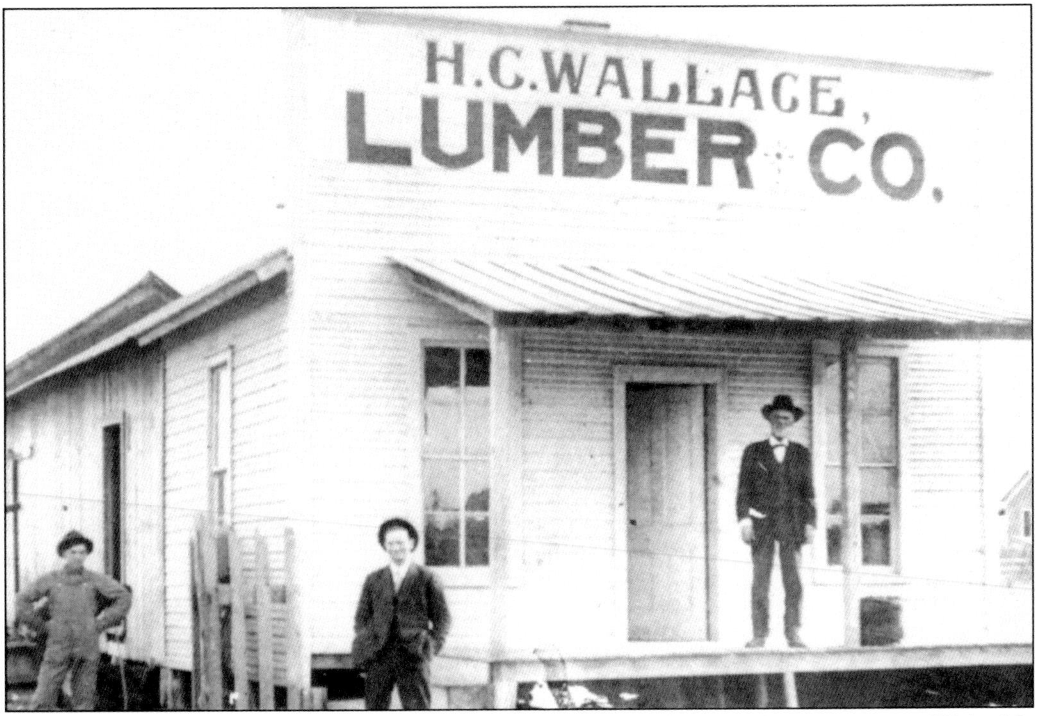

H.C. Wallace was living in Rockdale, Texas, when he heard about the new town of Kyle. He took the first train to cross the Colorado River to buy a site for a lumberyard in Kyle. In 1881, he loaded his merchandise into boxcars and moved his business to Kyle on Front and Austin Streets. He and his wife, Julia, were active in the Kyle Methodist Church and served the community in many ways. The photograph below shows Wallace behind his desk at the lumberyard on a winter day in 1899. (Both, courtesy HFP.)

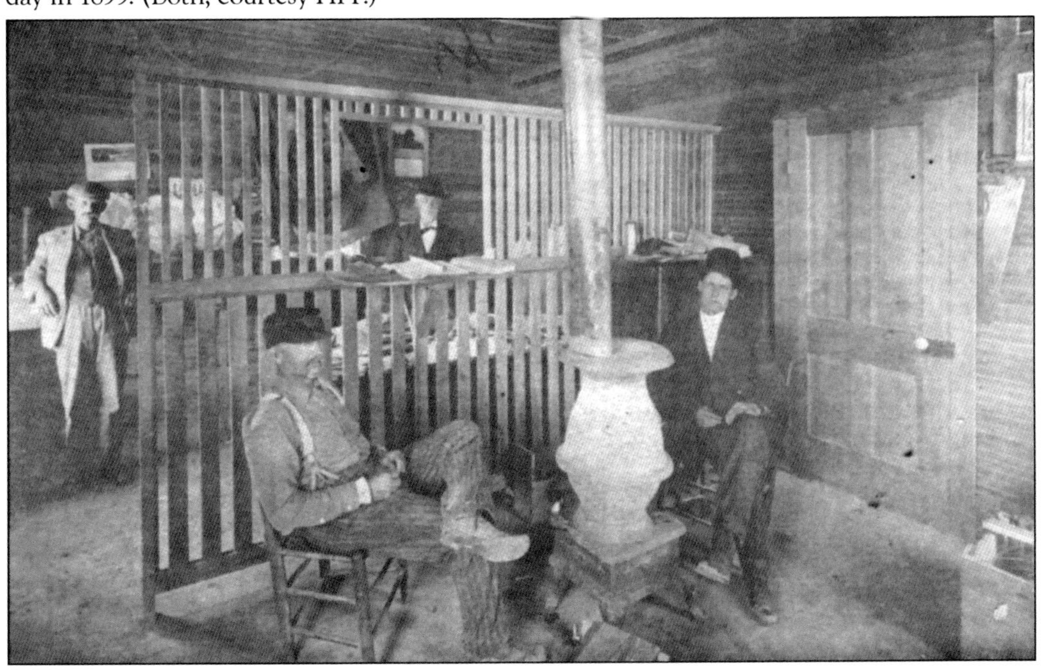

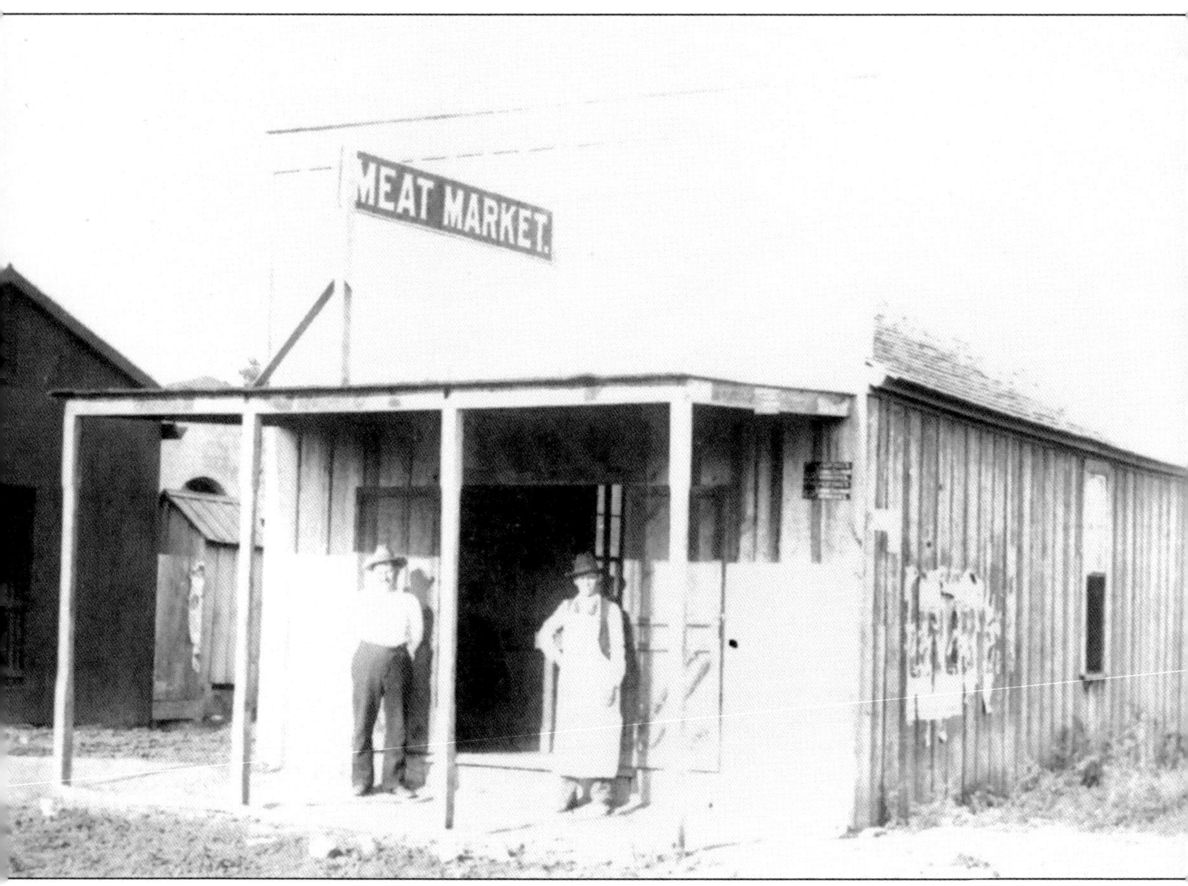

Founded in 1894 by Charles Thiele from New Braunfels, Thiele Meat Market—first on Center Street and later on Main Street—served the residents of Kyle for many years. The market had a huge chopping block where the meat was prepared, sawdust on the floor, and screen wire around the outside walls to keep out flies. A gasoline engine powered ceiling fans that cooled the area over the meat blocks. A cooler held 1,200 pounds of ice, which was hauled from San Marcos twice a week. Since country people came to town only on Saturdays, Thiele's son Nick sold meat to them from a horse and buggy (and later a Model T truck) three times a week. (Courtesy HCCM.)

The Kyle Methodist Church was organized in 1880 and constructed this building in 1887. The building was remodeled in 1929, and an addition was made in 1949. (Courtesy HFP.)

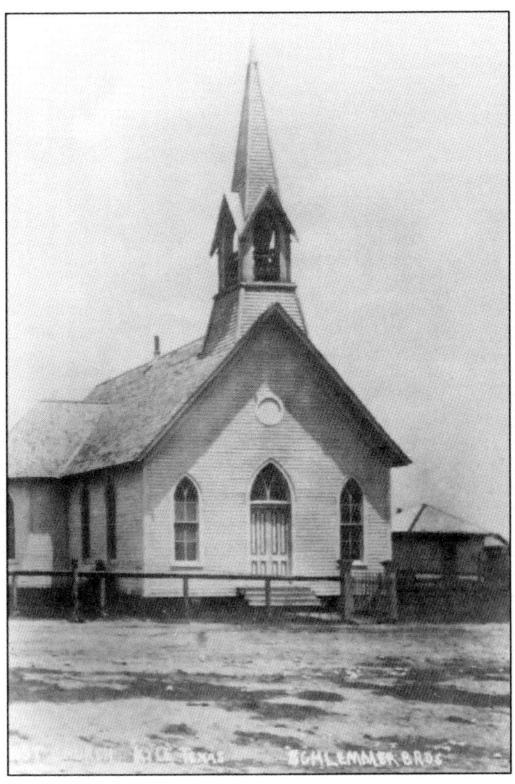

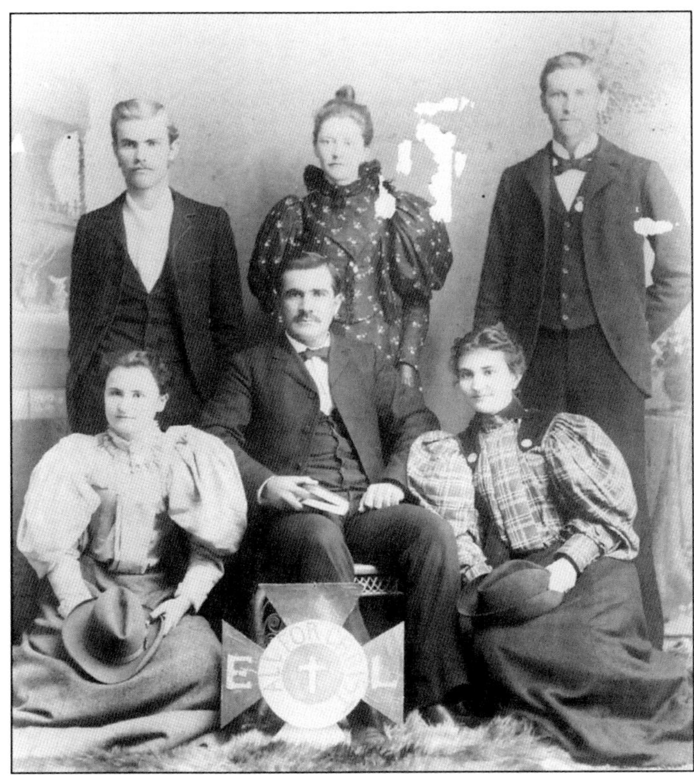

The Epworth League for young adults in the Methodist Church was an active group in Kyle. This 1895 photograph shows Rev. Sterling Fisher with the young people's group. From left to right are (first row) Jean Carpenter, Reverend Fisher, and Vance Word; (second row) Will Wallace, Stella Pickle White, and Ed Kyle. (Courtesy HFP.)

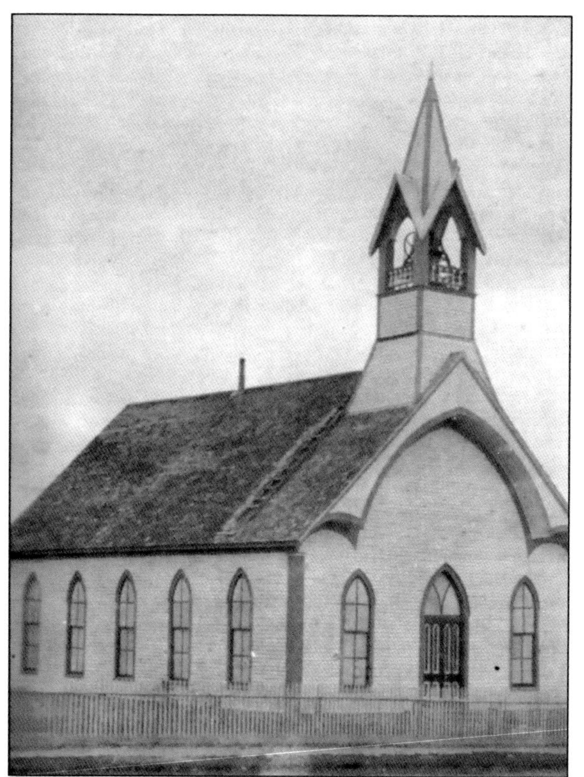

The First Baptist Church of Kyle was built in 1882 on land donated by the Texas Land Company. The wooden building was destroyed by fire in 1940, and most of the church's records were lost. For several years after the fire, the church met in the city hall. A new building was constructed in 1948. (Courtesy HFP.)

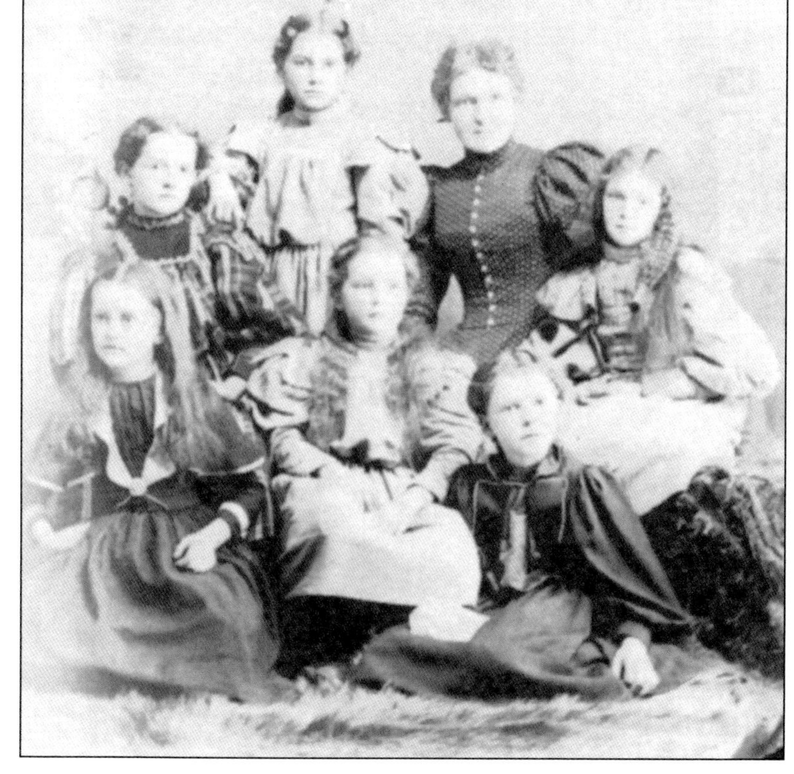

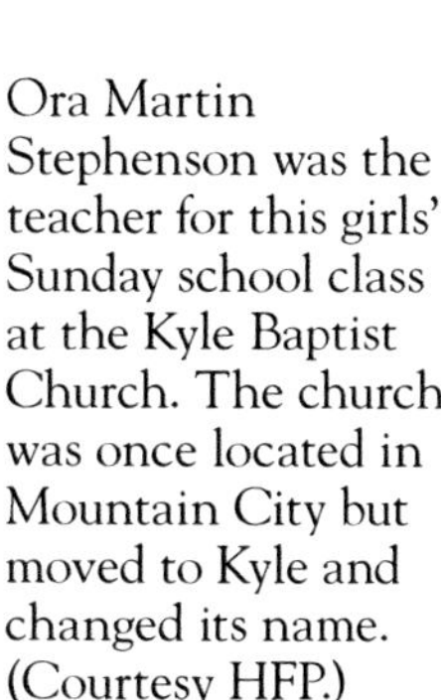

Ora Martin Stephenson was the teacher for this girls' Sunday school class at the Kyle Baptist Church. The church was once located in Mountain City but moved to Kyle and changed its name. (Courtesy HFP.)

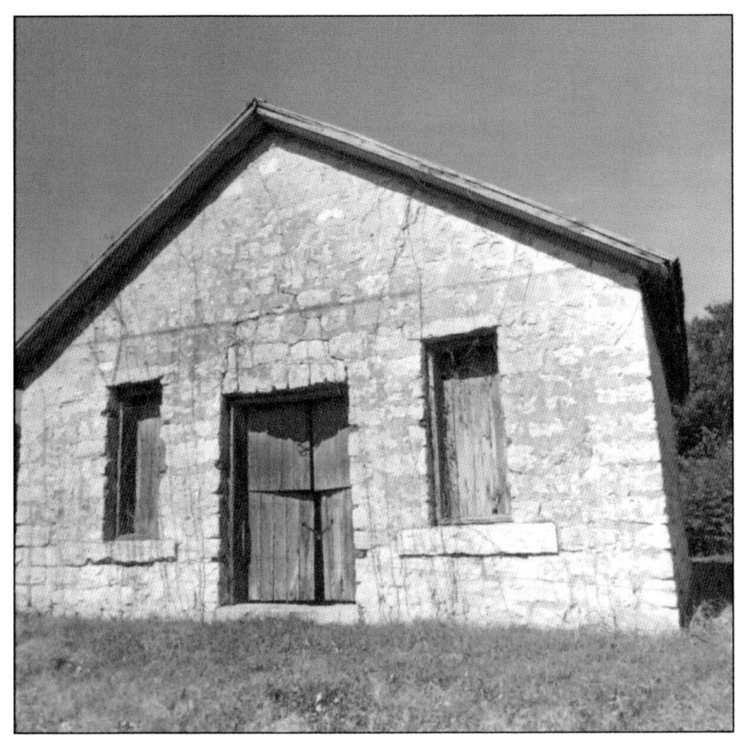

The Milk House, located on Hays Street, was used in connection with the creamery to store milk products. The building later belonged to rancher M.G. Michaelis III. (Courtesy HFP.)

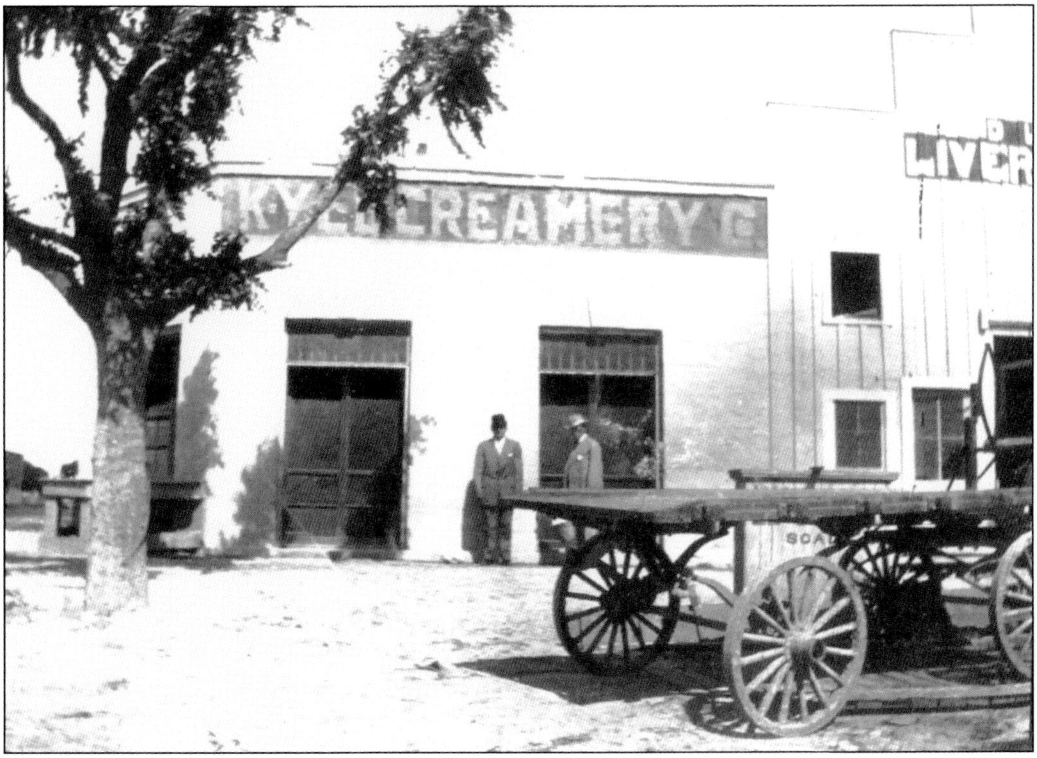

The creamery was operated in or near the building identified as the D.A. Young Building, which was the first rock structure built in Kyle. (Courtesy of Sharon Michaelis, City of Kyle.)

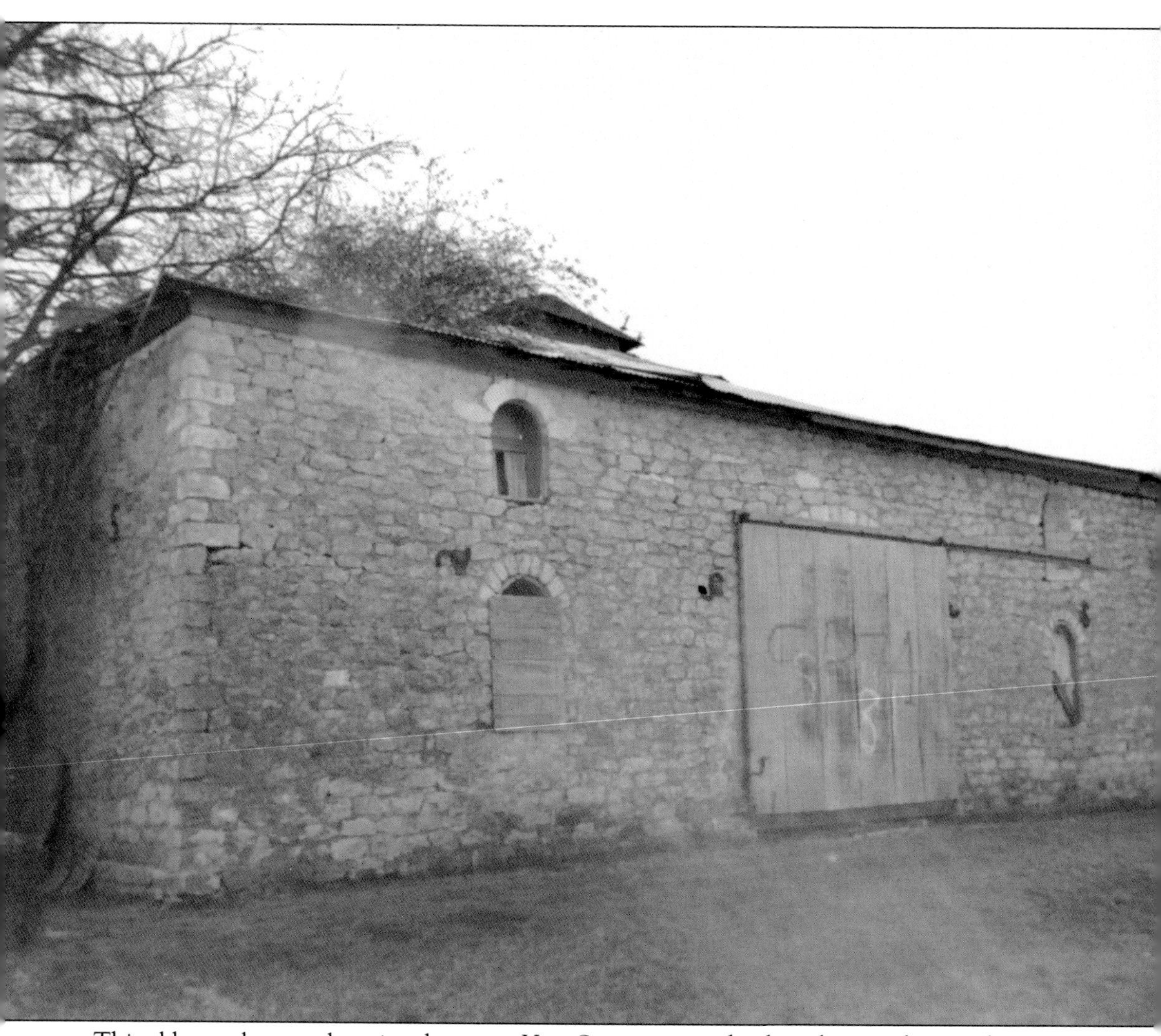

This old stone barn and carriage house on Hays Street was used to keep buggies for rental purposes. It was also used as the first automobile repair garage. It was owned by the Miller family until it was torn down in 2000. (Courtesy HFP.)

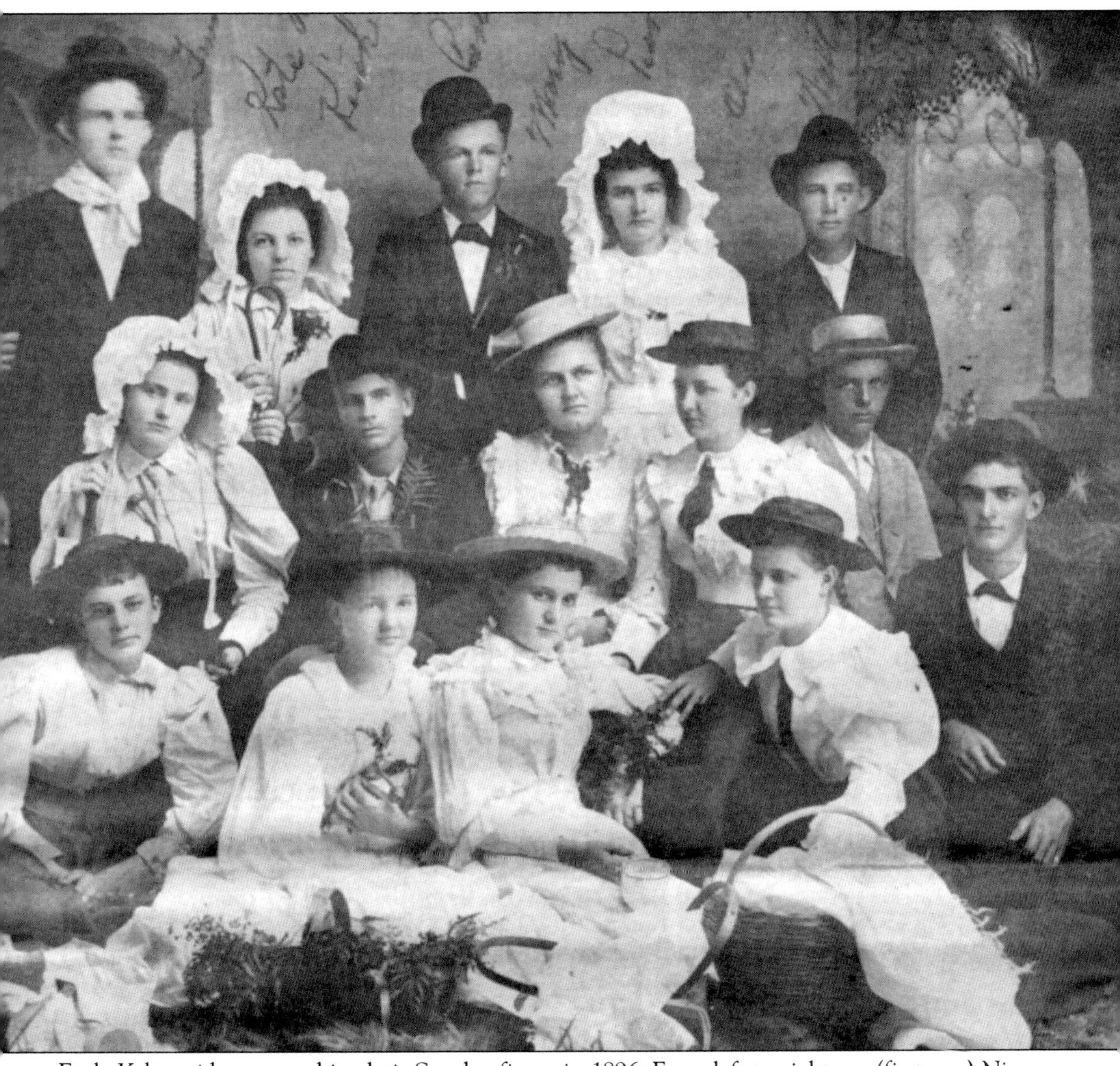

Early Kyle residents posed in their Sunday finest in 1896. From left to right are (first row) Nina Duty, Pearle Whisenant, Nette Carpenter, Sadie Groos, and Ad Groos; (second row) Fannie Wilson, Keith Wallace, Mary Storts, Ola Barbee, and Asa Chrostwaite; (third row) Elmer Martin, Kate McCarty, Carroll Donalson, Pearle Chrostwaite, and Walter Whisenant. (Courtesy HFP.)

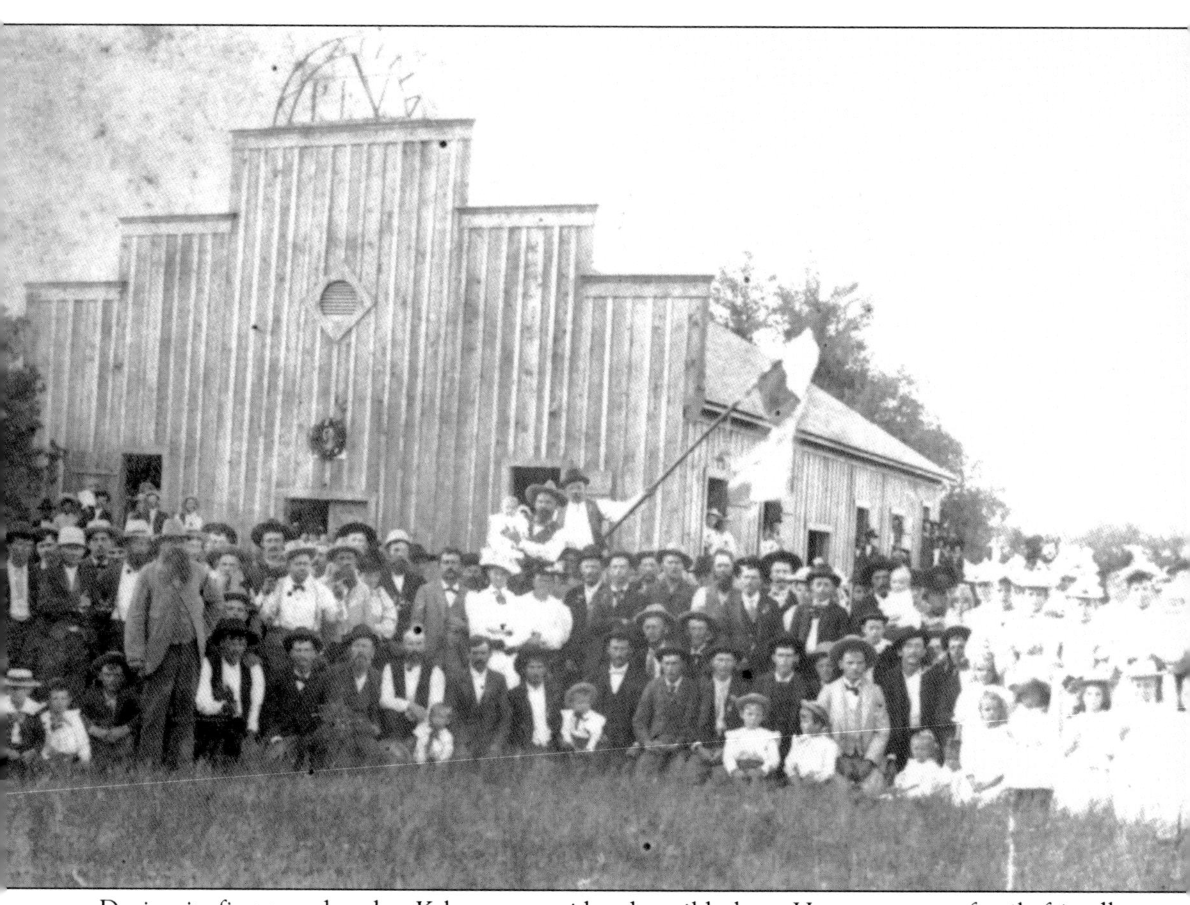

During its first two decades, Kyle was considered a wild place. However, more family-friendly entertainment was available at Plum Creek Hall between Uhland and Niederwald, west of present-day Highway 21. The hardworking German immigrants often enjoyed dancing there on Saturday nights. (Courtesy HCCM.)

Two

Kyle Family Contributions

Born in Tennessee in 1800, Claiborne Kyle arrived in Galveston, Texas, just as Congress made the offer to annex Texas in 1845. Kyle and his wife, Lucy Bugg, lived in Alabama and Mississippi before coming to Texas, settling first in Gonzales County, later in Austin, and finally in Hays County in 1847. There, they built the log house off Stagecoach Road, which has been preserved. Kyle became Hays County treasurer, a Texas state senator, and a representative in the House of Representatives during the Confederacy. He and Lucy had nine children, including five sons that served in Terry's Texas Rangers during the Civil War. All five survived the war, but Lucy died before they returned.

One of those sons, Fergus ("Ferg"), married Anna Elizabeth Moore before he left for the war. Their first child, Ellen, was born and died while Ferg was away. After returning, he and Lucy had eight more children, including Mary (who would be mayor of Kyle) and Edwin Jackson (dean of the School of Agriculture at Texas A&M and namesake of Kyle Field). Once he returned from the Civil War, Ferg served in the Texas Legislature and introduced the legislation that established the teacher's college in San Marcos, which became Texas State University. He also cosponsored the bill to purchase the Alamo in 1905, saving the monument from demolition. Along with his father-in-law, Judge David E. Moore, Ferg was instrumental in enticing the International–Great Northern Railroad to build the town that eventually took his name.

At Home July 10th 1854

My Dear Sir

Yours of the 6th Inst. is now before me, and I hasten to answer it. I was fearfull, that your getting into might aggravate your cough, but we must hope for the best, I do hope, that you will get intire releif by your constant attention to your use of water, dont give up, for I have every confidence, that you can be cured. Judge Cambell, is Still improving Mr McGonigale I am now looking for at my Home will Spend Some time with us in the Mountains, was glad to hear from Mr Wain, and that he was improving, had a good trip Home, Mr Moon met me at Mr Cherries, Came from his hogs very easy in a day, home, Billy has laid by the Crop, and Says he is Ready now to goe into the mountains, we have had Several heavy Rains Since you left, Crop is very good. I wish you to Say to D. Wippricht, that he must come and See me, also remembrance to Mr Captanjin, also to D. Happ, Say to the Doctor, that he must do his best on you, I wish the Doctor, to See Mr Digner, again for Me and See if Mrs D. will loane me her Goat, if She will do So I will return her with a half Maltese Goat,

I am anxious to improve my Goats, Speak a word to Mr Digner yourself, and Say to him I called to See him when I was at the Doctor but he was not at Home, no news in the neighborhood.

Written by Claiborne Kyle on July 10, 1854, this is a response to a letter from a sick friend. Kyle suggests remedies for treating the illness and sends his wishes for a recovery. He closes the letter with "howdy" from his wife, Lucy, and all of the children. (Both, courtesy of Jim Cullen.)

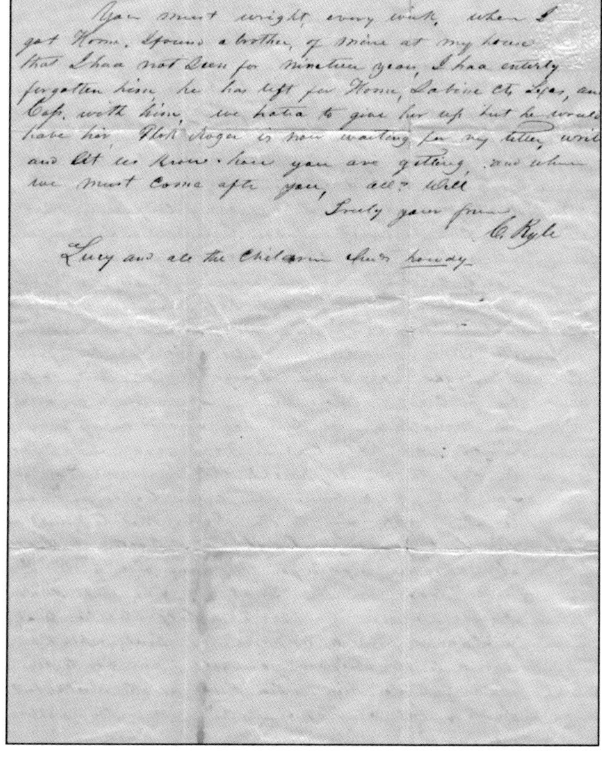

You must wright every week, when I got Home, I found a brother of mine at my house that I had not Seen for nineteen years, I had entirely forgotten him, he has left for Home, Sabine Co, Texas, and took Cap. with him, we hated to give her up but he would have her, Mr Rogers is now waiting for my letter, write and let us know how you are getting, and when we must come after you, all are well

Truly your friend

C. Kyle

Lucy and all the Children Sends howdy

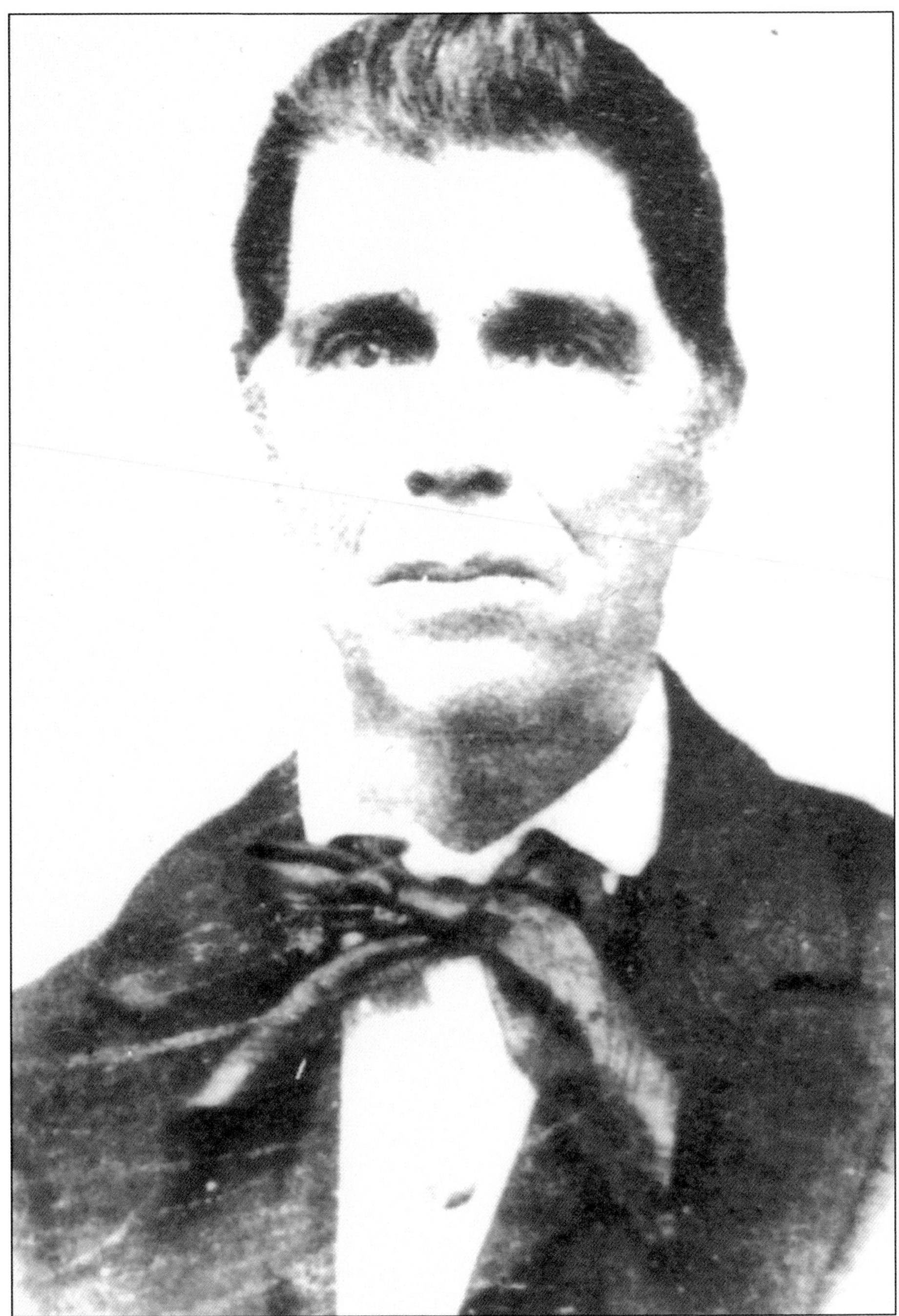

Claiborne Kyle was a political leader in the area of Hays County, where he settled in the middle of the 19th century. He was known as a shrewd politician, a man of excellent morals, a useful and worthy citizen, and a prosperous businessman. He served in the Mississippi Legislature before the family made a sudden move to Texas. Kyle had posted bond for his friend and state treasurer of Mississippi, Dr. Richard Graves. Graves absconded, forcing Kyle to liquidate the home, land, and slaves that he had inherited from his father and move to Texas to rebuild his fortune. (Courtesy of Jim Cullen.)

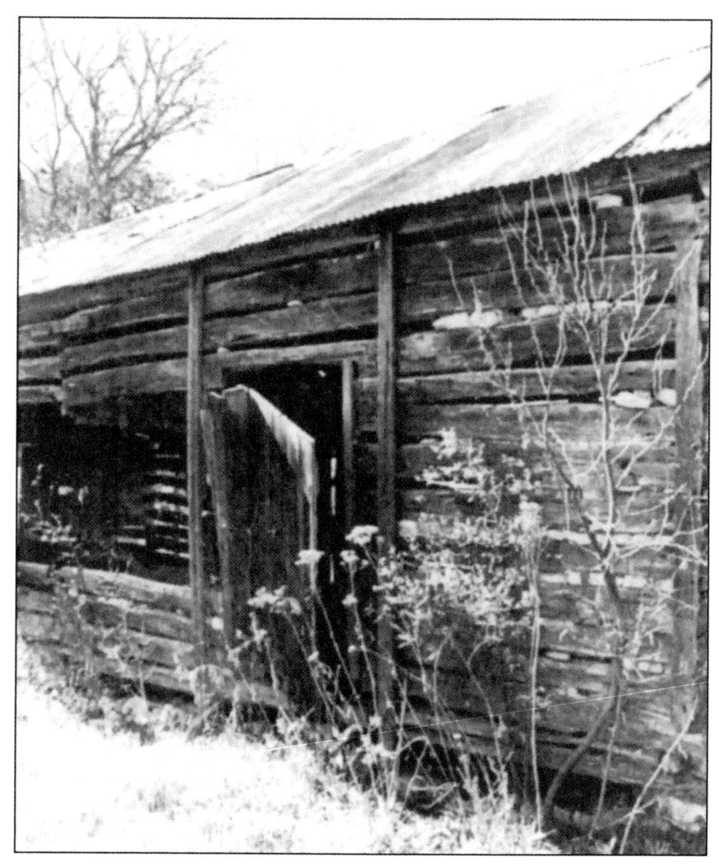

Built for his family by Claiborne Kyle around 1850, this double log house in the Blanco community near Kyle has four rooms with a dogtrot in between. The structure is 80 by 20 feet, built of hand-adzed cedar logs, square-notched at the corners and secured by wooden pegs. Believed to be the last remaining example of a four-pen, linear dogtrot log house in Texas, the Claiborne Kyle Log House was restored in 1982. It is open for visitors on designated days, and admission is always free. (Left, courtesy HFP; below, courtesy of Blanche Richmond.)

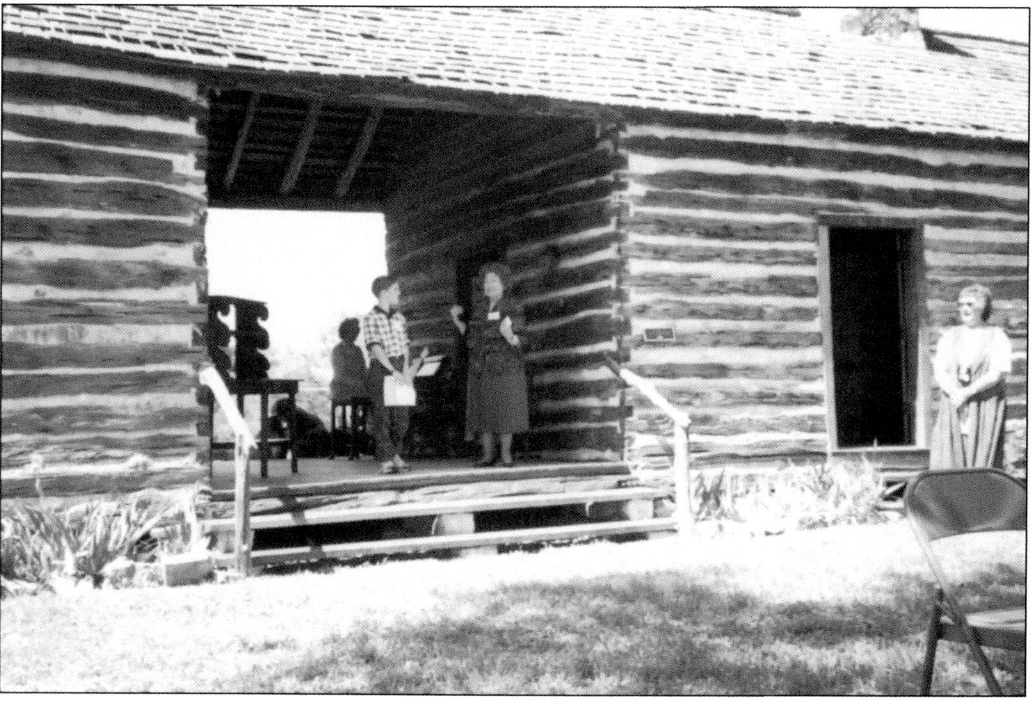

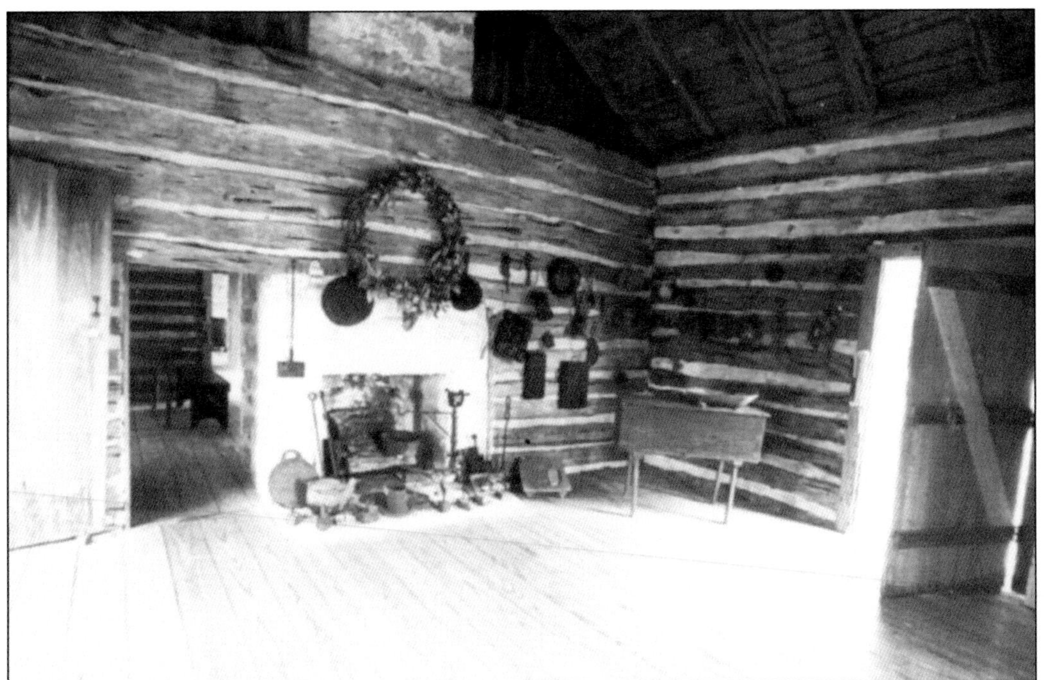

The Claiborne Kyle Log House is open from spring until fall, beginning with the Blooms over the Blanco open house celebration, which is held on the first Sunday after Easter each year. The log house is open the first Sunday of each month after Blooms over the Blanco from 2:00 to 5:00 p.m. Commission members are on hand to answer questions and lead informal tours. The open house season closes with the Claiborne Kyle Fried Chicken Dinner festivity, held the fourth Saturday in September from 11:00 a.m. to 2:00 p.m. Fresh chicken is cooked on-site and sold with beans, potato salad, pickles, rolls, dessert, and a drink for a nominal contribution. (Above, author's collection; below, courtesy HFP.)

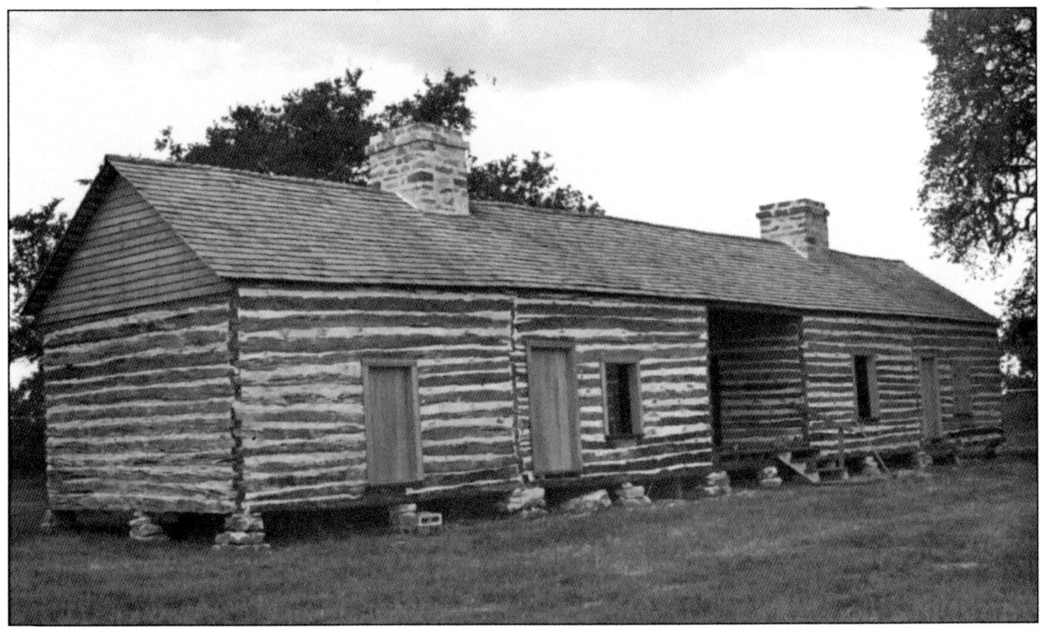

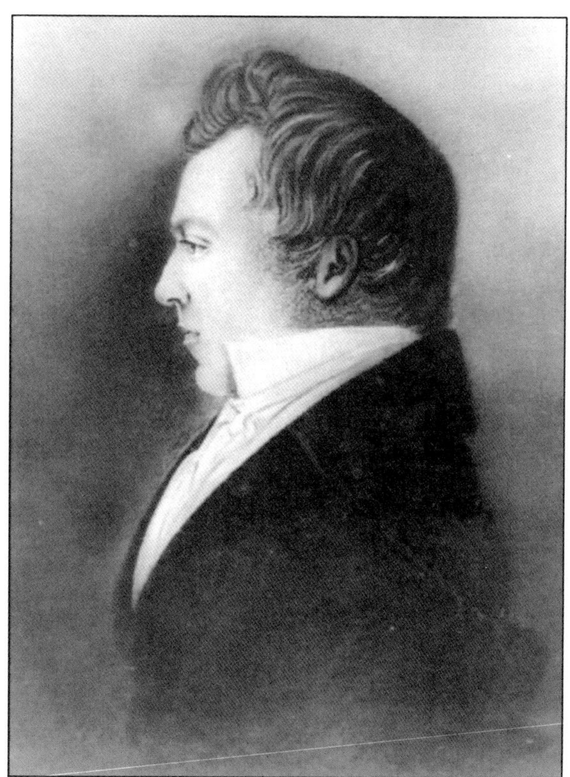

Judge David E. Moore purchased land near Claiborne Kyle in 1858 and later sold plots of this land to his daughters Annie (married to Claiborne Kyle's son Fergus) and Mary Ellen. When the International–Great Northern Railroad sought a site for a new town on its rail line, the Moore family deeded 200 acres of land. (Courtesy of Jim Cullen.)

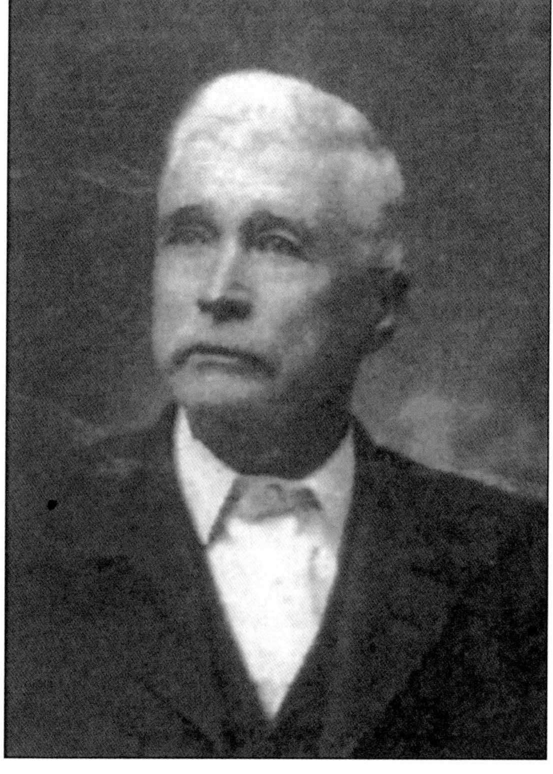

The second son of Claiborne and Lucy Kyle, Fergus ("Ferg"), moved to Hays County with his family. He joined Terry's Texas Rangers at the outbreak of the Civil War, shortly after his marriage to Anna Elizabeth Moore. Like his father, Ferg was interested in politics and served in the Texas Legislature after the war. Capt. Ferg Kyle died in 1906. (Courtesy HFP.)

Anna Moore Kyle had nine children with her husband, Fergus. The first child, Ellen, died when her father was off fighting in the Civil War. Since the Kyle family's financial holdings were depleted by the Civil War, Fergus's marriage to Anna brought assets to the family. (Courtesy HFP.)

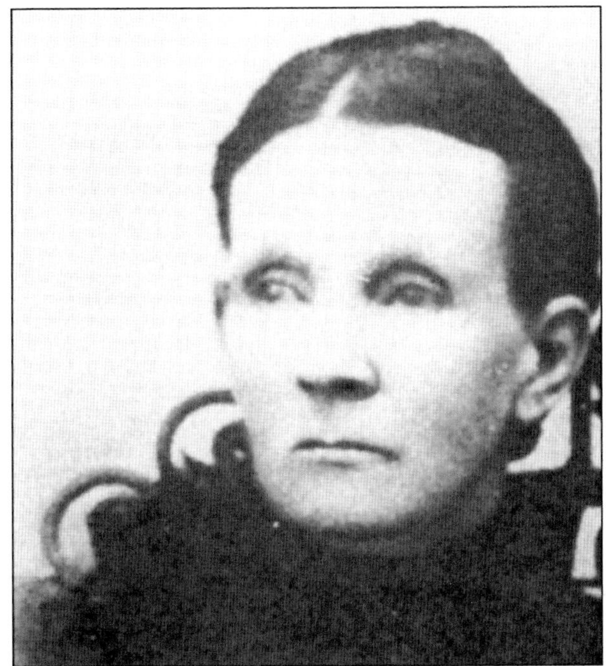

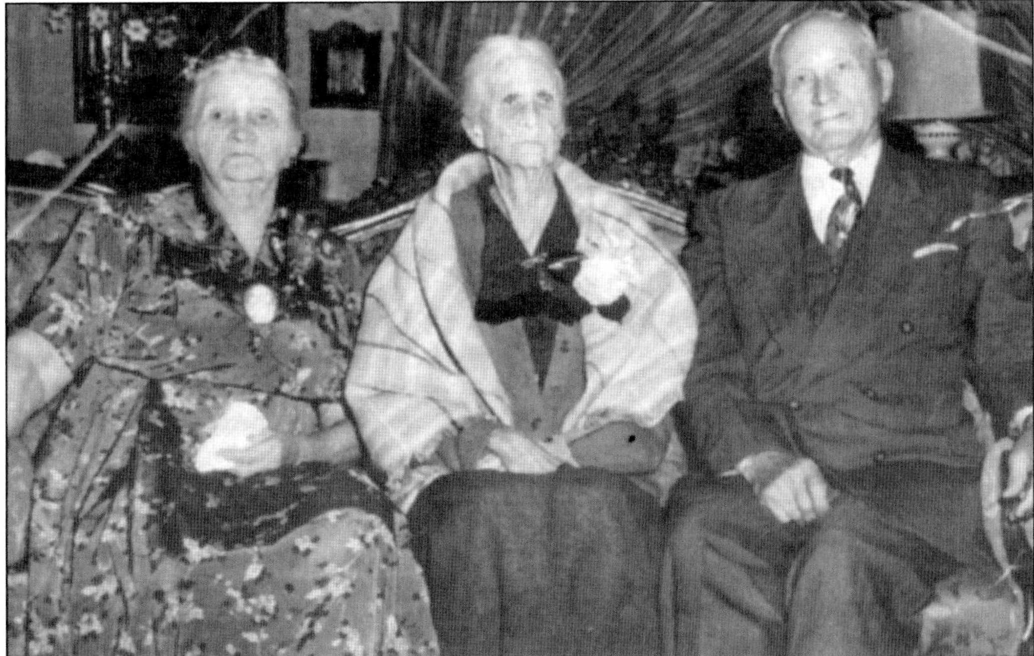

In 1937, Mary Kyle Hartson ("Miss Mary," center) was elected mayor of Kyle by a write-in vote. She held the position for nine years, from ages 72 to 81. During her term in office, a municipal water system was built, the fire department was updated, a new school was constructed, and the town was cleaned in general. From 1943 to 1946, women filled seven of the nine city offices, gaining nationwide attention, including a picture in *Life* magazine. This photograph shows Hartson on her 90th birthday with Rosa Kyle Good and her brother, Edwin Kyle. Hartson died in 1956 and is buried in the Kyle Cemetery. (Courtesy HFP.)

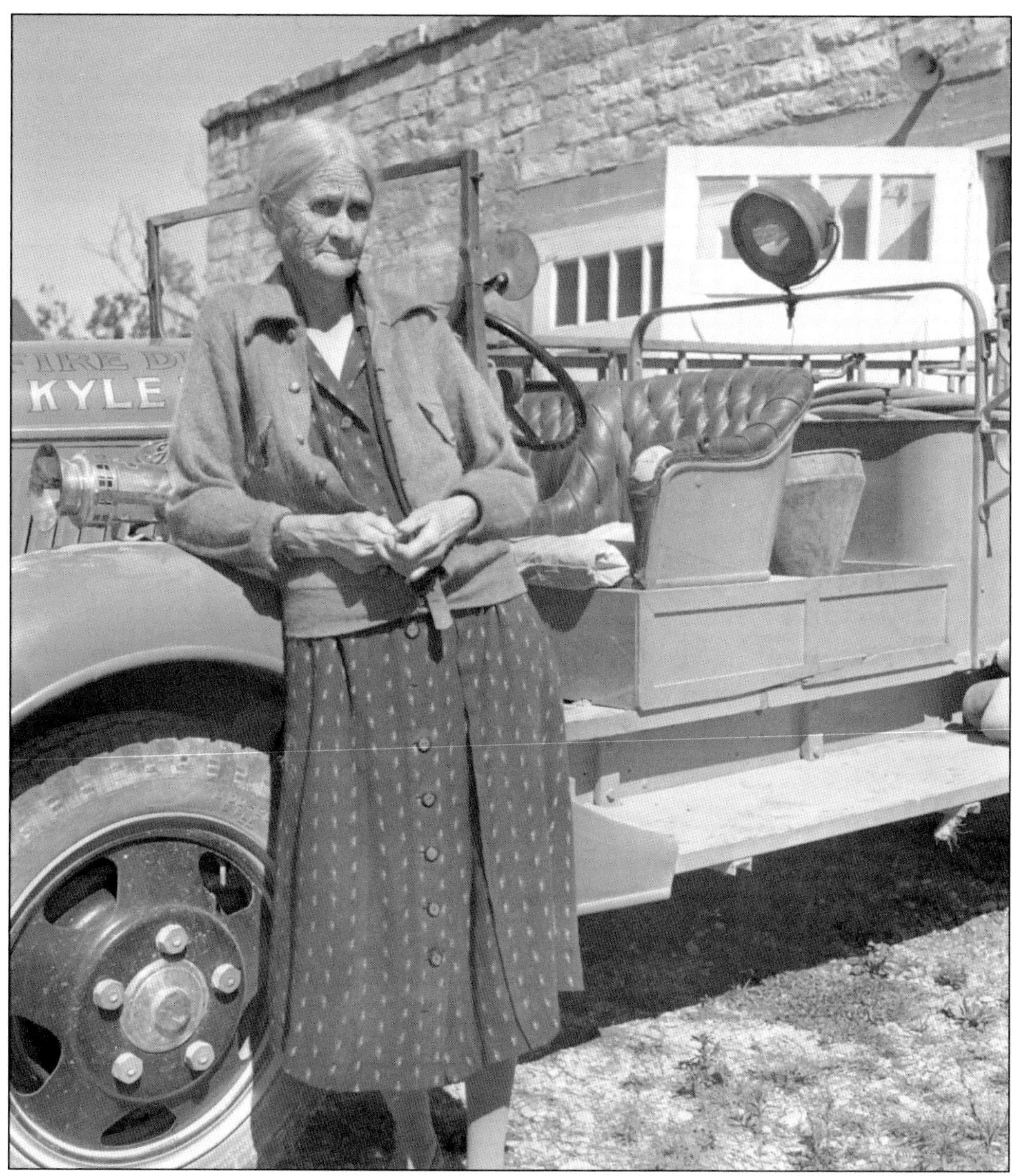

Mary Lucy Kyle was the second child of Fergus and Anna Moore Kyle, born after her father returned from the Civil War in 1865. She attended school at the Blanco Chapel and later at the seminary in Kyle. She attended Sam Houston State Normal College in Huntsville and then taught school in Kyle and later in Taylor, Texas. In 1891, she married streetcar engineer George Hartson of Dallas. The Hartsons lived in Dallas and Laredo before they moved in 1900 to Avino, Mexico, where George Hartson was an electrical supervisor for a mining syndicate. When her husband was killed in an industrial accident the next year, Mary Kyle Hartson moved back to Kyle with her two young children and gave birth to a third child. Widowed with three children, Hartson was appointed postmistress of Kyle shortly after she returned in 1901. She served in that role until 1923. Family influence secured the position for her, but her personal efficiency held it through both Democratic and Republican administrations. (Courtesy of the Neal Douglass Collection, Austin History Center, Austin Public Library,)

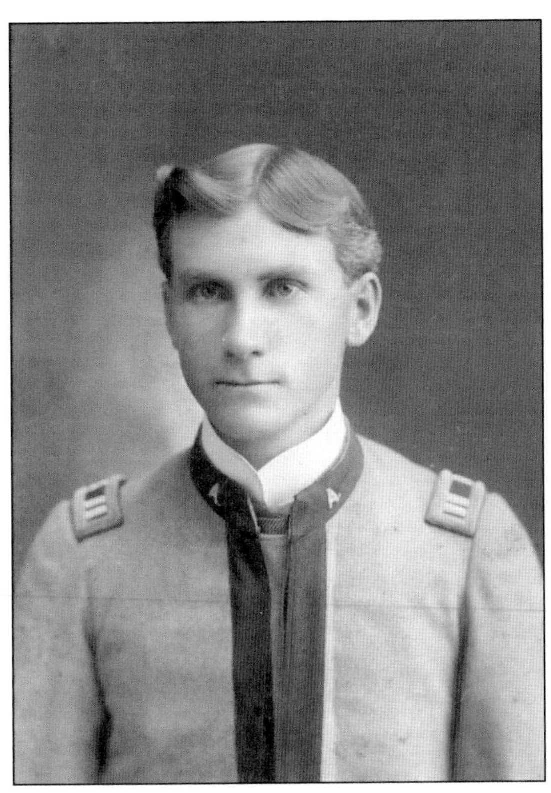

Edwin Jackson Kyle, son of Fergus Kyle, graduated from Texas A&M in 1899, after serving as the first student commander of the corps of cadets. After graduate studies at Cornell University, Edwin Kyle joined the faculty at Texas A&M in 1902 and served the university as a professor of horticulture, dean of the College of Agriculture, and chair of the Athletic Council until his retirement in 1944. The football stadium at Texas A&M, which was first constructed with his assistance, was named Kyle Field in his honor. Pres. Franklin Roosevelt named Kyle ambassador to Guatemala in 1945. Kyle died in 1963. (Both, courtesy of the Cushing Memorial Library and Archives, Texas A&M University.)

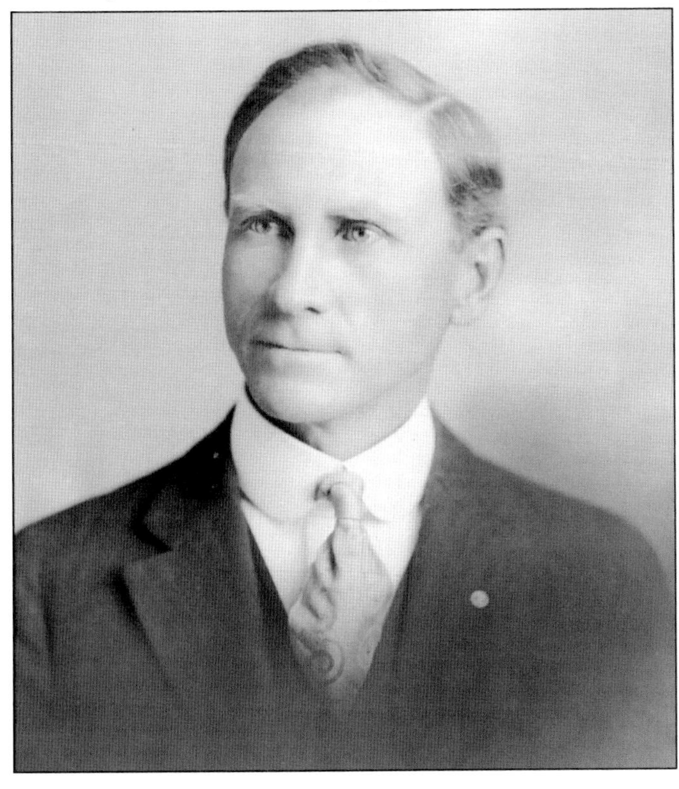

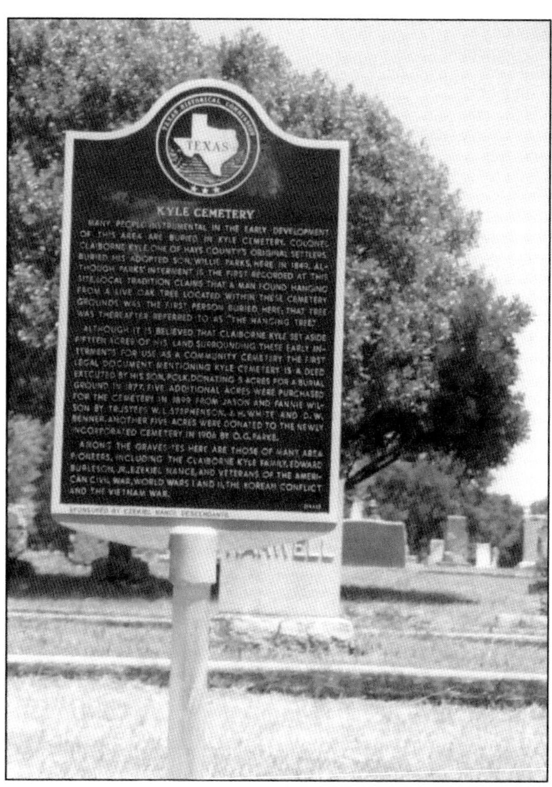

It is believed that Claiborne Kyle set aside 15 acres of land near his home for a community cemetery. Kyle's adopted son, Willie Parks, was the first burial recorded here, although local tradition claims that a man found hanging from a live oak tree within the cemetery grounds was the first person buried. Many members of the Claiborne Kyle family, as well as Edward Burleson Jr., Ezekiel Nance, and other Kyle-area pioneers, are buried in the Kyle Cemetery. (Courtesy HFP.)

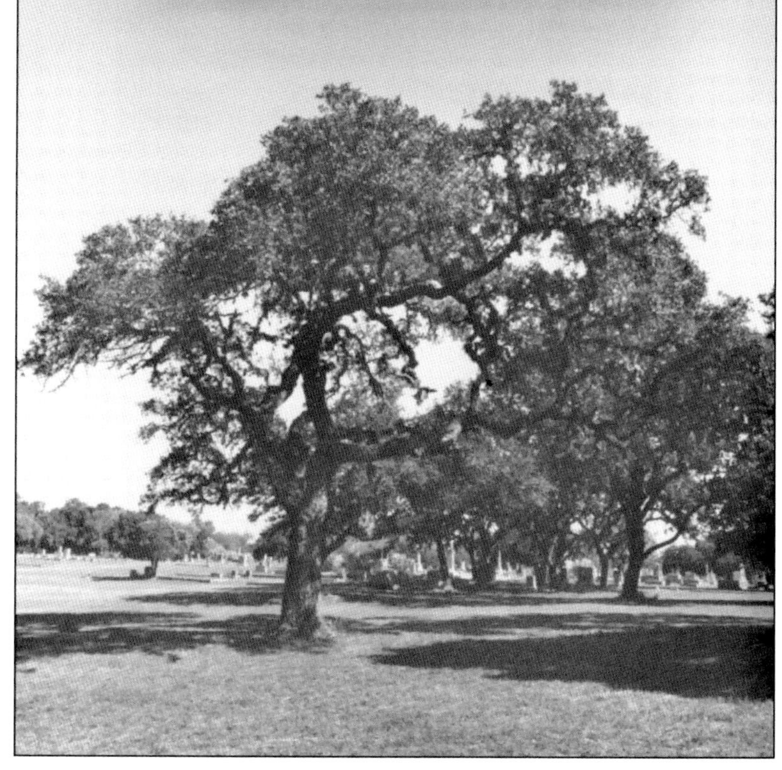

Sometime in the late 1840s, long before the town of Kyle came into existence, cowboys from the Kyle Ranch were rounding up stray cows when they discovered a man hanging from a limb of a live oak, about a quarter-mile from Col. Claiborne Kyle's home. Not knowing the man's identity or why he had been hanged, they cut the body down and buried it beside this tree in an unmarked grave. The tree is now known as the Hanging Tree. (Courtesy HCCM.)

Three

Kyle in the Early 20th Century

The turn of the century brought changes to the 21-year-old town on the railroad line. In 1906, Kyle incorporated as a village and began planning for the construction of a city hall on the town square. The first laws passed by the new city council addressed several issues: fines for driving an automobile faster than 10 miles per hour in the city limits; fines for running mules, horses, hogs, or cattle in the city limits; and fines for working or hunting on Sundays. Existing businesses grew, and new ones were established, including a bottling plant, an oil mill, and a newspaper. Additional churches were formed, including the Christian Church in 1905 and the Catholic Church in 1909. A new school building was constructed, more teachers were hired, and different subjects were made available to students. Kyle residents entertained themselves with parades, horse racing, and other pursuits unknown a generation before. World War I took some young men away to serve their country, including school principal Henry Hendricks, who enlisted before the end of the 1916–1917 school year. The war with Germany created issues for the German immigrants, who were still conducting church services in their native language and speaking German in their homes. By the first decades of the 20th century, Kyle citizens took on leadership positions in the business and community life of their hometown, including those born to the German immigrant families.

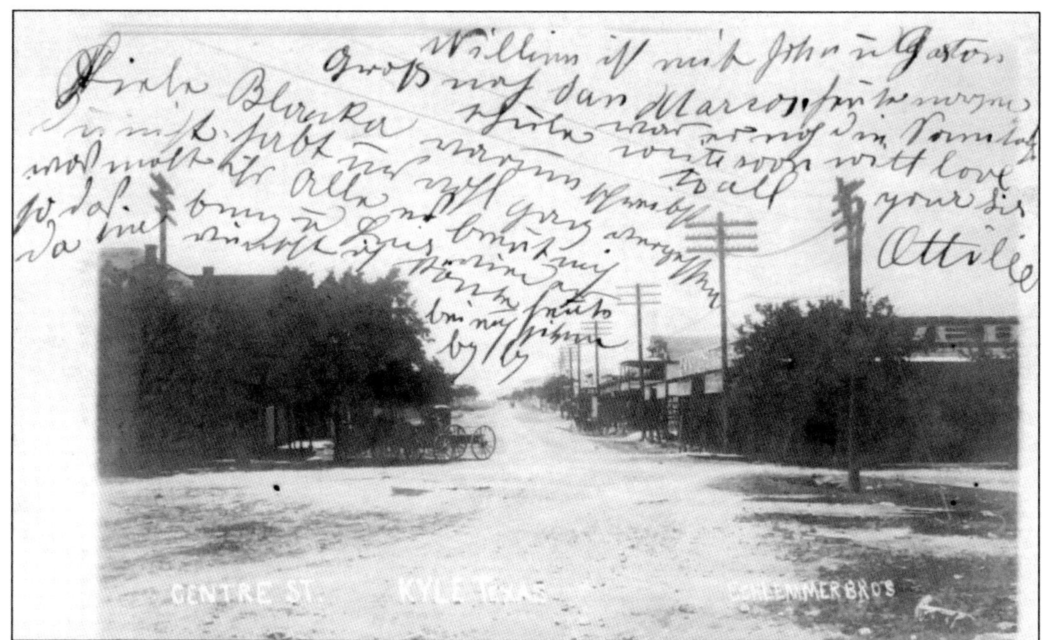

By the beginning of the 20th century, postcards were a popular way for businesses to share town images and for people to communicate with friends and family. As this photographic postcard of Center Street indicates, postcards did not contain a place for a message but only for the address and stamp, resulting in people writing their message on the photograph. (Courtesy of Robert Frizzell.)

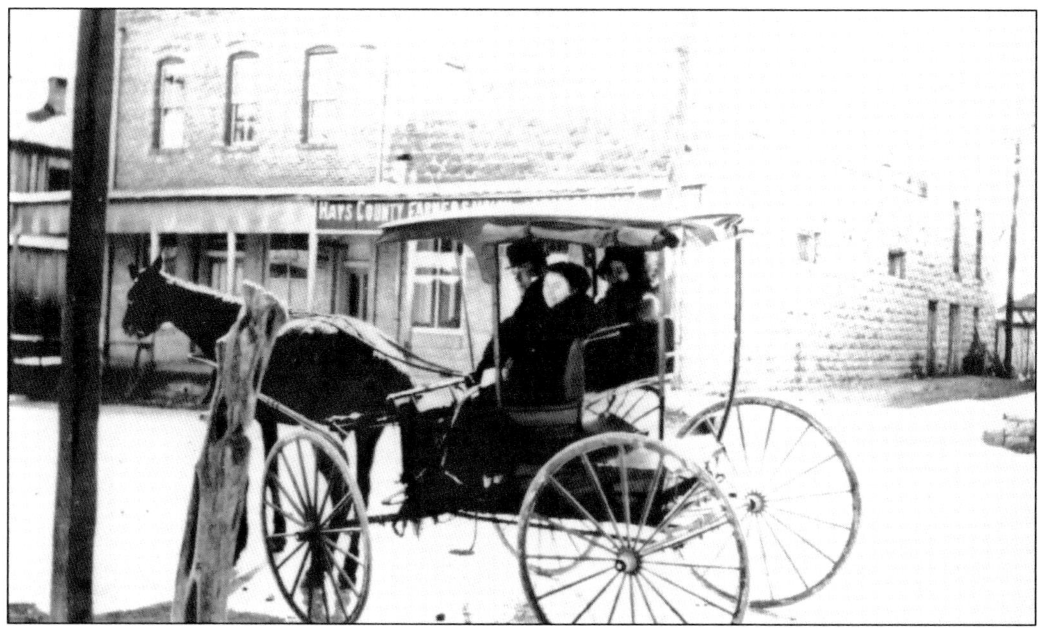

Early in the 20th century, the horse and buggy was still the primary means of transportation in Kyle. This photograph shows visitors or shoppers in downtown Kyle. (Courtesy of Sharon Michaelis, City of Kyle.)

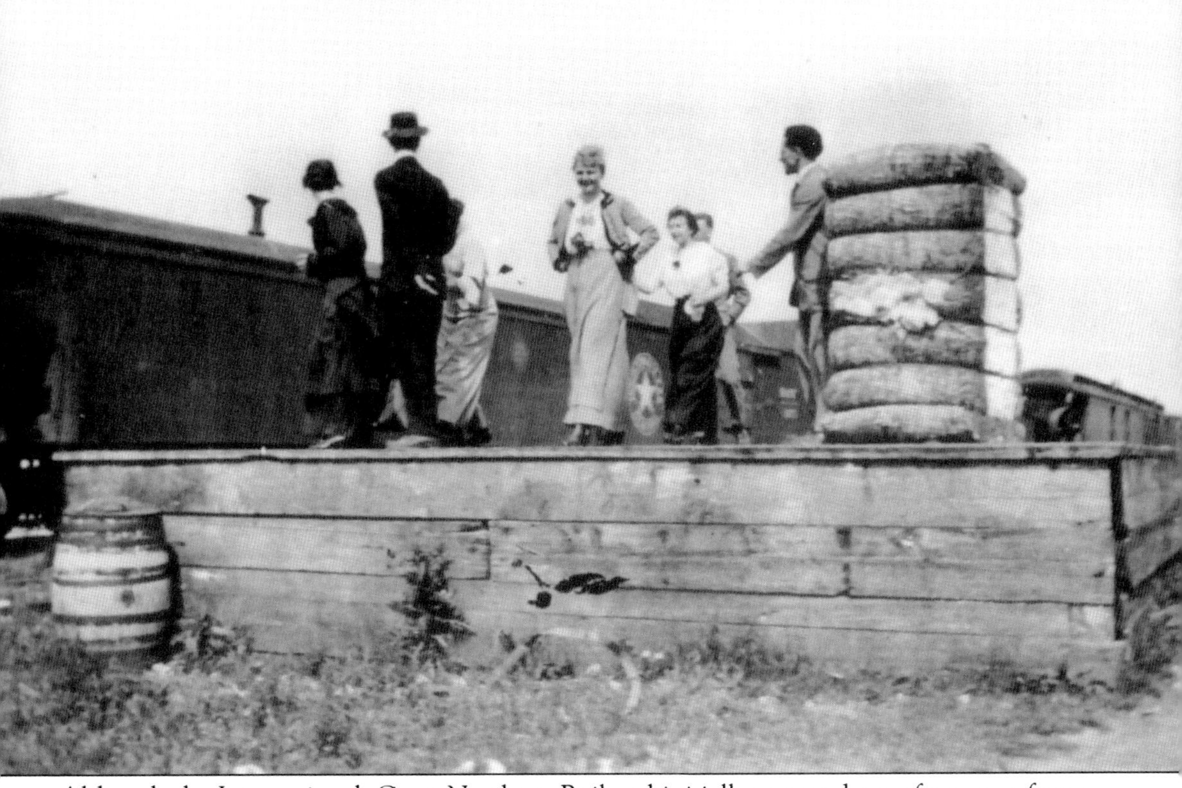

Although the International–Great Northern Railroad initially operated out of a tent, a frame building was soon constructed to serve as a depot. This building was in the center of Center Street and burned in October 1916. It was rebuilt on the same site but moved the next year to its present location. Shipping cotton from the fields surrounding Kyle was an important part of the local railroad business. At one time, most of the cotton from the six gins in and around Kyle was shipped from the Kyle Station—from 3,000 to 5,000 bales each year. (Courtesy of Sharon Michaelis, City of Kyle.)

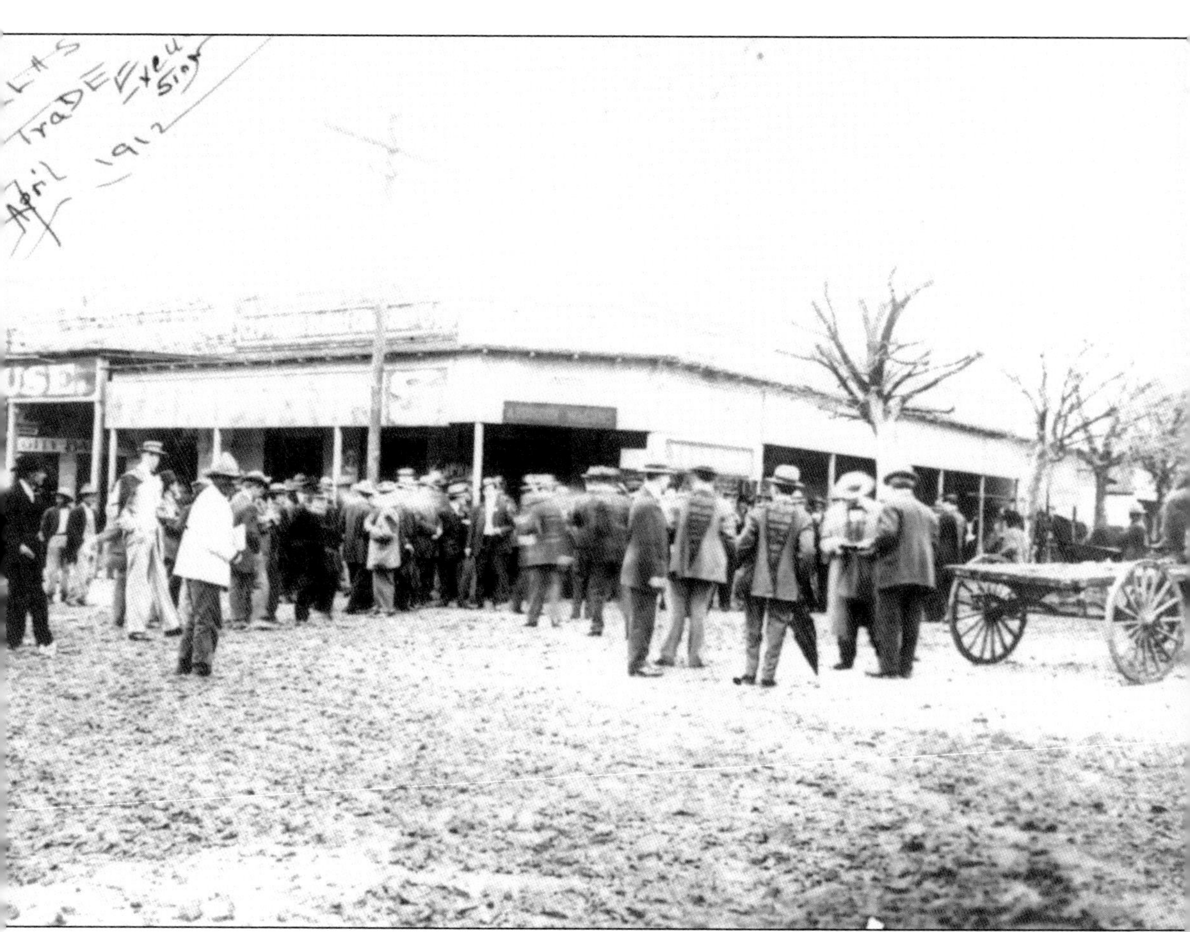

In addition to patronizing local retail businesses, Kyle citizens also were able to buy products and wares from salesmen who came by train from Dallas to show new merchandise. This photograph shows the Dallas Trade Excursion on April 12, 1912. (Courtesy HCCM.)

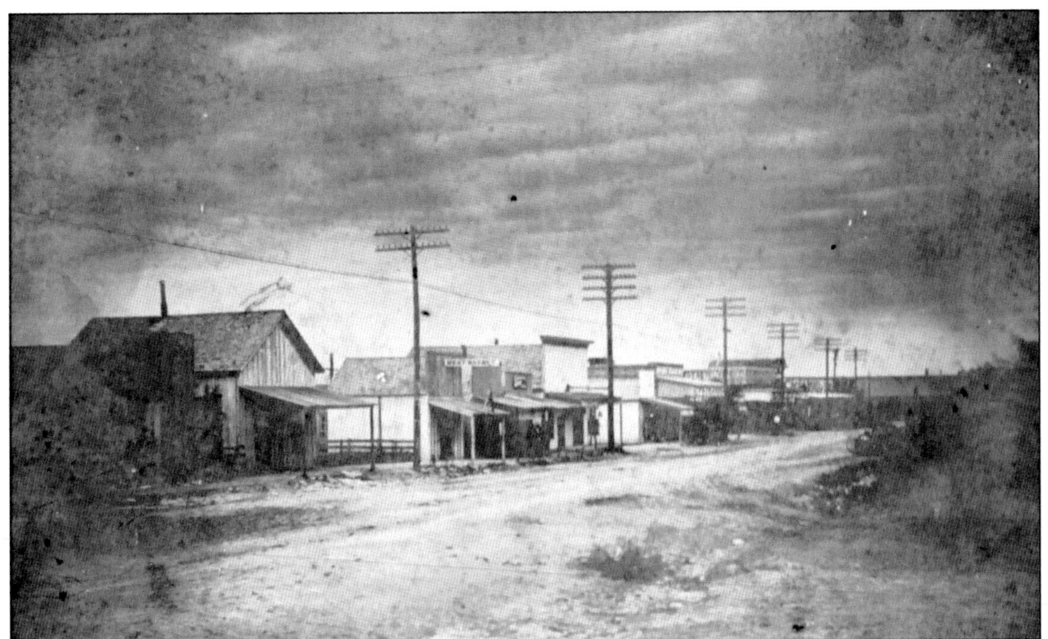

This view of Center Street shows another angle of the businesses in Kyle in 1907. (Courtesy HFP.)

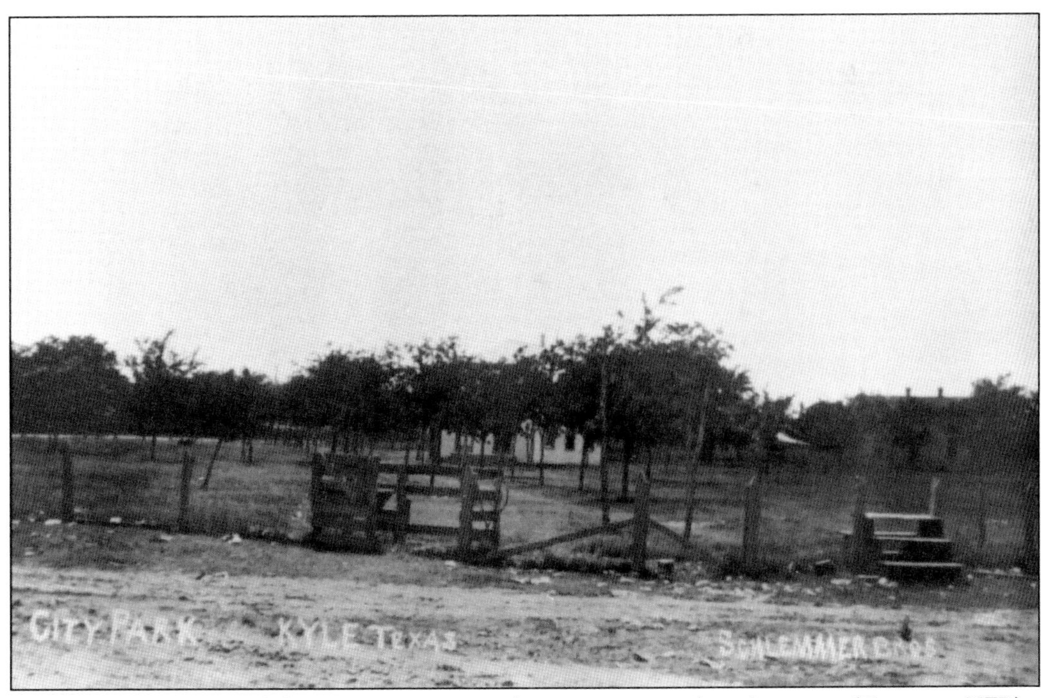

In 1907, the City Park did not appear to provide many options for relaxation. (Courtesy HFP.)

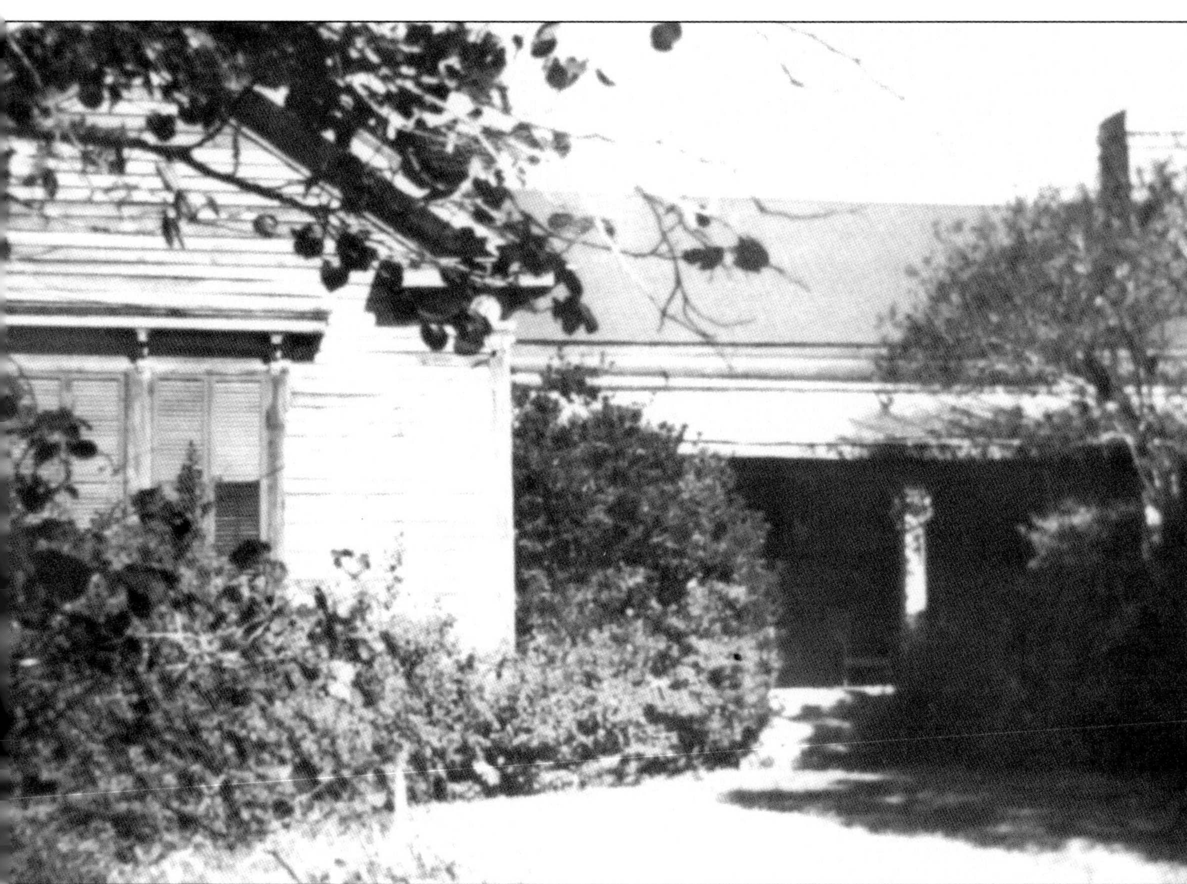

Although Kyle was primarily a farming community with retail businesses to serve farmers' needs, there was some industry in the new town as well. Maj. Ezekiel Nance, who had operated a gin in the Blanco community, established the first cotton gin in Kyle in 1881. Nance was a progressive, visionary man whose efforts were important in the development of Kyle. His home is pictured. (Courtesy HCCM.)

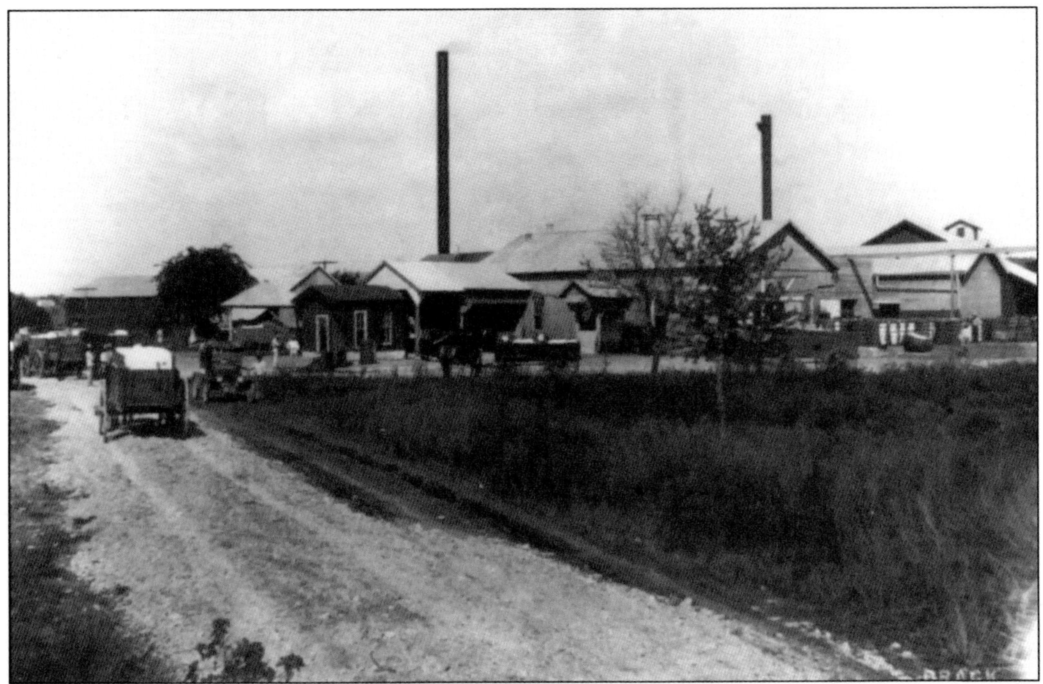

A cottonseed oil mill was organized as part of the cotton gin. The mill occupied 10 acres and had a capacity of 25 tons of cottonseed each day. Business increased until 1925, when a drought, tornado, and hailstorm resulted in crop failure. That year, the machinery was sold, and the mill closed until 1937. (Courtesy HCCM.)

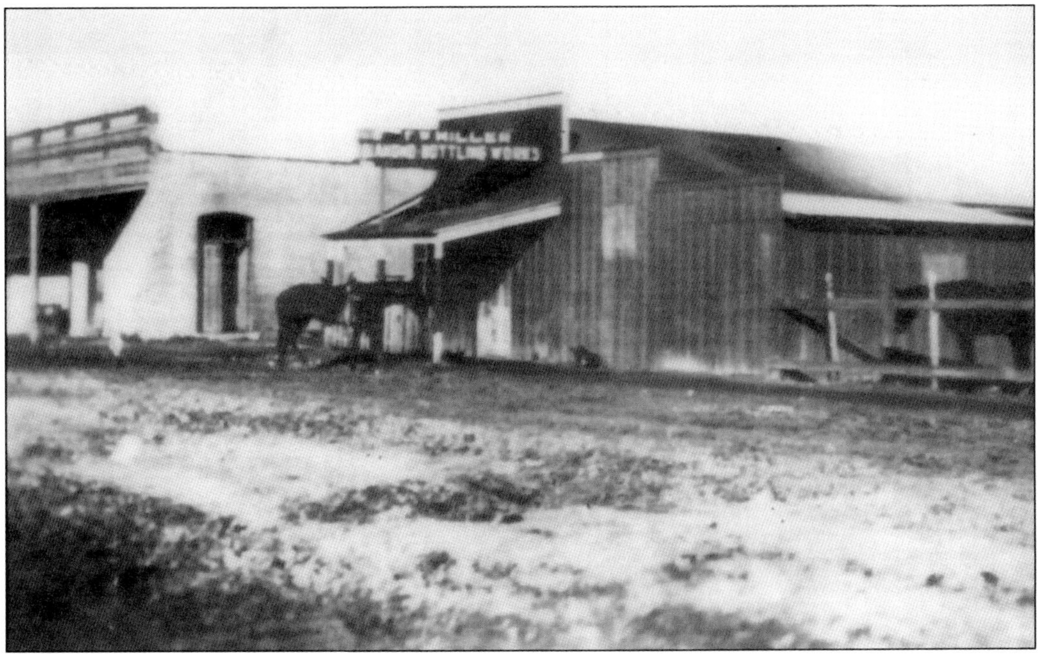

Around 1900, brothers Oscar and Fritz Miller operated a bottling company in Kyle, first called Diamond Bottling Works. At the same time, there were at least two other local bottlers—L.A. Hoffman and Borchert & Groos. (Courtesy of Jim Cullen.)

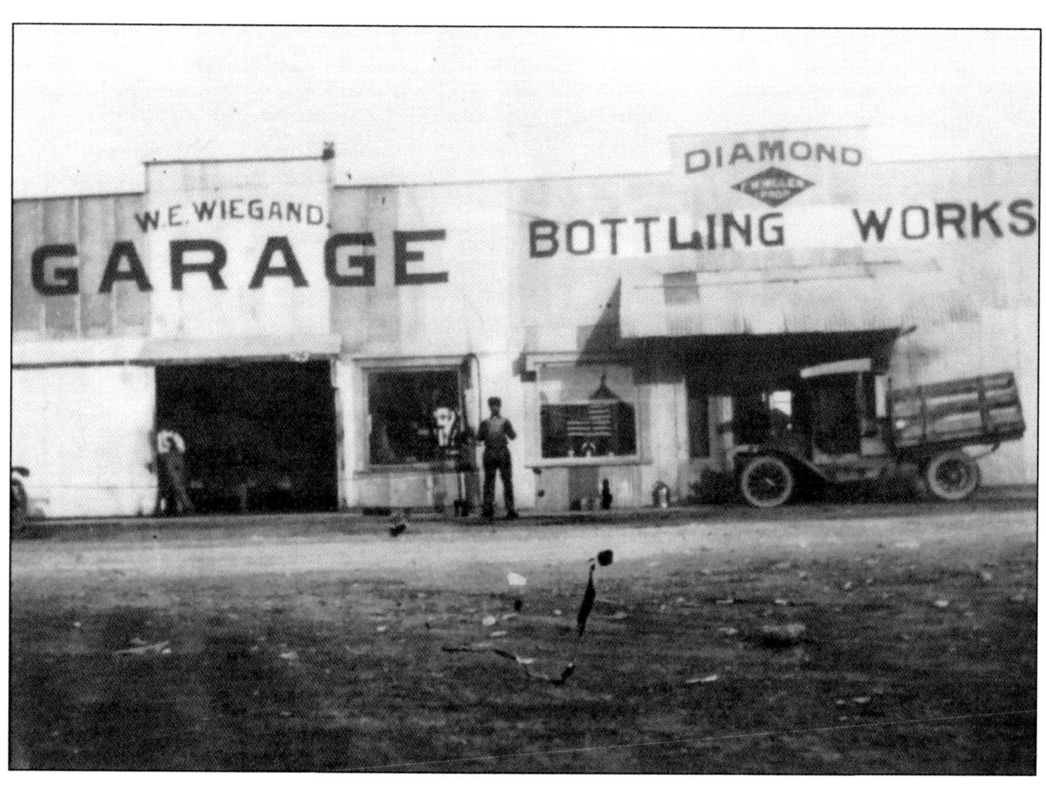

The Millers were the most successful of the Kyle bottlers and eventually became the Coca-Cola franchisees for parts of Hays, Blanco, and Caldwell Counties. The business was originally on the east side of South Main Street but later moved to the southern portion of the 200 block. (Both, courtesy of Jim Cullen.)

Diamond Bottling Works

F. W. MILLER, PROPRIETOR

BOTTLERS OF DR. PEPPER, IRON BREW, COCA-COLA, CASCADE GINGER ALE AND ALL KINDS OF SODA WATER

HEADQUARTERS FOR HAY'S CITY MINERAL WATER. FILTERED WATER AND SYRUP USED. PURITY GUARANTEED

TELEPHONE NUMBER NINETY-NINE

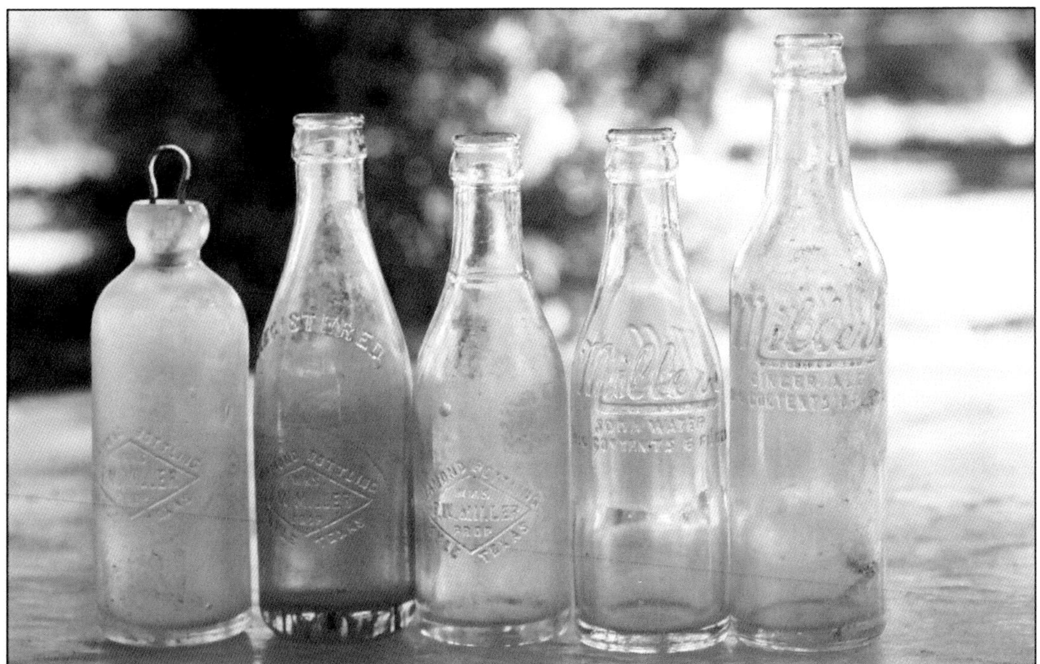

These bottles survive from the Fritz Miller bottling operation in Kyle. From left to right, they are a Diamond Bottling Works "Hutchinson" bottle from pre–bottle cap days (late 1890s–1910); Diamond Bottling Works bimal crown top, where the glass neck and lip were applied separately (first bottle to use a "crown" or bottle cap); Diamond Bottling Works bottle, made by the automatic bottling machine (1915–close of plant in 1927); Miller's Soda Water, which would have contained any of the company's many flavors; and Miller's Ginger Ale. (Courtesy of Jim Cullen.)

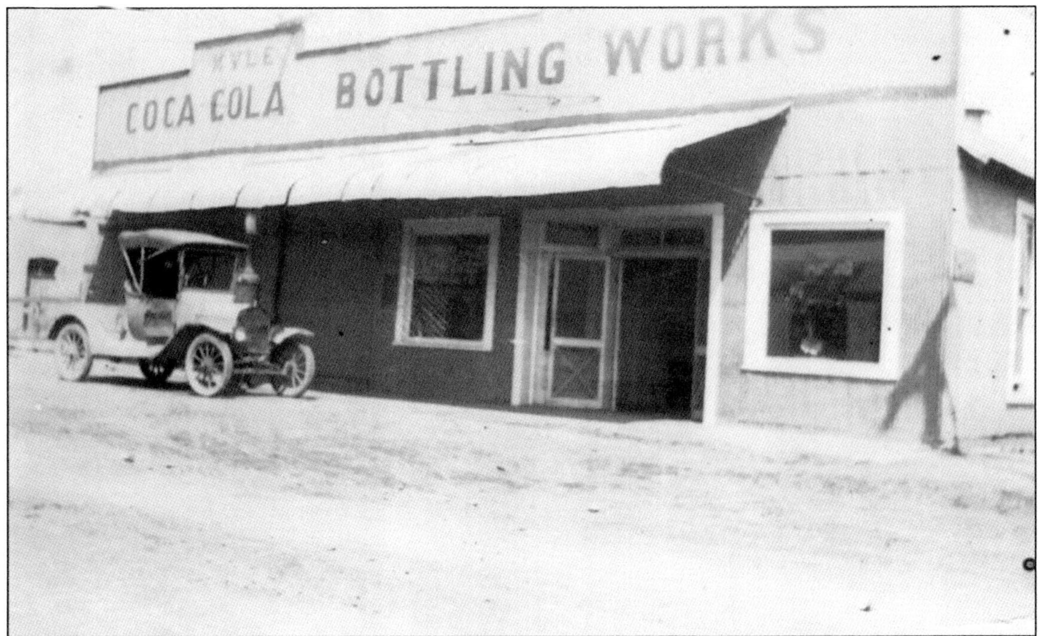

The first building for the Coca-Cola bottling plant was shared with W.E. Wiegand's garage until 1915. (Courtesy of Jim Cullen.)

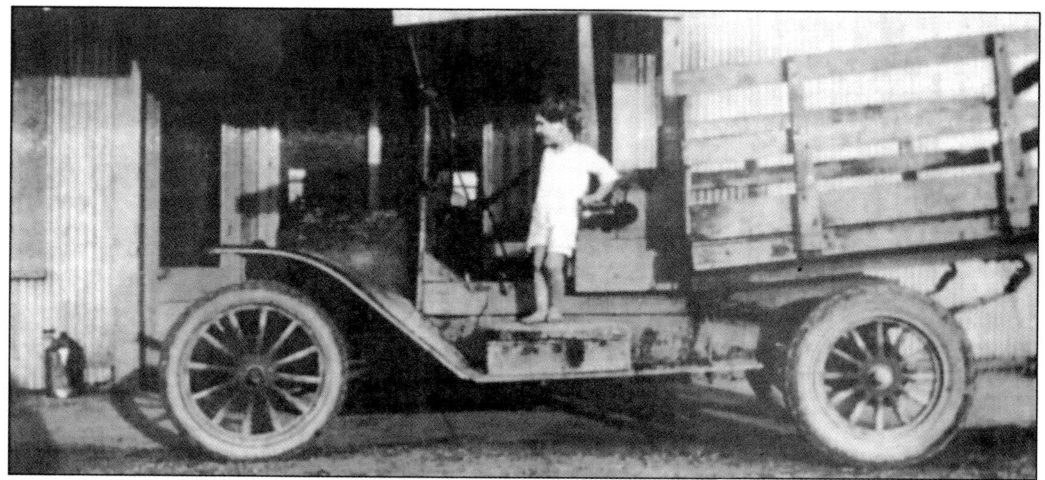

Fritz W. Miller Jr. is sitting on one of his father's delivery trucks in front of the bottling company building. Deliveries were made to Hye, Johnson City, Round Mountain, Mount Gaynor, Henly, Driftwood, and Dripping Springs. Since roads were not paved, delivery men often could not climb steep hills with fully loaded trucks. (Courtesy of Jim Cullen.)

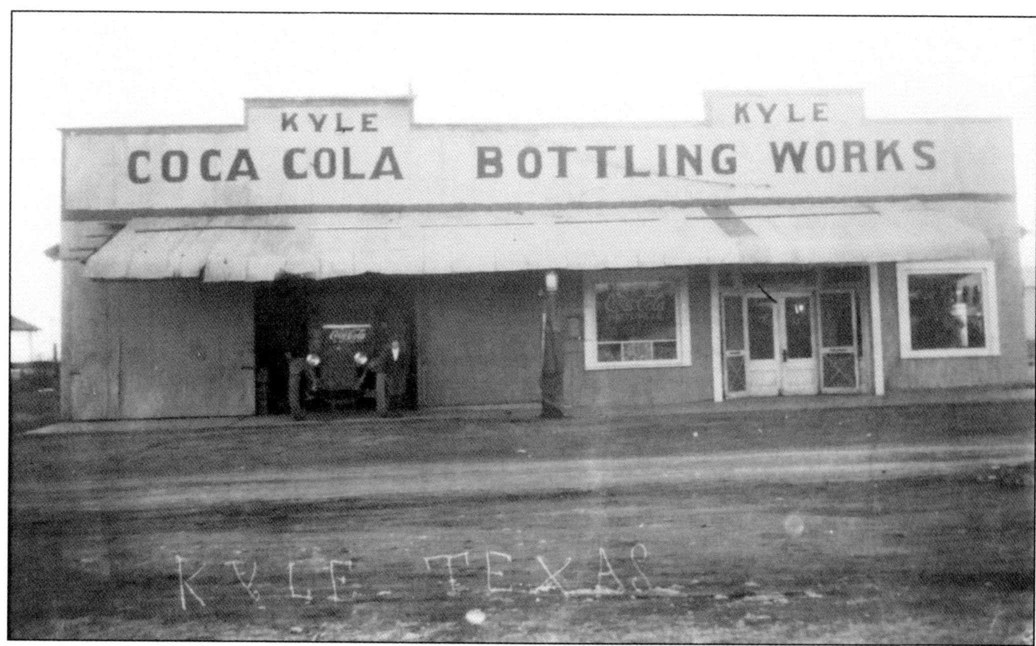

Until Miller sold his business to San Marcos Coca-Cola bottler A.C. Feltner in 1927, he made annual appearances at the Camp Ben McCulloch reunion, often bringing his bottling machine and carbonator to use water from the springs to bottle drinks for the encampment. (Courtesy of Jim Cullen.)

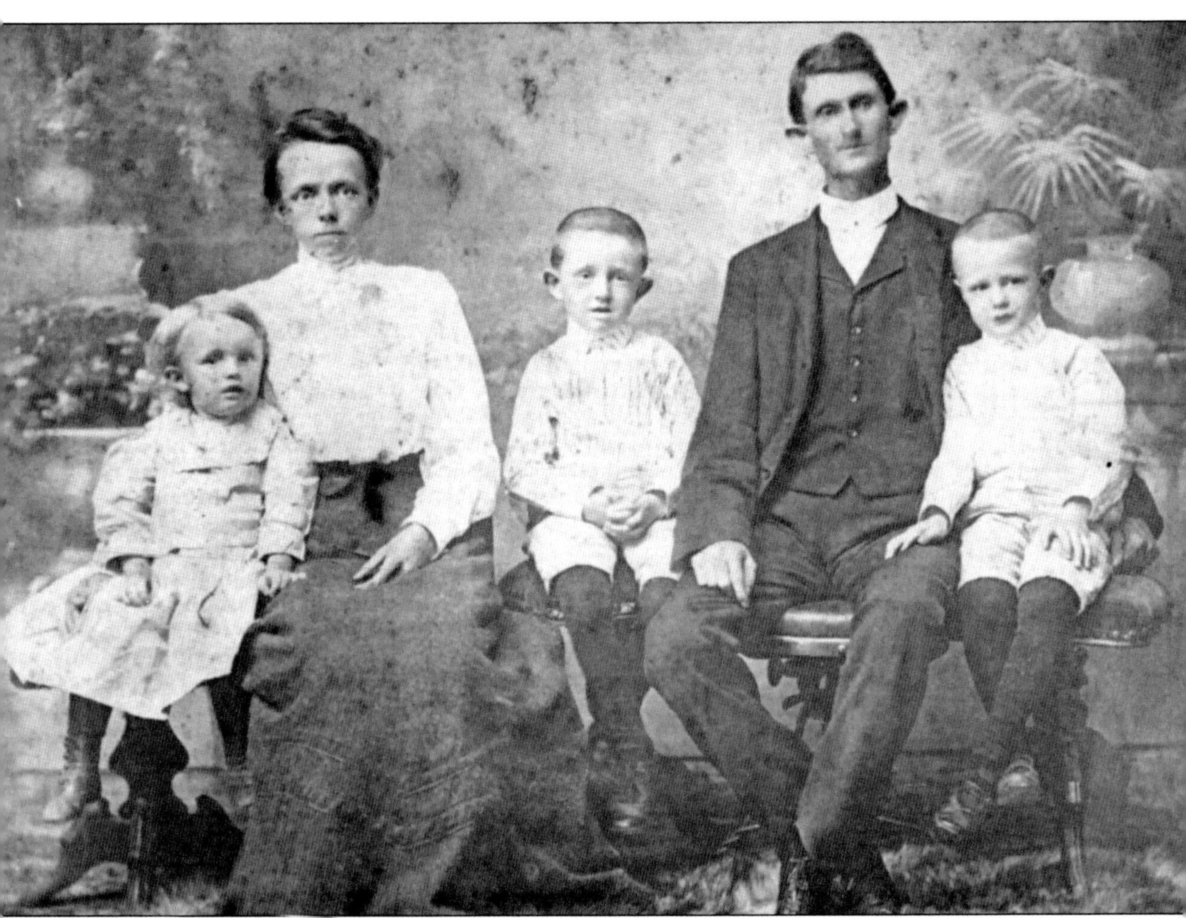

Thomas Fletcher Harwell, pictured here with his young family, founded the *Kyle News* in 1903 and printed the paper using equipment he had bought from two men who had unsuccessfully tried to establish the *Hays County News* in Kyle. This 1905 photograph includes Harwell, his wife, Annie Lee Turner Harwell, and sons Don Lee, Turner, and Tom. (Courtesy HFP.)

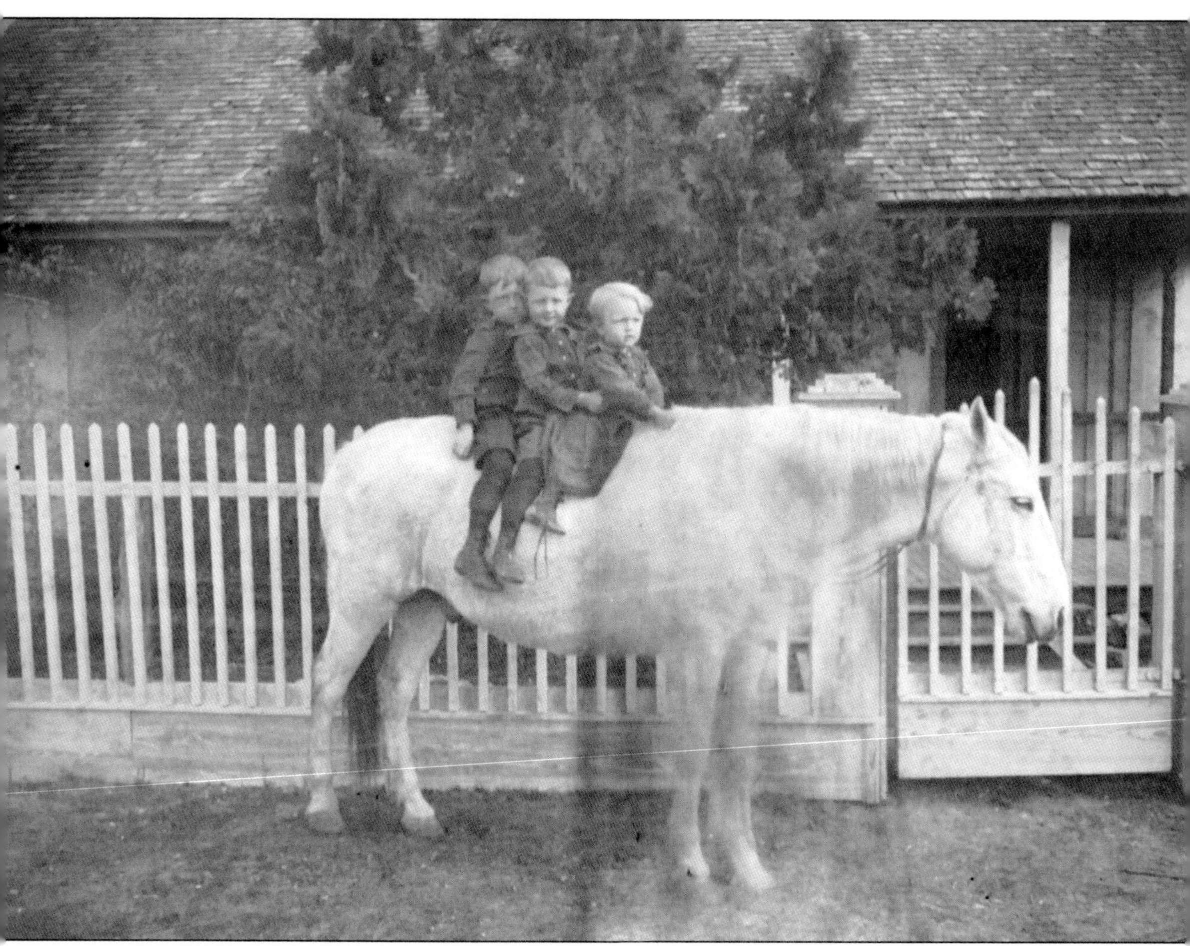

Pictured on a horse with his brothers, Young Turner Harwell grew up in the newspaper business. Younger brother Tom died of influenza in 1918 while serving in World War I, and brother Don Lee became a Methodist minister, leaving Turner to carry on the family journalistic tradition. He bought the paper from his father in 1925. Father and son wrote most of the material, sold advertisements, ran the business, and distributed the paper. The *Kyle News* was operated for 50 years by the Harwell family until it was sold in 1954 to Bob Barton and Moe Johnson. Turner continued to write for the paper for until his death 40 years later. (Courtesy HFP.)

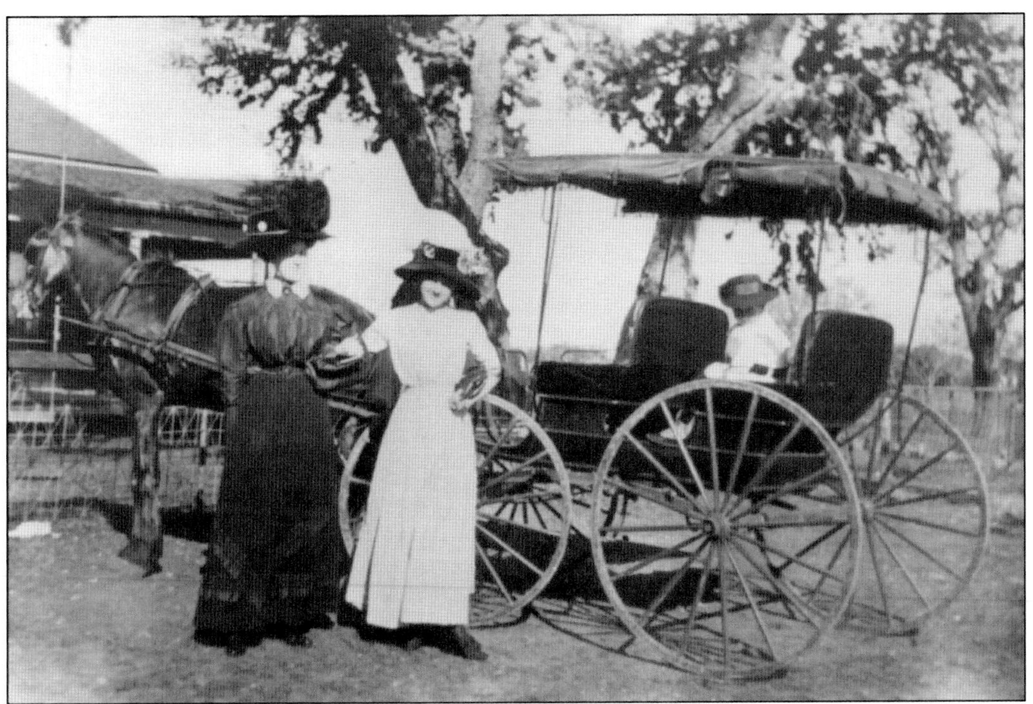

These photographs of the Michaelis Ranch show (above), from left to right, Anna Louise "Lillie" Michaelis, Corinne Huettig, and M.G. Michaelis Jr. around 1911. The photograph below features Natus Sledge, Kyle's rural mail carrier, at the Michaelis Ranch. In the carriage are, from left to right, Ada Hellmuth, Corinne Huettig, and Marguerite Hellmuth. (Both, courtesy HCCM.)

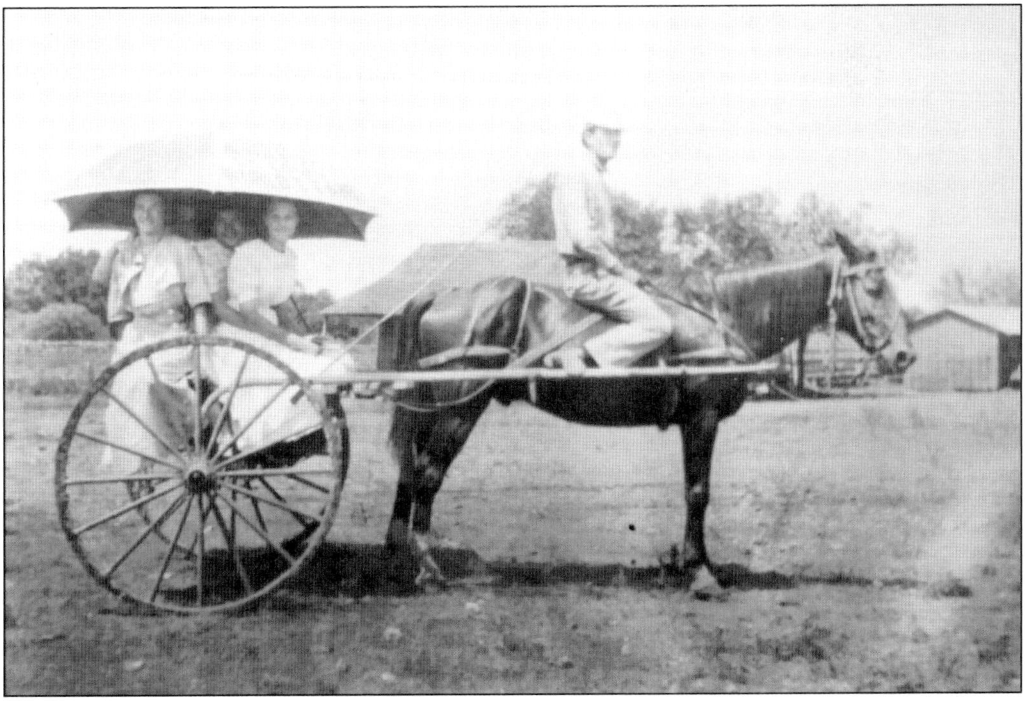

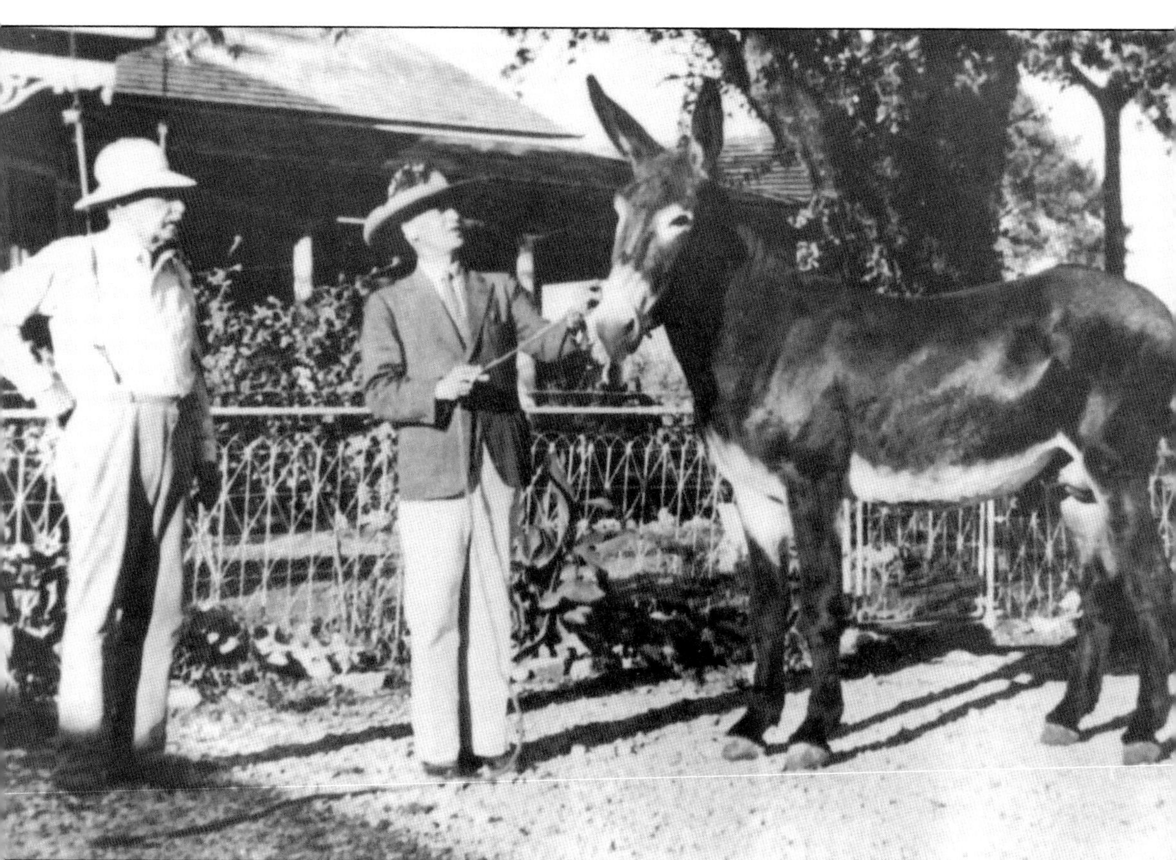

Although all kinds of businesses came to Kyle in the first few decades of its existence, the economic staple continued to be farming and ranching. One of the most famous ranches in the Kyle area is the Michaelis Ranch. In the 1890s, M.G. Michaelis Sr. began raising Shorthorn and Hereford cattle at the Kyle Ranch. His son M.G. Jr. had ranched in Mexico since 1924 and acquired two Charolais bulls, which were sent to the Kyle Ranch to breed with the Shorthorns and Herefords. The elder Michaelis also bred donkeys. In the above photograph, Michaelis and Dr. Schreuder, brother-in-law of Dr. Albert Schweitzer, trade hats after the purchase of donkeys for the Union of South Africa. (Courtesy HCCM.)

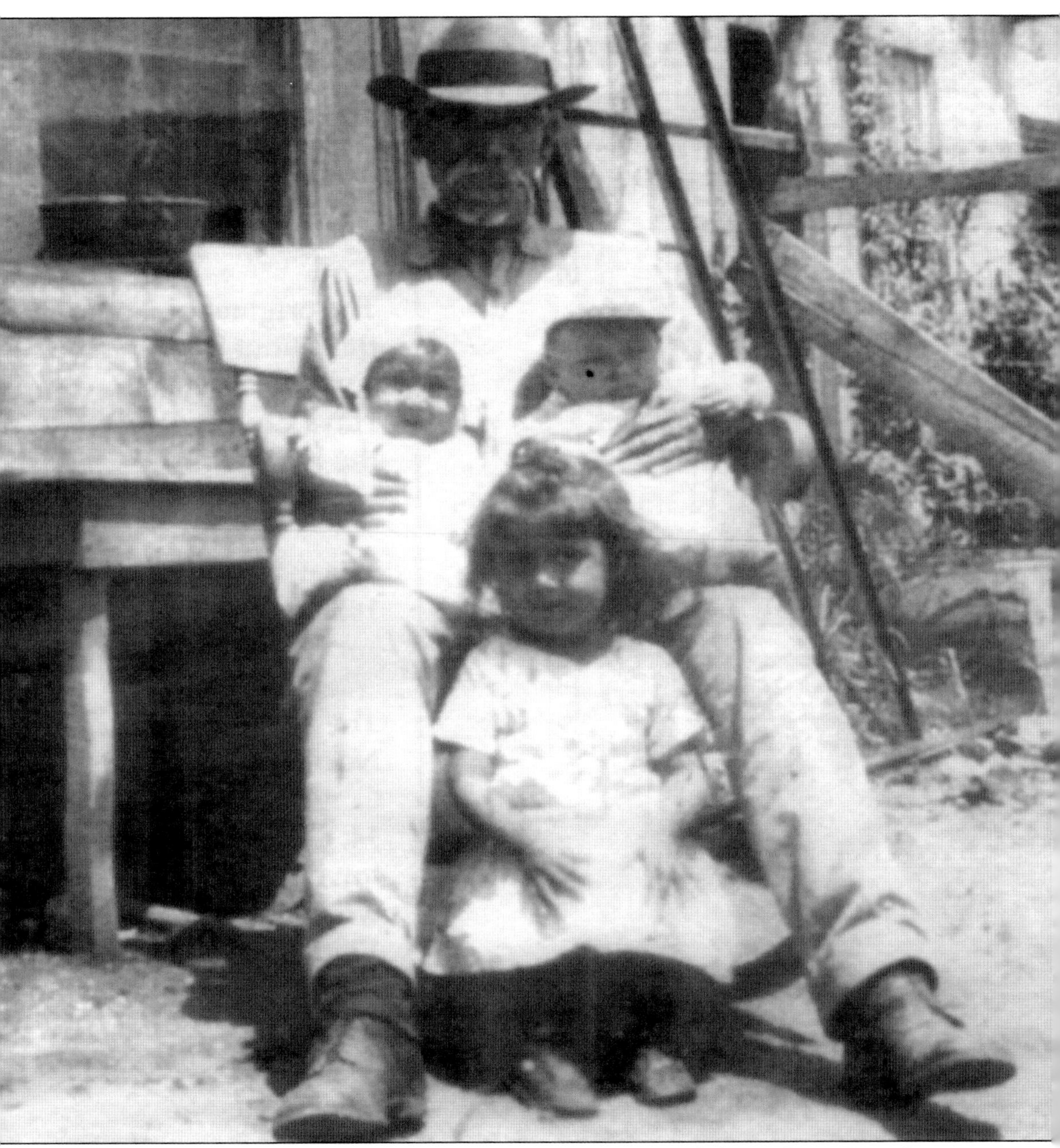

Shoemaker Agapito Ortunio Sr. sits with his grandchildren. From left to right are Juan Ortunio Jr., Toribia Ortunio, and Agapito Ortunio (son of Hilario Ortunio). Ortunio's shop was located on Miller Street near Front Street. The Ortunio family was among the first families to settle in Kyle. (Courtesy HFP.)

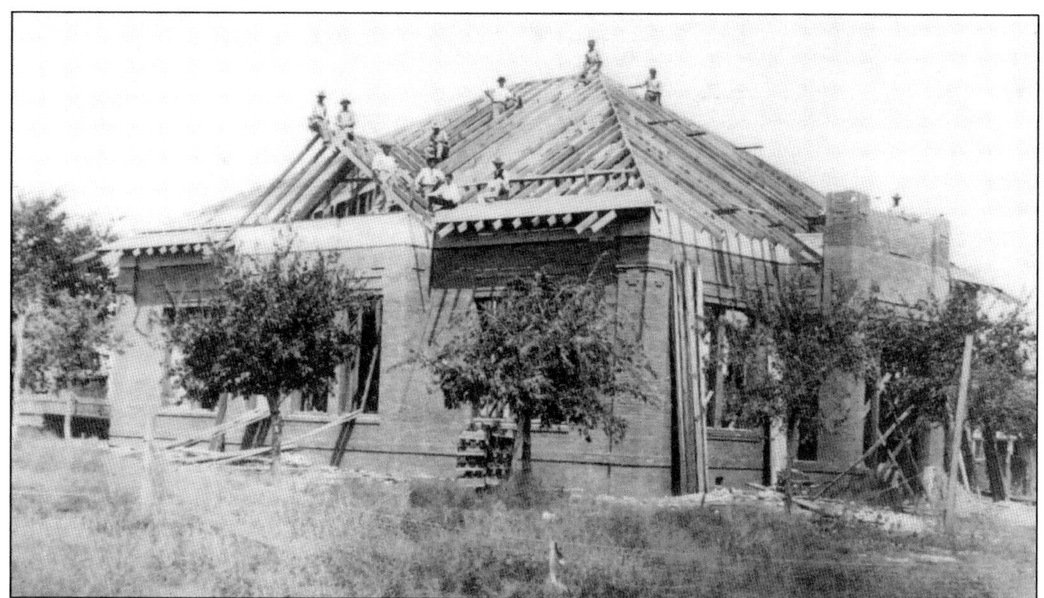

One of the first actions of the city government after Kyle was incorporated as a village in 1906 was to investigate the possibility of building a city hall. The county donated $500, and donations paid for the rest of the project. In March 1912, the council awarded a contract to Millhollon Brothers for $6,100 to construct the building. Controversy surrounded the floor of the building. One group wanted it flat so seats could be removed for dancing. Opponents (mainly Baptists and Methodists who opposed dancing) argued for a slanted floor to give the audience a better view of the stage. The slanted floor won but was replaced in a later remodeling project. Since its completion, the building has served as a community center. For many years, opening ceremonies and school graduations were held in the building, which was then configured as an auditorium. (Both, courtesy HFP.)

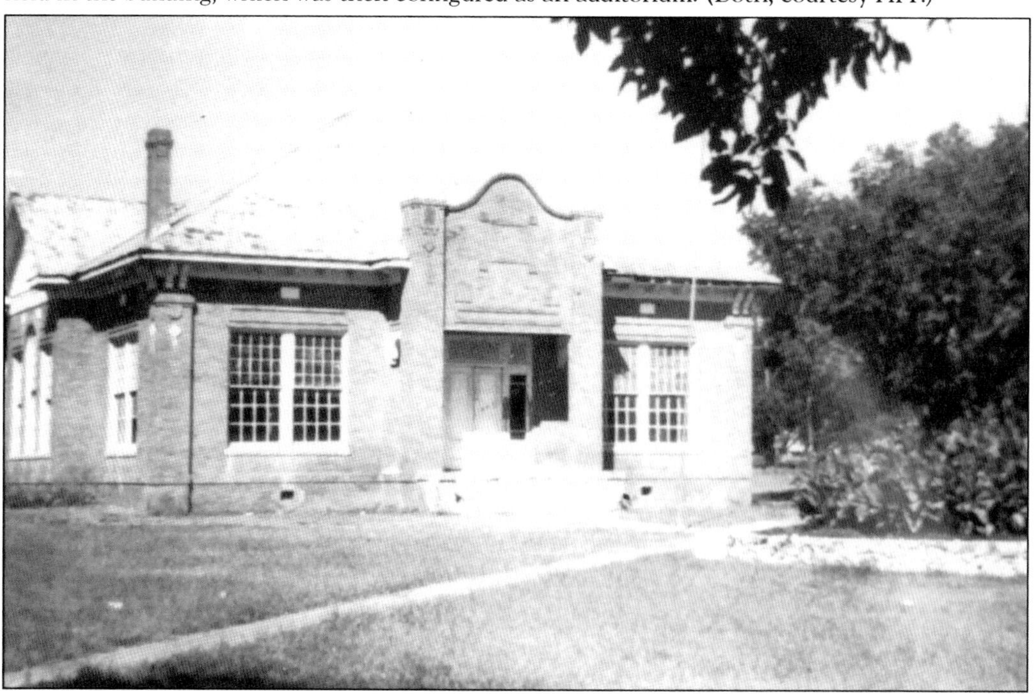

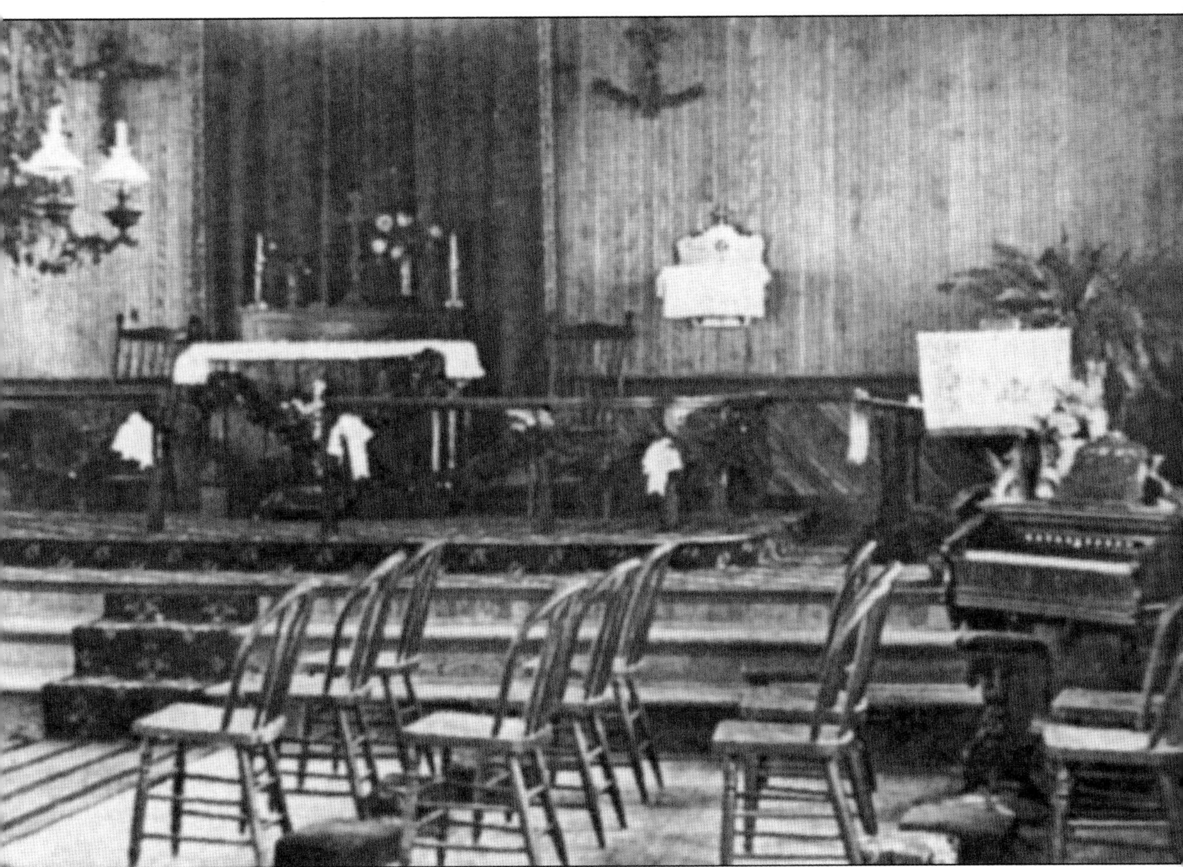

Although several churches were established in Kyle's early years, more were created in the early 1900s. In 1905, the Kyle Christian Church was formed, with 10 charter members. Since the congregation was small, they did not employ a pastor or have a building but met in city hall. In 1913, they purchased a building that had been constructed in the 1880s after being started by the Presbyterians then sold to the Episcopalians before it was completed. The Episcopal congregation was too small to continue, so they sold the building and disbanded. The Christian congregation moved the building to Center Street, a block west of the square. By 1935, membership had decreased, so the building was sold in 1944. The photograph above shows the interior of the church associated with three denominations. St. Anthony's Catholic Church was founded in 1909 by the Claretian Fathers from San Antonio. Fire destroyed the original building and all records in 1917, but the church was rebuilt in 1922. (Courtesy HCCM.)

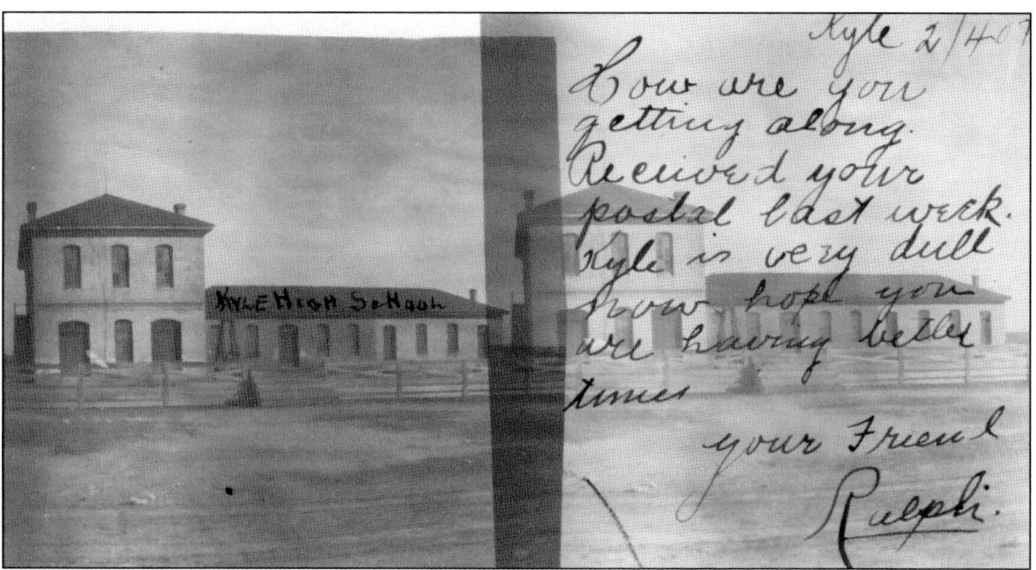

This postcard shows the first public school built in Kyle. Double printed, this card had no place for the message to be written, so the user wrote over the photograph (and described Kyle in 1907 as "very dull"). The structure shown here was constructed around 1890 and was used until 1910, when it was torn down to make room for a larger and more modern school building. (Courtesy of Robert Frizzell.)

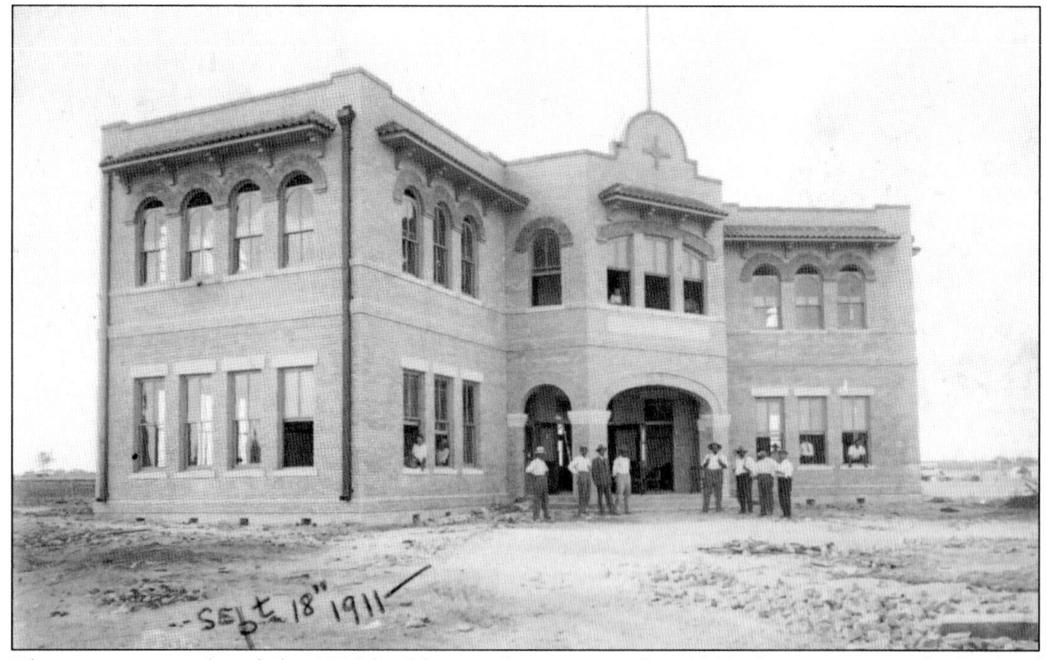

This structure replaced the 1890 building and was opened in 1911. A notation on the back of this photograph identifies the man in the white panama hat as R.J. Sledge Sr., which is not likely, since Colonel Sledge died in 1900; however, it could be R.J. Sledge Jr. The man with both hands on his suspenders is identified as Will Stevenson and the man with one hand on his suspenders as Toalson. This structure was used until 1938, when it was torn down and its materials sold to help pay for the new building. (Courtesy of the Word family.)

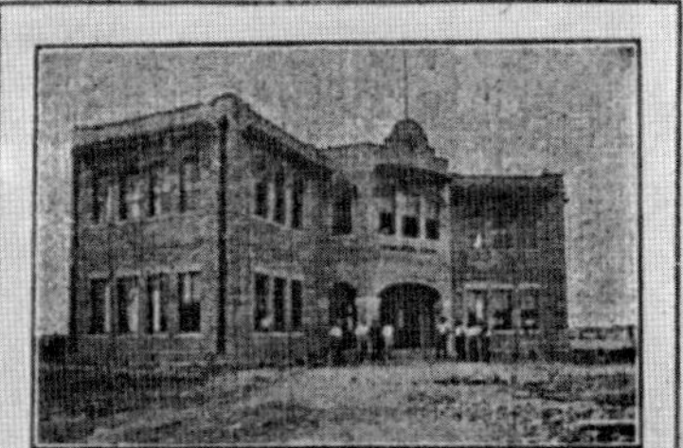

SCHOOL BOARD: E. C. WOO[illegible] Pres. J. W. TOMPKINS, Sec. CHARLES THIELE

KYLE PUBLIC SCHOOL

FACULTY

HENRY R. MOORE, Principal

MISS BELLE SCHMIDT MISS MAGGIE GROOS MRS. H. R. MOORE

MRS. J. B. STEPHENSON, Piano MRS. J. W. CHILDS, Voice MRS. EUGENE B. LUDER, Expression

Kyle, Texas

January 21st.

Mr.. Mill C.[illegible]ngold.

Chicago Ill.

Dera Sir;-I have a letter from you ,containing photo, and some splendid testiminals. In answer to a search by me for a teacher in the subject of Agriculture and other subjects.

Your recommendations seem quite effecient, ~~and~~ in every thing except agriculture , which you failed to say how ~~k~~ long you had been studying. and whether or not you had any special preperations in that line.

In way of explanation I will say that under the new state law in Texas we are allowed a special appropriation for our school if we will secure a teacher of special training in agriculture and fulfill a few other requirements, and sta~~r~~t up a dept. of agriculture in our school.

Now we habve met the requiremetnt' in every thiing except the teacher and are anxious for a teacher for that department, who has had at least two years expeni training in agriculture. So if you have had two years experience in agriculture, and have a certificate in that subject please answer this by telegram. Yours truly Henry R. Moore.Prinl

Have had fully two years special training
also taught two years agriculture
accredited on life Certificate
~~answer by telegram~~
Telegram decision at once

This undated letter is a response from the principal at Kyle High School to an inquiry from a man in Chicago seeking a job as an agriculture teacher. The applicant's handwritten response indicates that he has the required experience and certification for the position. (Courtesy of Jim Cullen.)

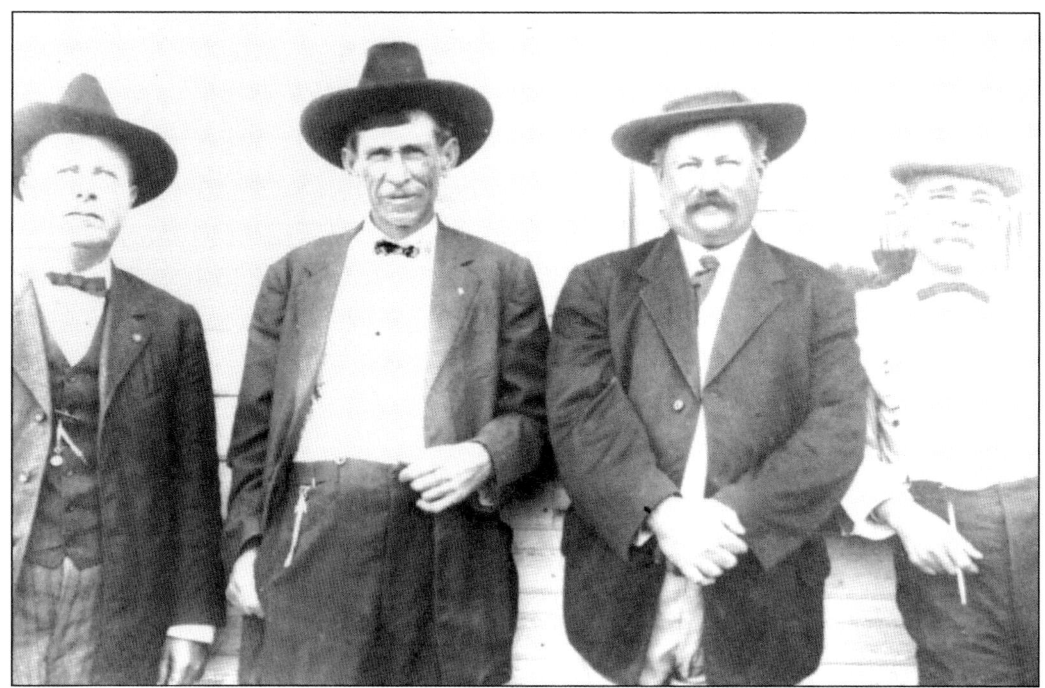

School board members whose names appear on the letterhead on the previous page are pictured here. From left to right are M.W. Rogers, Hays County School Board; E.C. Woods; Charles Thiele; and J.W. Tompkins, Kyle School Board. (Courtesy HCCM.)

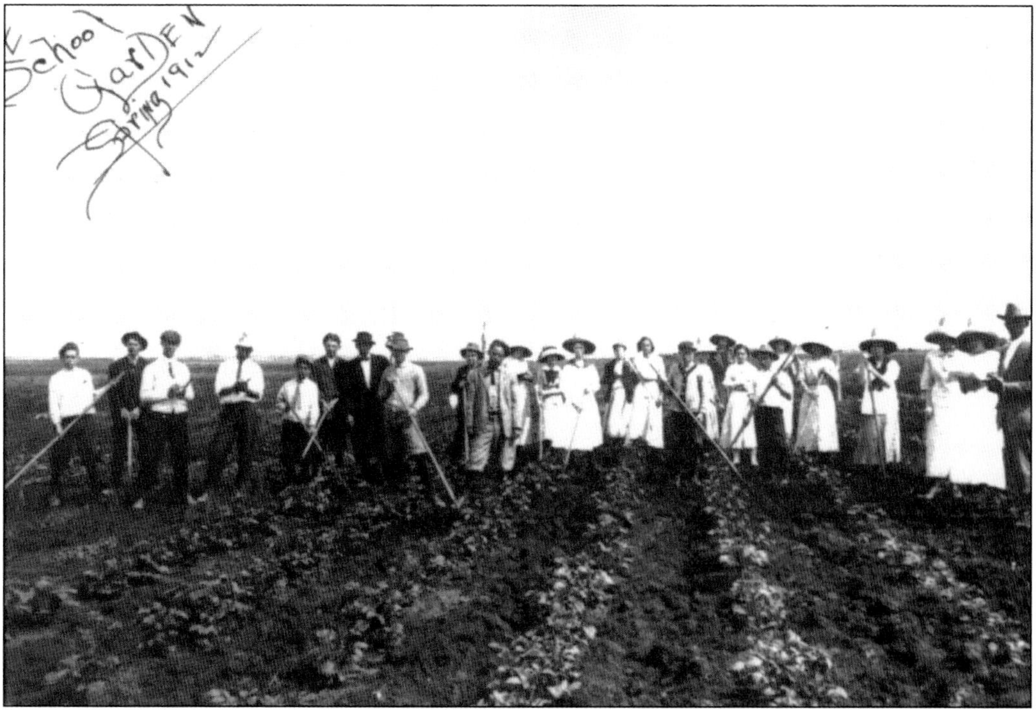

Although this photograph is labeled "School Garden, Spring 1912," other sources indicate that it is in fact the agriculture class from the high school working fields east of Kyle. (Courtesy HCCM.)

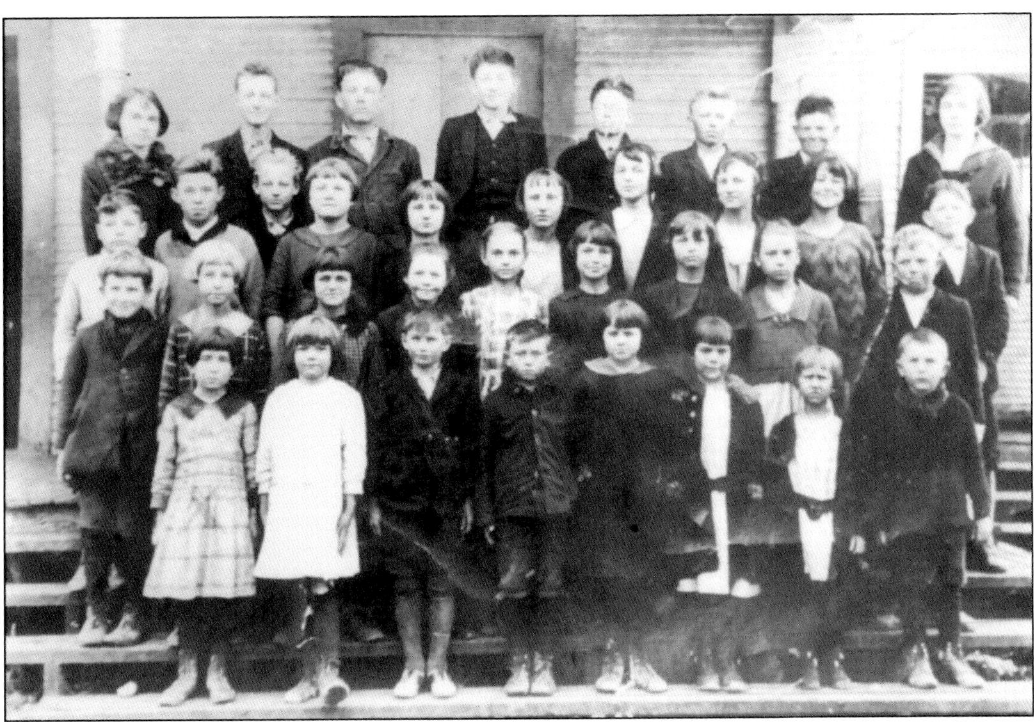

Hemphill School opened in 1891 to serve primarily the children of the German immigrant families who lived around the Pecan Springs area east of Kyle. Most children spoke German everywhere but in the classroom. A new building was constructed in 1920 and offered classes for children through nine grades. Students wanting to go to high school attended school in Kyle. The class pictured is from the 1924–1925 school year. (Courtesy HFP.)

Parents or Guardians Please Read

On or before the first Wednesday of each school month this report will be filled out by the teacher and sent to you for inspection. If not presented at the proper time, kindly notify the teacher.

If a pupil receives C or D on any subject, it should be made a matter of immediate inquiry. Possibly it is to be attributed to lack of study, to too many outside engagements, to irregularities in attendance, or to some cause which may be removed or corrected.

Special attention is called to the serious consequences of **Irregular Attendance.** The loss of even a portion of a daily session often proves to be a serious interruption to progress, and tends to produce a lack of interest in the school work. Excuses showing good cause for the absence or tardiness should always be sent promptly to the teacher on the return of a child to school. Neglect of this may cause the child to be sent back home for the excuse.

We suggest that you talk over this report with your child each time it is received, and if it has any peculiar needs which are indicated to you by the marks on this card, that you confer with the teacher or superintendent regarding it.

In making out these reports and criticisms the teacher has no other motives than to benefit the pupil, and give parents accurate information as to the progress of their children; and parents are urged to co-operate in every way with the teacher, that each month might show improvement.

Parents will please examine carefully each month's report, and sign name at bottom of page two, and return to teacher.

Frieda E. Hofheinz
Principal or Superintendent.

Hemphill
NAME OF SCHOOL

Rte 3 Kyle
POSTOFFICE

1922-1923
TERM

Frieda E. Hofheinz
PRINCIPAL OR SUPERINTENDENT

NAME OF PUPIL

DEPARTMENT 8th GRADE

TEACHER

IMPORTANT TO PARENTS

Reports are sent out at the end of each month. Please note progress and standing of your children, commending or reproving accordingly.

See that lessons are prepared at home. Earnest co-operation on the part of parents will greatly aid the work of the teacher.

EXPLANATION OF MARKS

A—90-100 Excellent. C—70-80 Passable.
B—80-90 Satisfactory. D—Less-70 Unsatisfactory.

Every unexcused absence deducts 5% from attendance and 1% from each recitation of that day.

An average of 70 is required, both for maintaining a grade and for promotion at end of Term.

Certificate of Promotion

(TO BE FILLED OUT AT END OF TERM)

The above named pupil having maintained the average of 88 is hereby promoted to the Ninth Grade for next Term.

Frieda E. Hofheinz
SUPT. OR PRIN.

TEACHER

Date May 15/1923

This report card from the Hemphill School indicates the high expectations for students and their school participation. (Author's collection.)

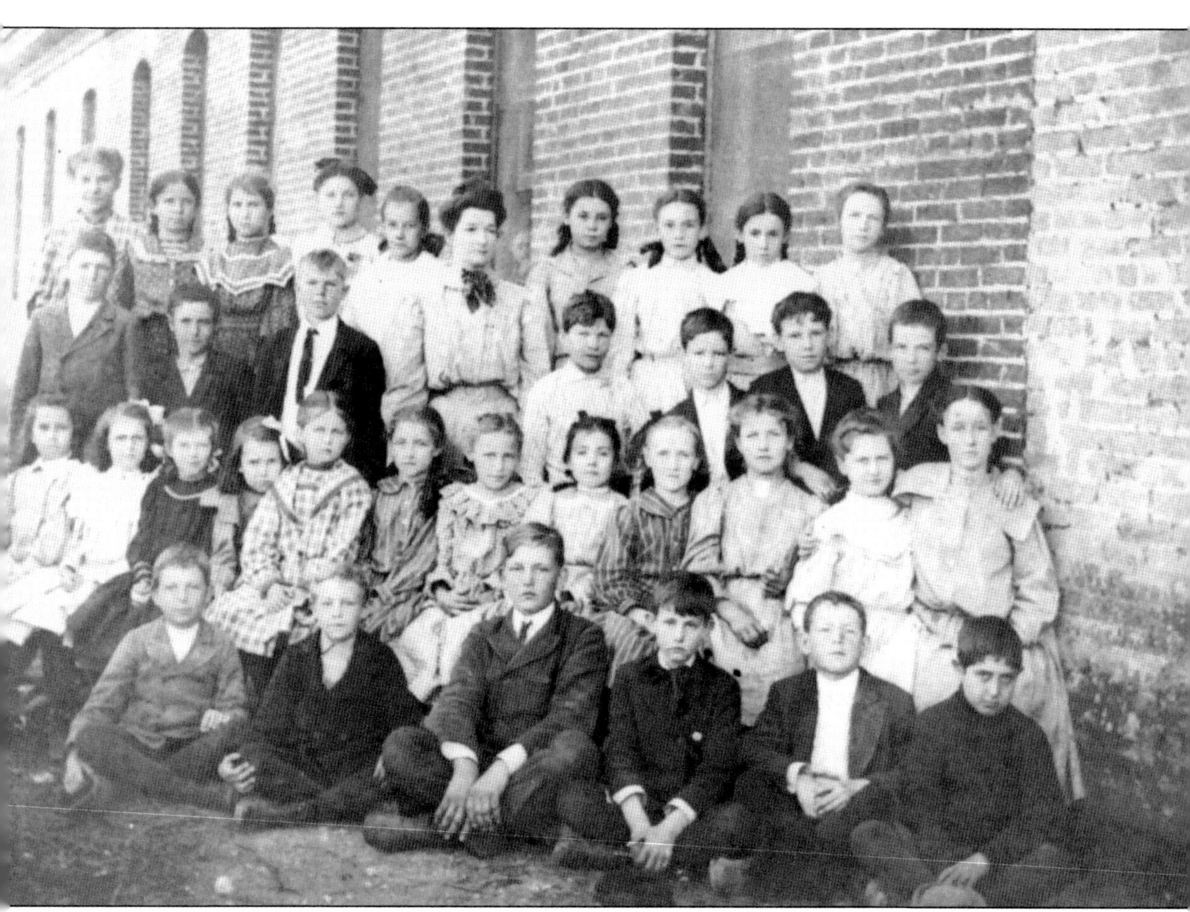

Belle Schmidt had a long career as an educator in Hays County, including serving as the county school superintendent for Hays County in the 1930s. She is pictured here with her class in the early 1900s. (Courtesy HCCM.)

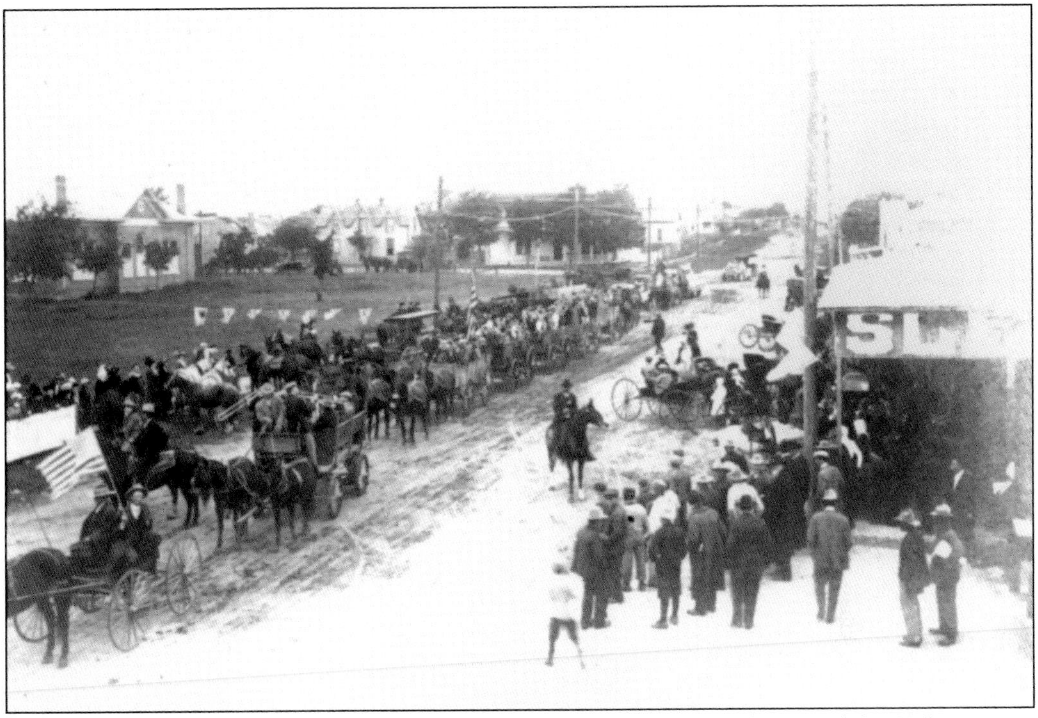

Billy Allen and T.F. Harwell led one of Kyle's many parades in the early part of the 20th century. The city hall is on the square to the left. (Courtesy HCCM.)

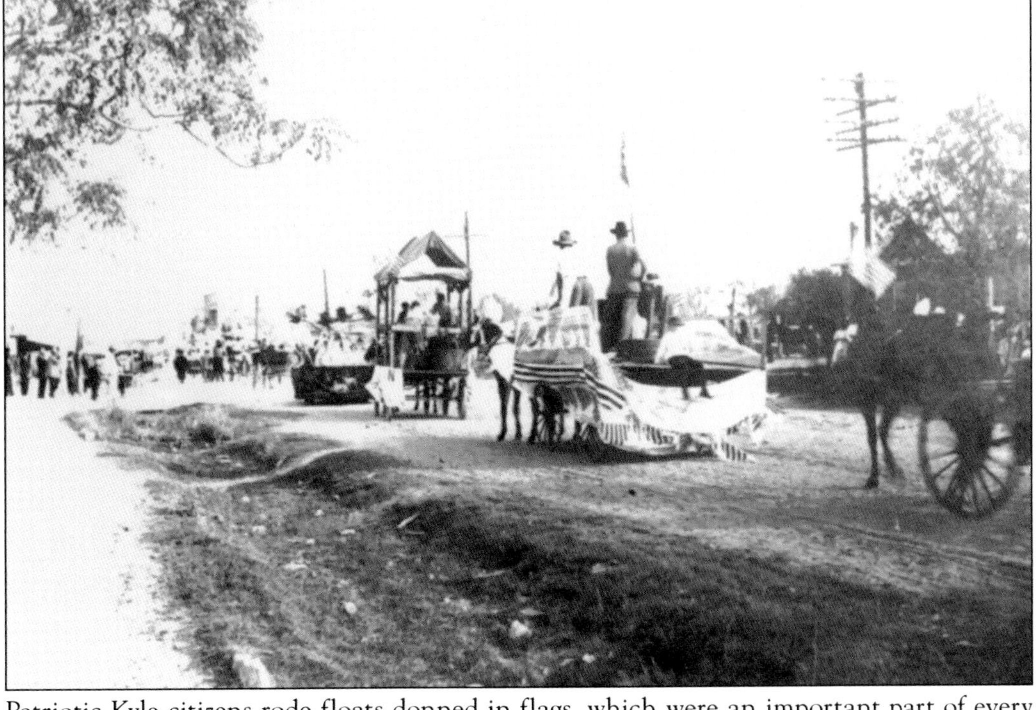

Patriotic Kyle citizens rode floats donned in flags, which were an important part of every parade. (Courtesy HCCM.)

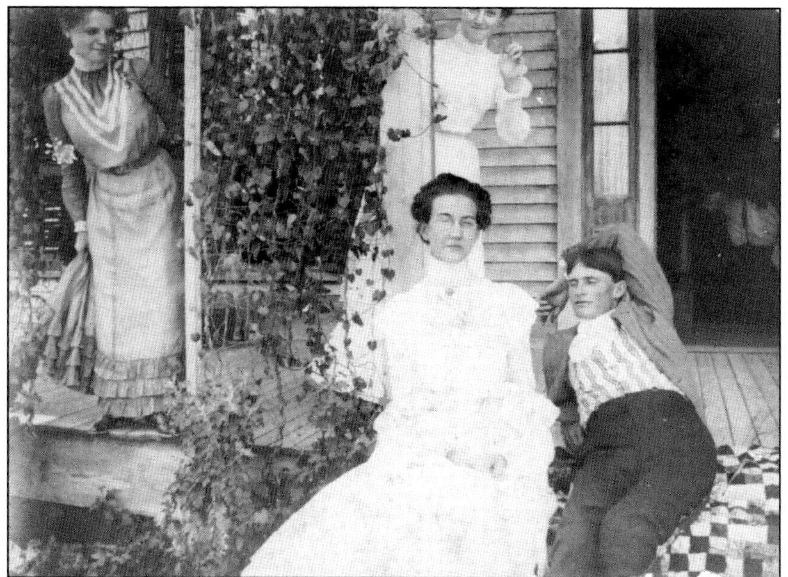

People in early 1900s Kyle found entertainment in a variety of ways. These people seemed to be posing for a photographer for fun. (Courtesy of the Word family.)

No. 38277

The Jockey Club

CERTIFICATE OF FOAL REGISTRATION

1903.

This is to certify that the Bay Filly named "All Wool" by Gallantry out of Remnant foaled May 5th 1903 is duly registered by The Jockey Club.

Marks: Star

Secretary.

Registrar.

Issued to O.G. Parke, Kyle Texas

New York Nov 2nd 1903

CERTIFICATE TO BE PRESERVED AND TRANSFERRED TO THE PURCHASER IF THIS HORSE IS SOLD.— RECORD TRANSFER ON REVERSE SIDE.

Other Kyle residents found excitement in horse racing. The O.G. Parke family managed a track on their property and built stables where they bred and trained race horses. They also had a polo track closer to town. This registration with the Jockey Club in New York indicates that Parke's involvement in the racing business extended beyond his track in Kyle. (Courtesy HCCM.)

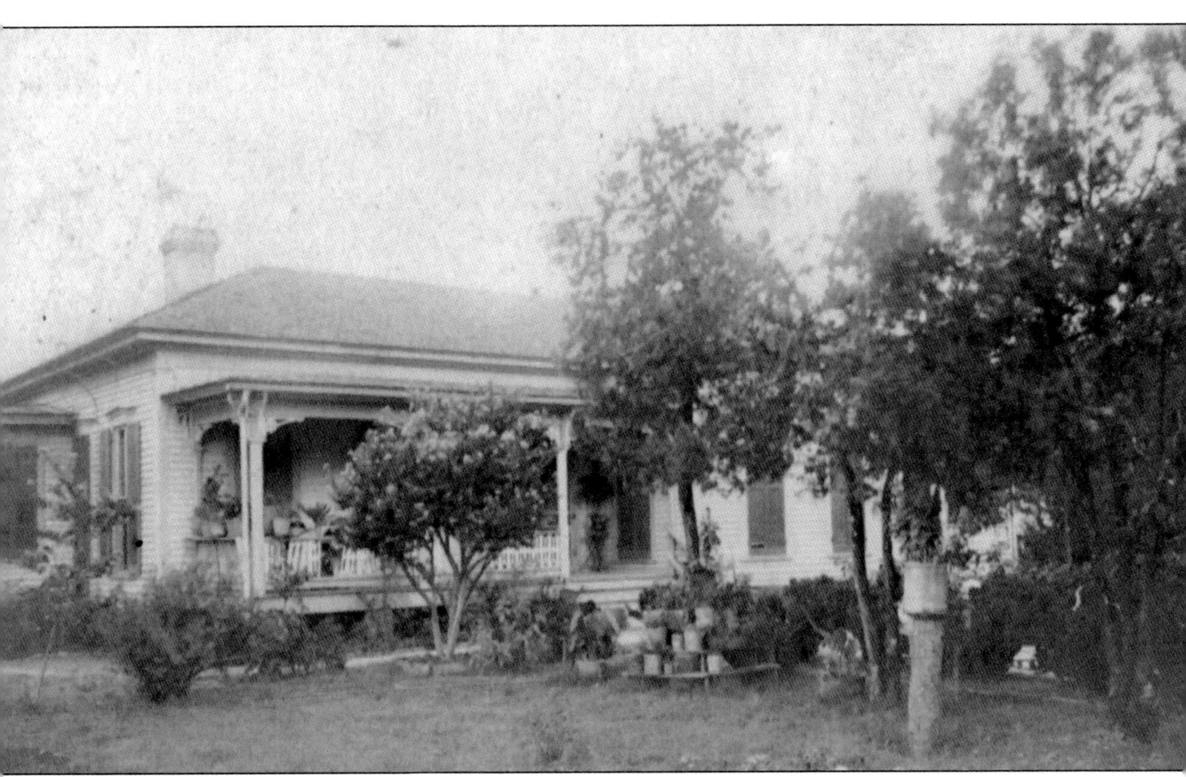

Although this photograph was labeled "Calk House," another source identified the home as that of Charles Thiele, and still others name it the Sanders House. This home has been converted into commercial office space today. (Courtesy of the Word family.)

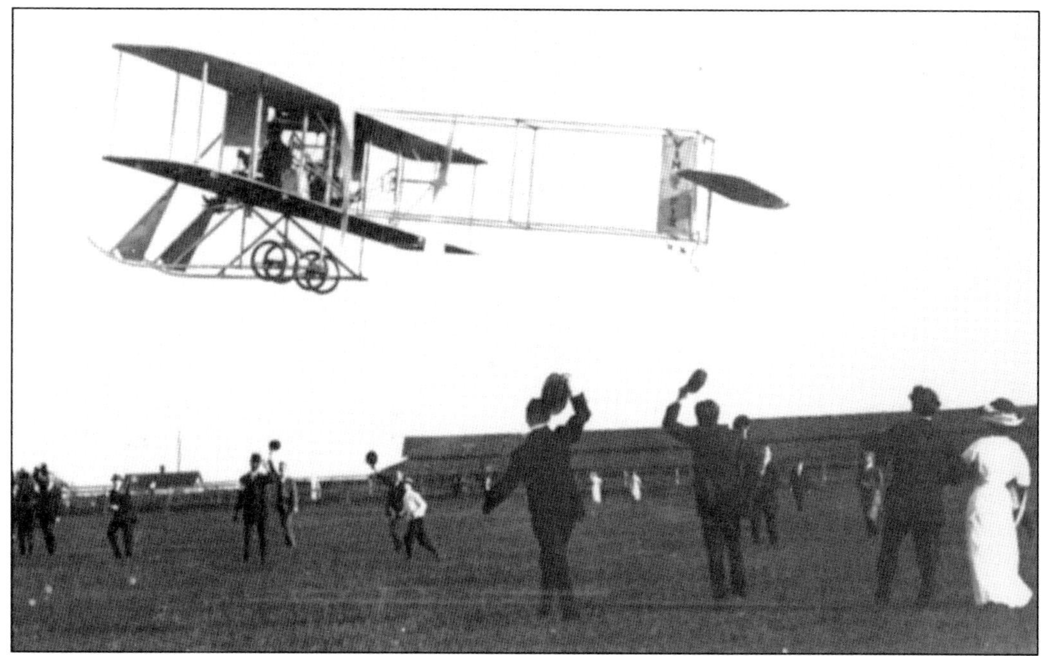

The big excitement in Kyle in the early 20th century was the landing of the Vin Fiz airplane as a part of its cross-country flight in October 1911. The plane, piloted by Cal Rogers, was flying from New York to San Antonio and then to the West Coast to promote the Vin Fiz grape drink. (Courtesy HFP.)

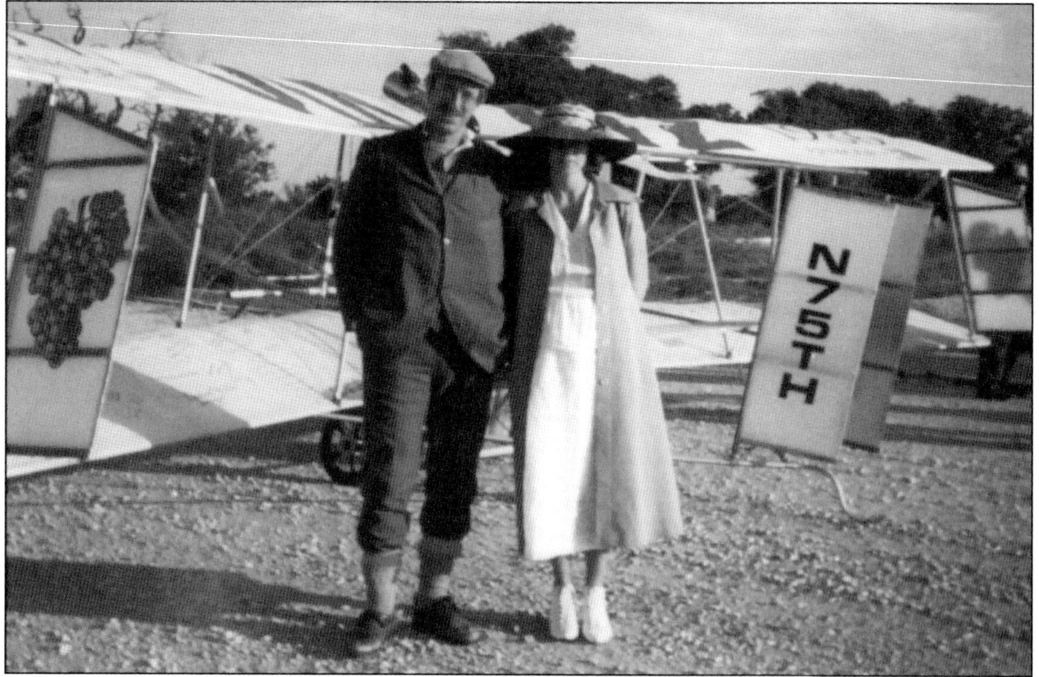

A reenactment of the Vin Fiz landing in Kyle was held on the 75th anniversary of the event in October 1986. Pictured in period clothing in front of the replica plane are Jim Lloyd and Mrs. Lloyd. (Courtesy of Blanche Richmond.)

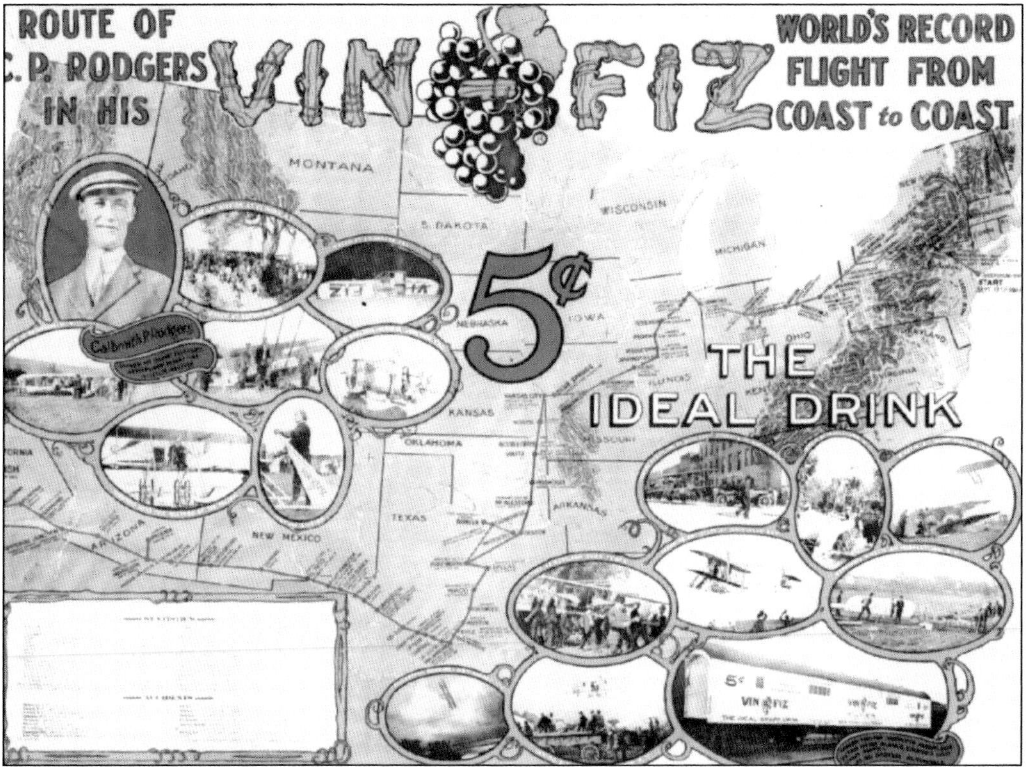

This poster traces the route of the plane across the country. Sadly, Rogers was killed in a crash not long after he reached California. (Courtesy HFP.)

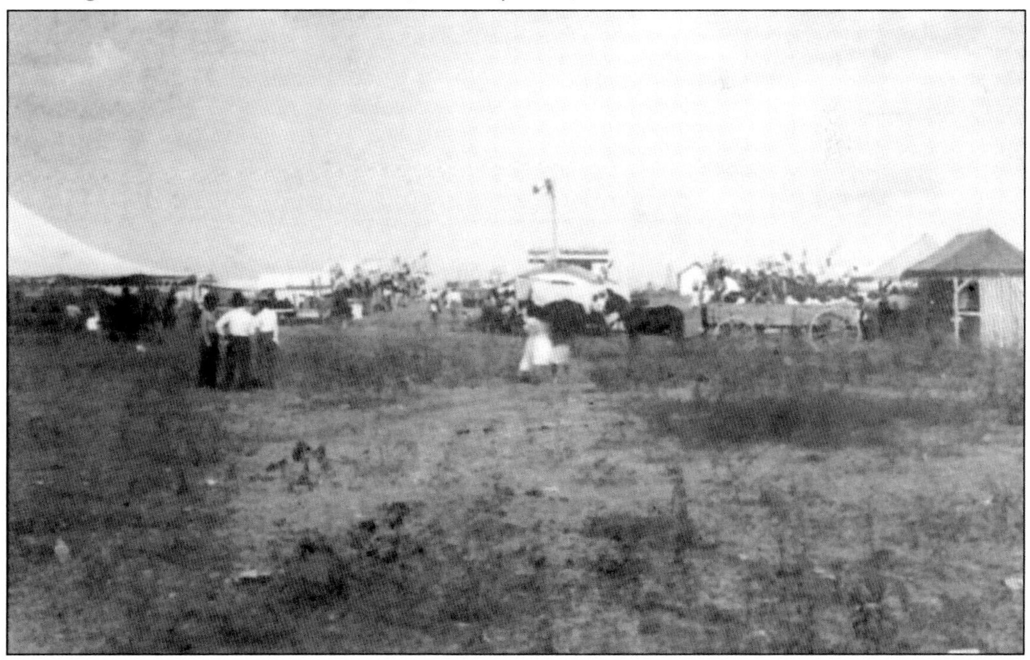

This view of a festival in City Park shows that the people in Kyle had opportunities to enjoy themselves in the town. (Courtesy HFP.)

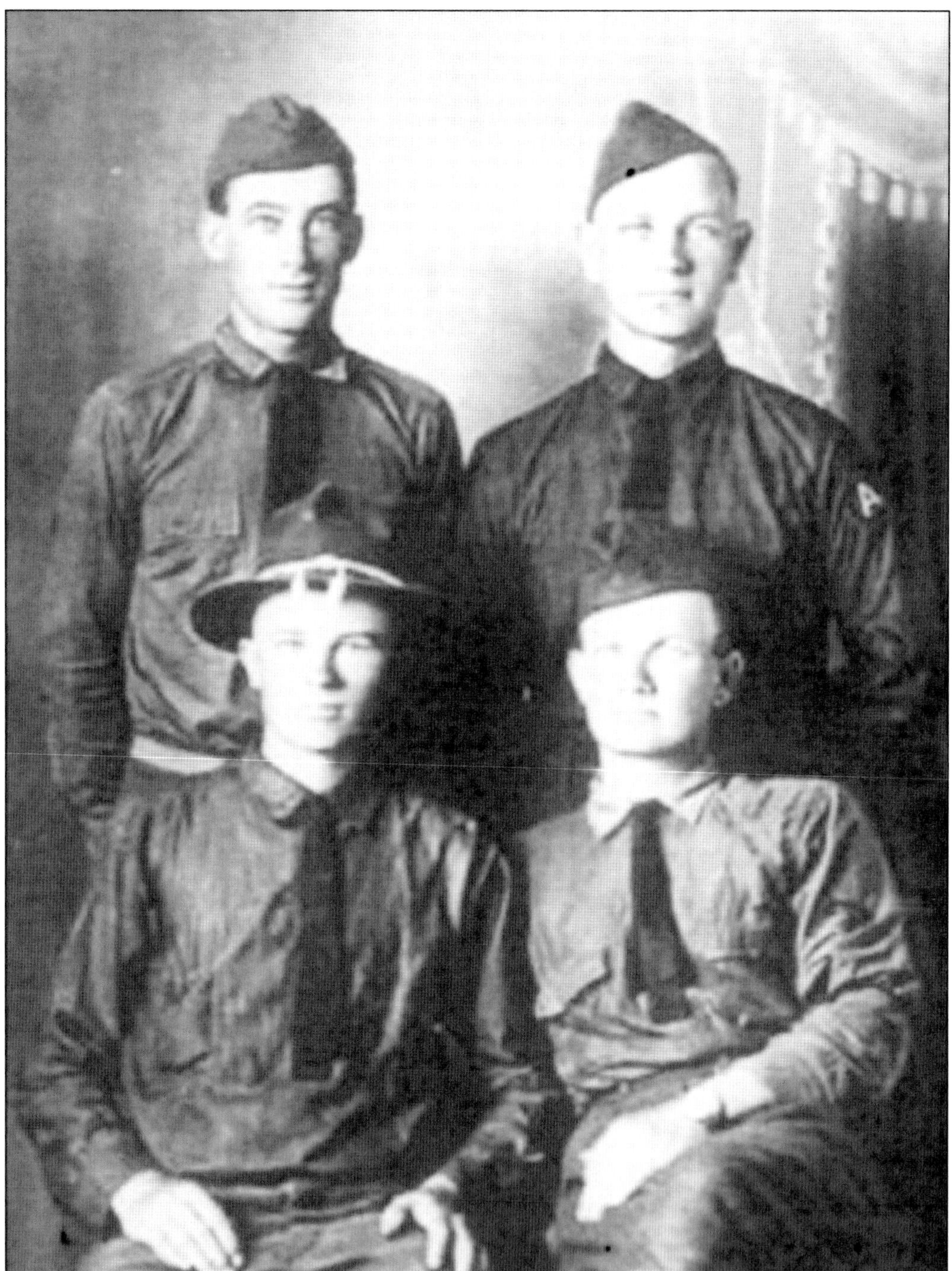

Certainly, the most significant national event of the first three decades of the 20th century was World War I. Several young men from Kyle served in the war, including these men from the German Baptist Church who went to war against the homeland of their ancestors and saw their parents' native language banned from church. From left to right are (first row) Arthur Schmeltekopf and William Wiegand; (second row) Willie Schmeltekopf and Walter Hill. (Courtesy IBC.)

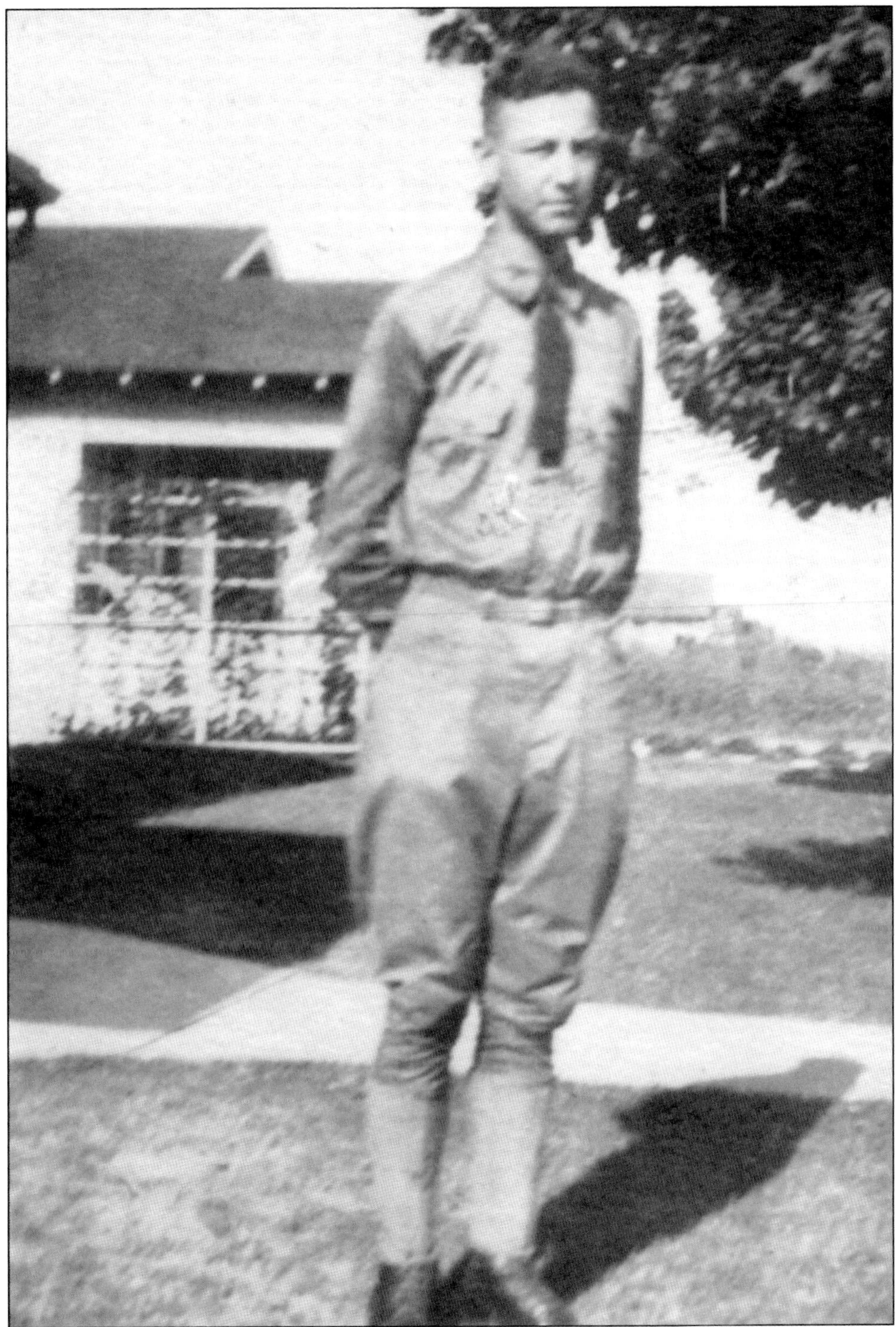

In 1926, Lex Word, a veteran of World War I, founded the Bon Ton store in Kyle. Son of Mamie Sledge Word and William Alexander Word, Lex was born in Kyle in 1896. Sadly, his father died of blood poisoning before he was born. Here, Lex is pictured in his corps of cadets uniform at Texas A&M. (Courtesy of the Word family.)

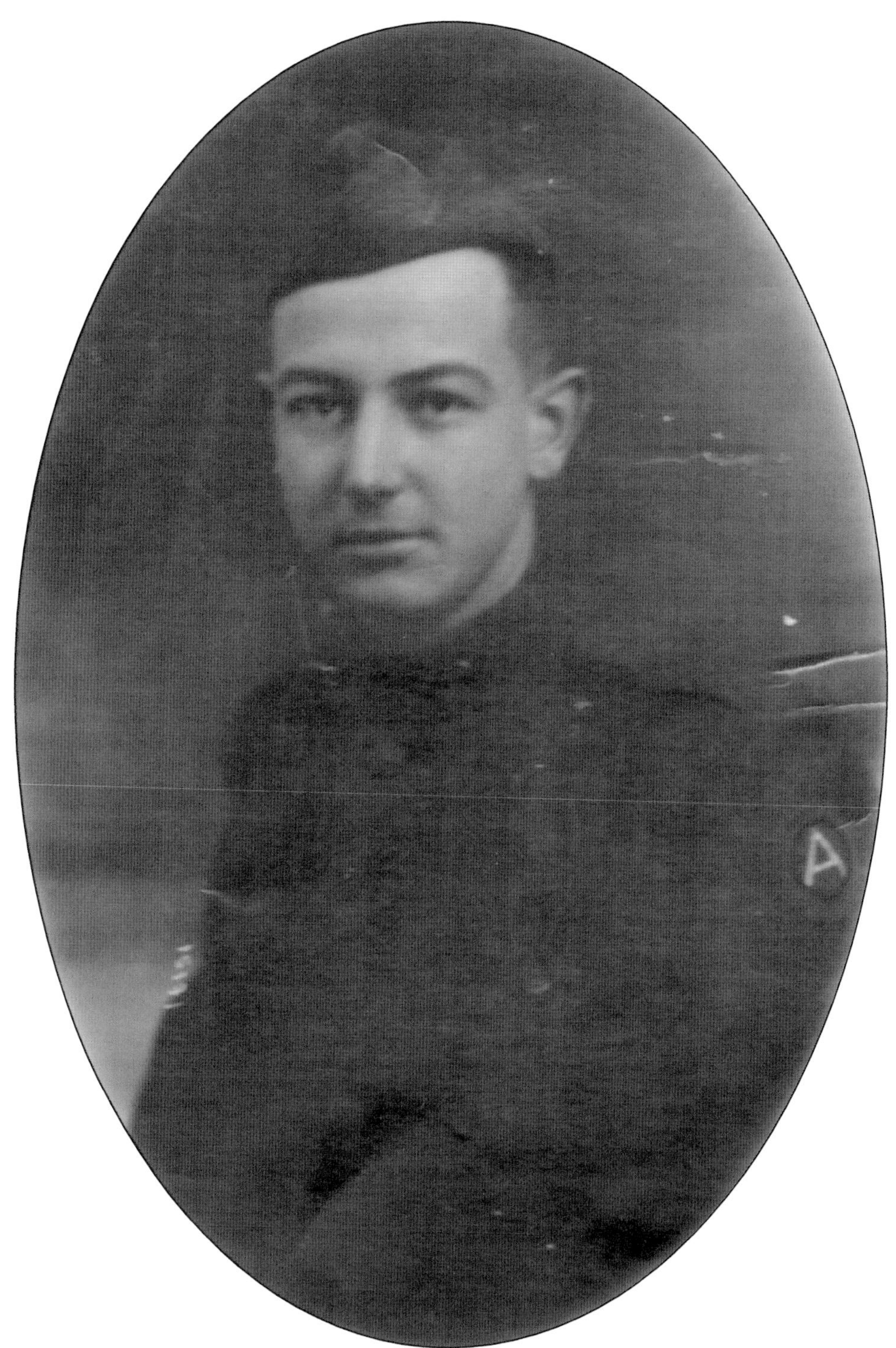

In addition to the Bon Ton, Word was involved in the Kyle State Bank, a chicken hatchery and feed store, and an implement company with a variety of partners. Word is shown here in his World War I uniform in Germany in 1919. The Hays County Appraisal District building is named for Word. (Courtesy of the Word family.)

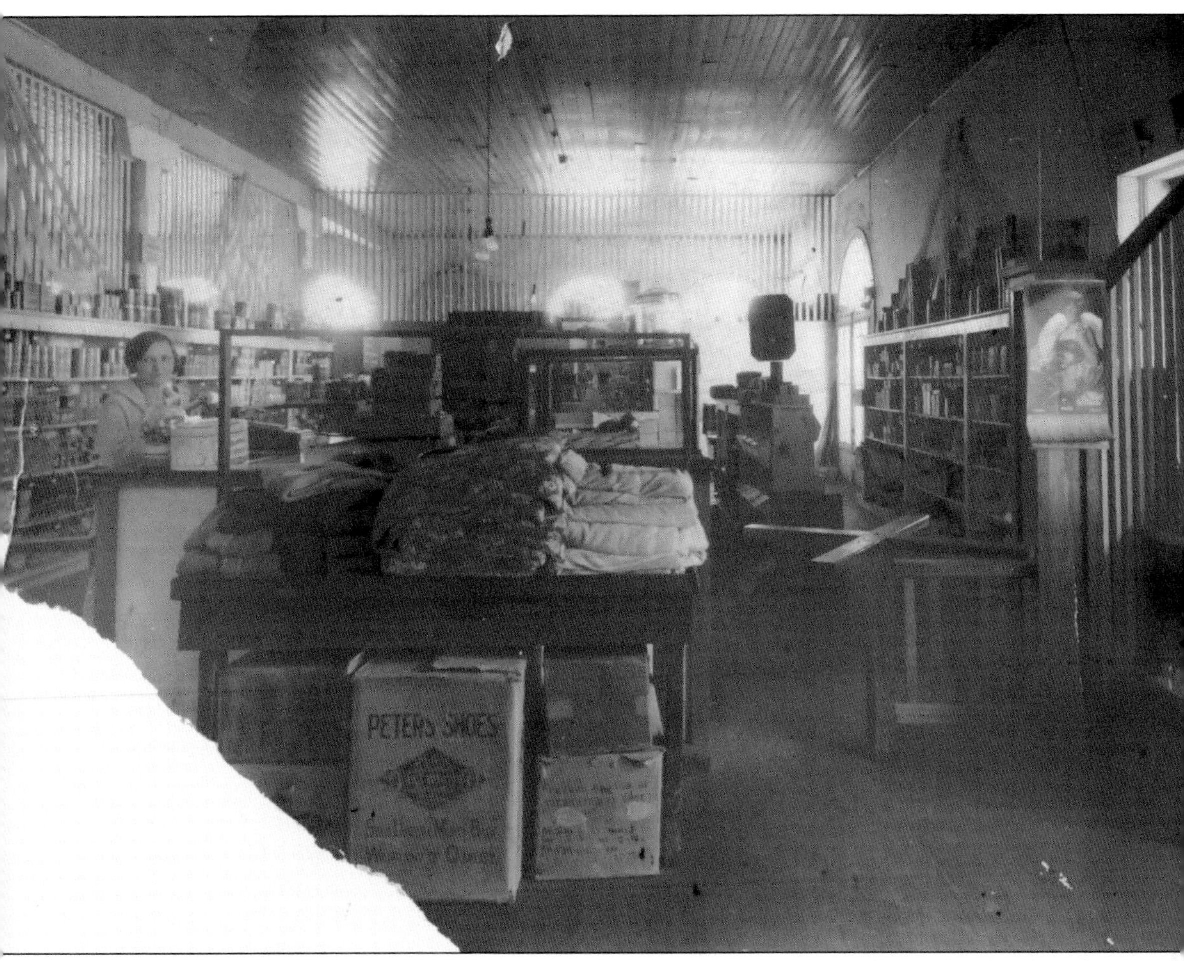

This photograph shows the interior of the Bon Ton store in 1926. Arthur Schmeltekopf and Ruth Chesser are the pictured employees. Founded by former employees of the R.J. Sledge store, the Bon Ton provided many young men from Kyle with business experience, including Adolph Hill, Leslie Hill, Lee Sturdivant, Ernest Morgan, and Cecil Bales. (Courtesy of the Word family.)

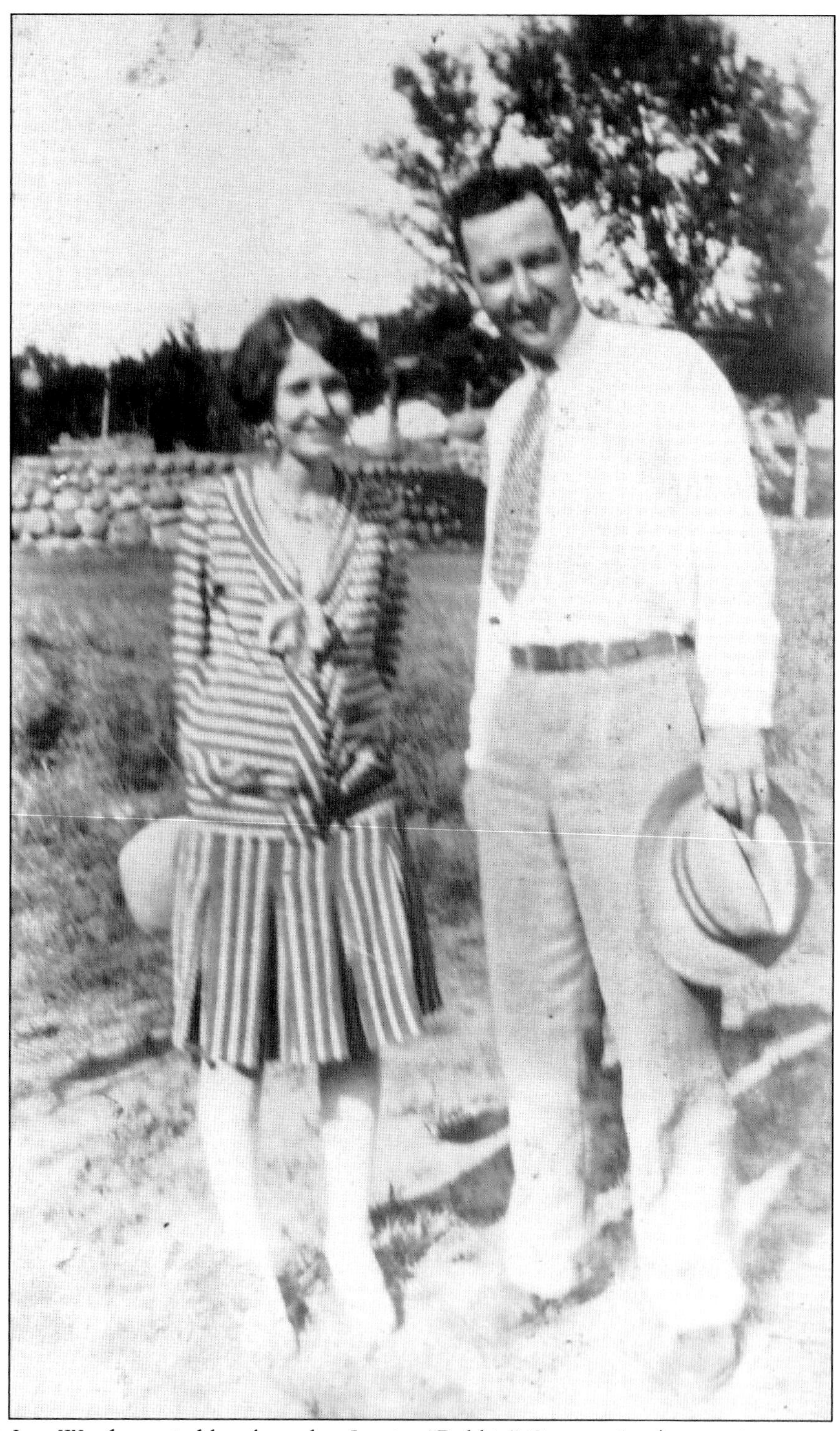

In 1929, Lex Word married local teacher Louise "Bobbie" Gossett. In the ensuing years, Bobbie Word was involved in improving the quality of life in Kyle. One of these enhancements was the establishment of the Kyle Community Library. (Courtesy of the Word family.)

Four

Notable Kyle Residents

In its 135 years of existence, Kyle has been the home to thousands of good people, many of whom have had successful personal and professional lives. During these years, however, a few individuals have attained great success in a variety of fields. Pulitzer Prize–winning author Katherine Anne Porter (then named Callie Russell Porter) came to live in Kyle with her grandmother Catherine Ann Skaggs Porter in 1892 after her mother died in childbirth, leaving Callie's father with a two-year-old daughter and a newborn son. Porter lived in Kyle in her grandmother's home on Center Street until she was a teenager. The home has now been restored and is the site of the Katherine Anne Porter Literary Center. Rhodes Scholar Terrell Sledge was born in Kyle in 1904, graduated from Kyle High School and the University of Texas, and then studied at Oxford University from 1926 to 1929. Because his father died during his time at Oxford, Sledge returned to Kyle to help run the family business. Before his untimely death at 51, Sledge ran for the US Senate and published a progressive newspaper called *The People's Business*. Cecil Carlton "Tex" Hughson was born in nearby Buda but moved to Kyle when he was five years old. An outstanding athlete at Kyle High School, after graduation in 1933, Hughson attended the University of Texas, where he was an All–Southwest Conference pitcher. In 1937, Hughson signed a contract with the Boston Red Sox and spent the next 11 years with that organization, although his baseball career was interrupted by service in World War II.

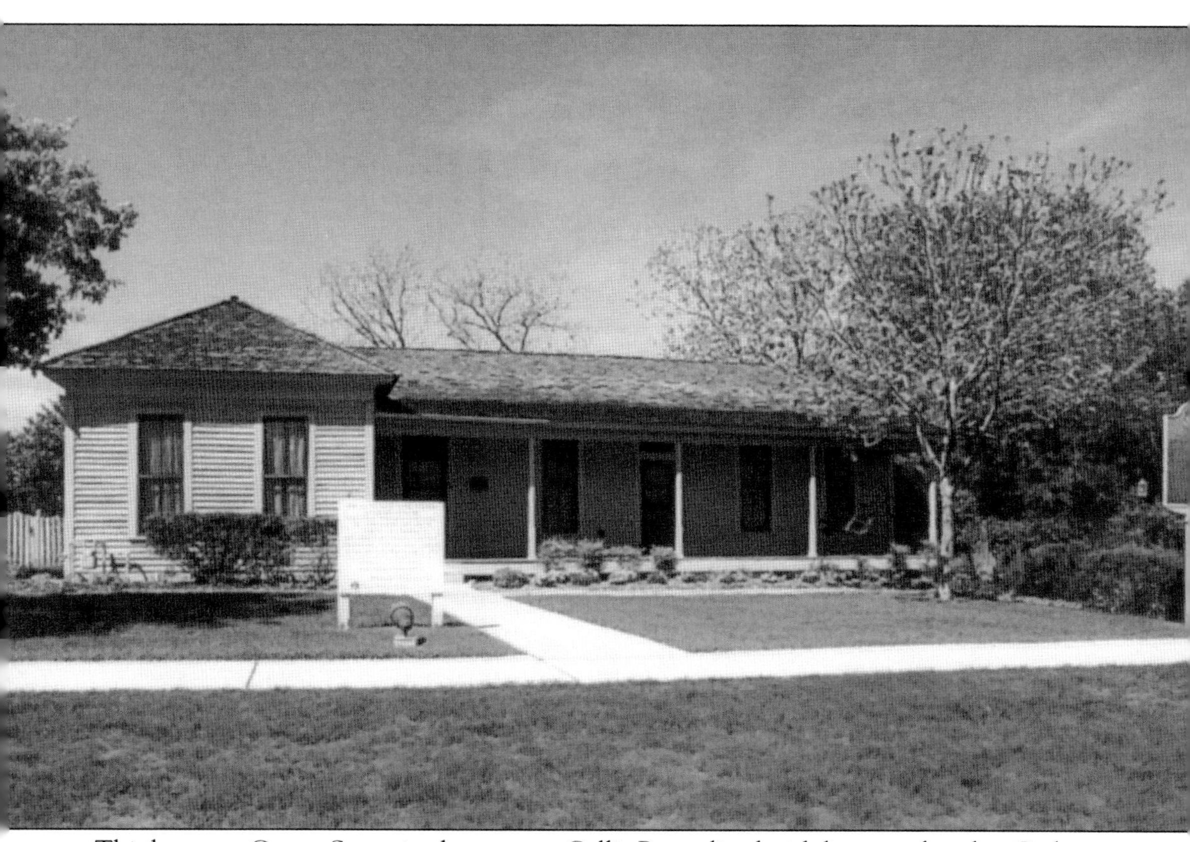

This home on Center Street is where young Callie Porter lived with her grandmother Catherine Ann Porter (called "Aunt Cat" by Kyle residents), whose name she eventually adopted. As a young child, Callie was interested in writing and drama, and she performed her own plays on the gallery of the house. In 1997, the home was restored and leased to Texas State University. The Katherine Anne Porter Literary Center is currently housed here and hosts a Visiting Writers Series and an Artist in Residence program. The Katherine Anne Porter Literary Center and the restoration of the home have received substantial funding from the Burdine Johnson Foundation. (Author's collection.)

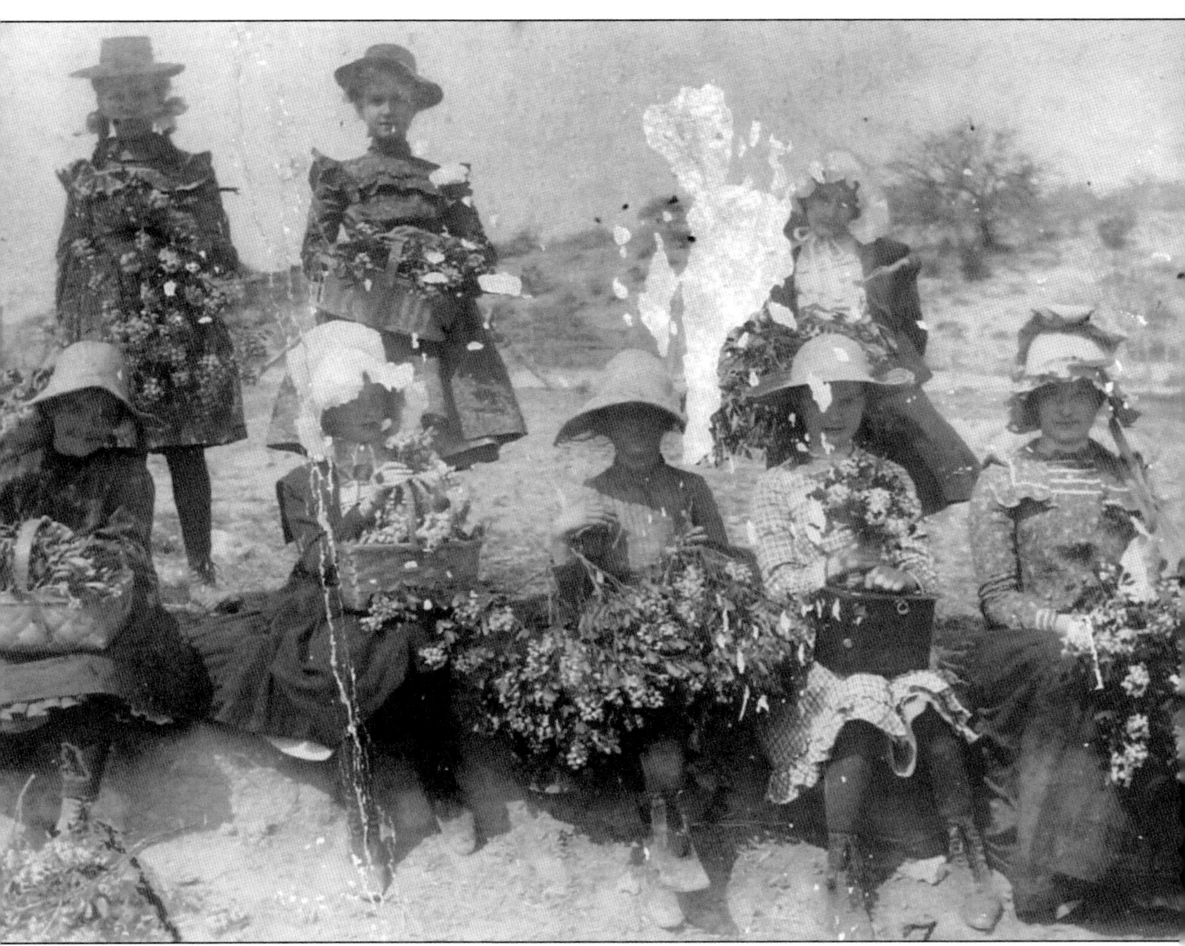

Katherine Anne Porter is pictured with her Kyle classmates. One of her classmates was Erna Schlemmer, whose nephew Curt Engelhorn would fund the initial operation of the Katherine Anne Porter Literary Center after the home was restored in 1997. Other classmates pictured with Porter are Mary Groos, Nita Schlemmer, Katie Weatherford, Mary Alice ?, and "daughter of the Methodist pastor" Abby Graham, along with teacher Belle Schmidt. Porter died in 1980 and is buried in Indian Creek next to her mother. (Courtesy of the Kyle Public Library.)

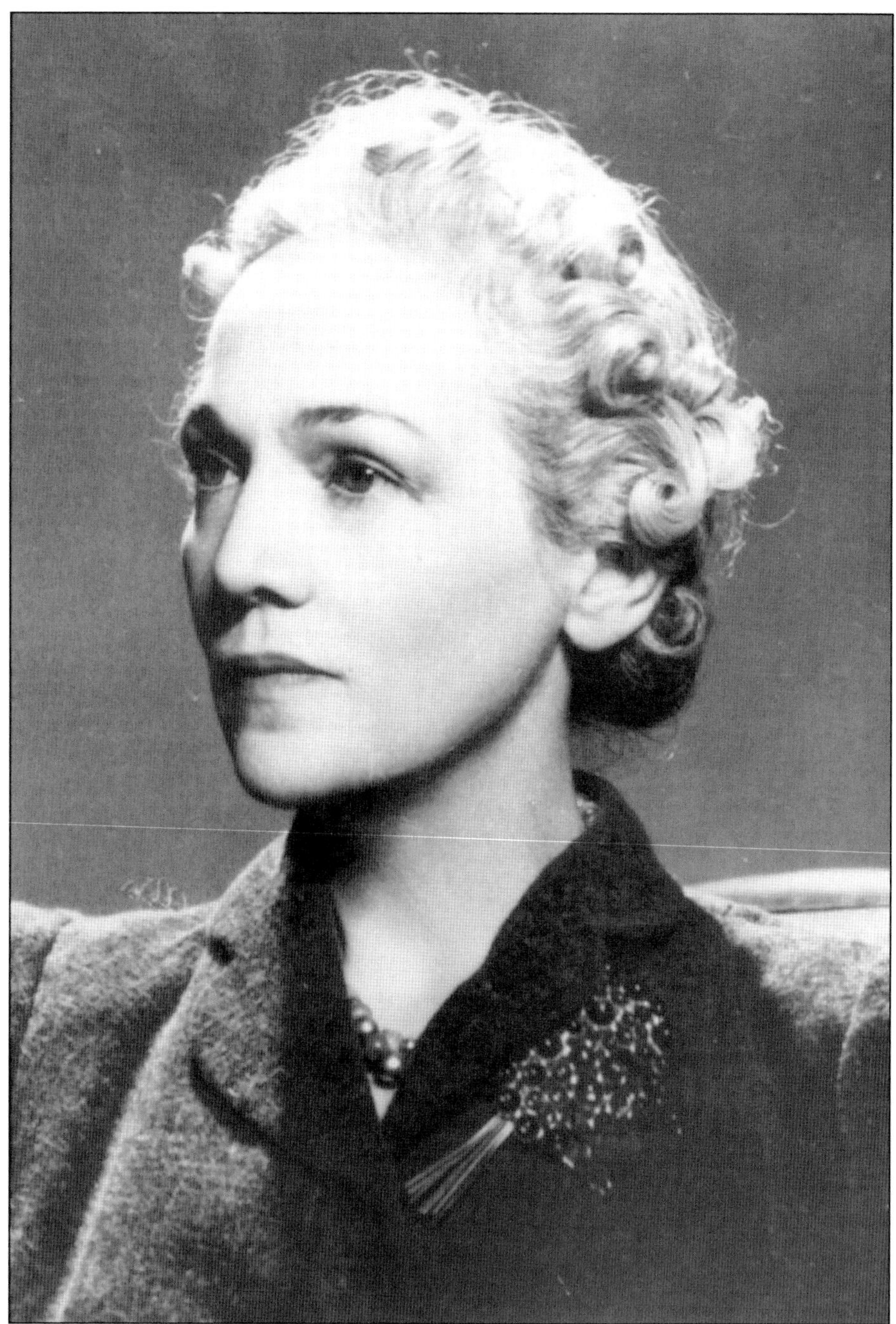

Katherine Anne Porter was born in 1890 in Indian Creek, Texas, but moved to Kyle at age two with her father and newborn brother. The family later moved from Kyle to San Antonio after her grandmother's death in 1901. Porter used Texas scenes and experiences from her childhood to inspire her writing but rarely returned during her adult life. She won the National Book Award and the Pulitzer Prize for her book of collected stories in 1966. Her only novel, *Ship of Fools*, was made into a movie, bringing her national acclaim. (Courtesy of the Katherine Anne Porter Literary Center.)

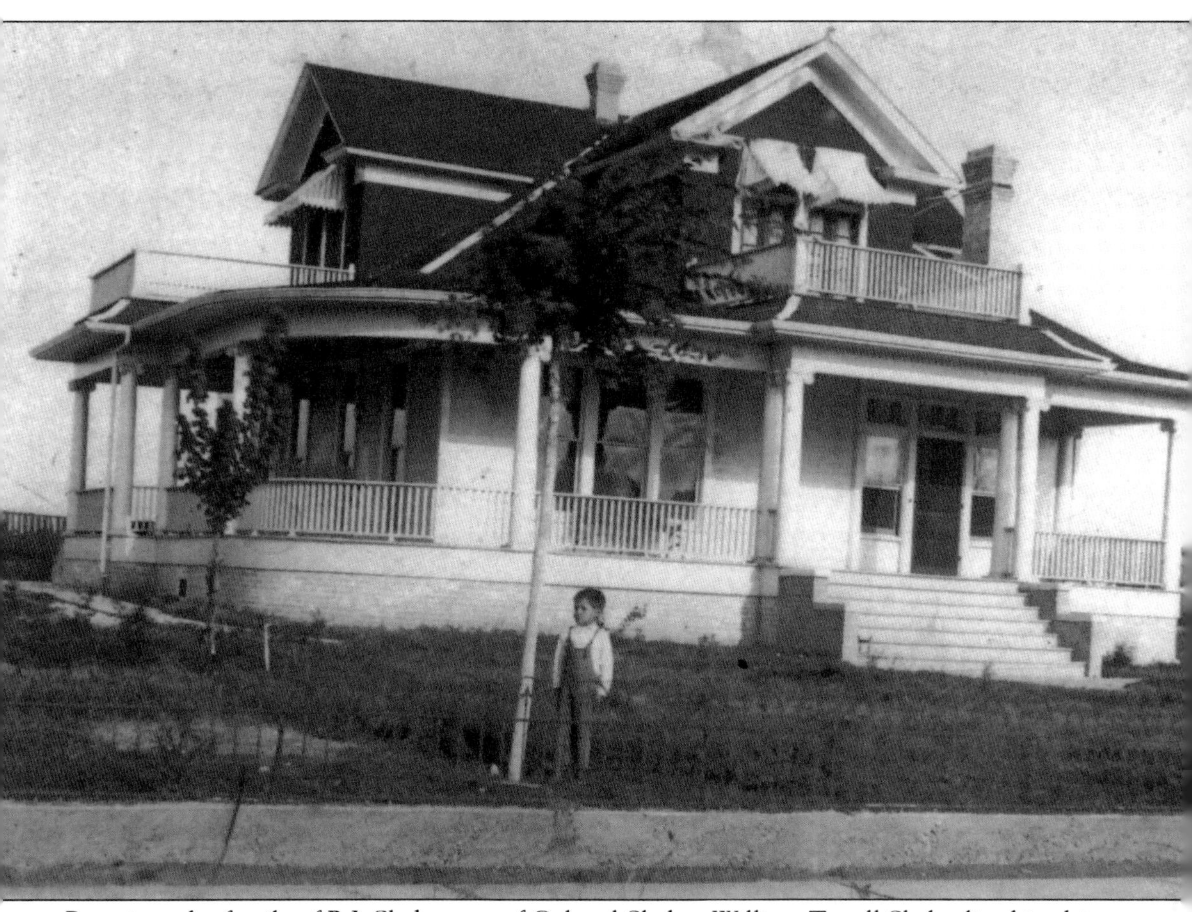

Born into the family of R.J. Sledge, son of Colonel Sledge, William Terrell Sledge lived in this home from the time it was built in 1912 until his death in 1955, except for the years he spent at college in Austin, at Oxford as a Rhodes Scholar, and in the military during World War II. Between the time he returned home from Oxford and left for war, Sledge worked in his family's store, raised cattle, hosted a radio show, sold advertising for WOAI in San Antonio, repossessed cars, and taught English at Kyle High School. This home still belongs to the Sledge family. (Courtesy HFP.)

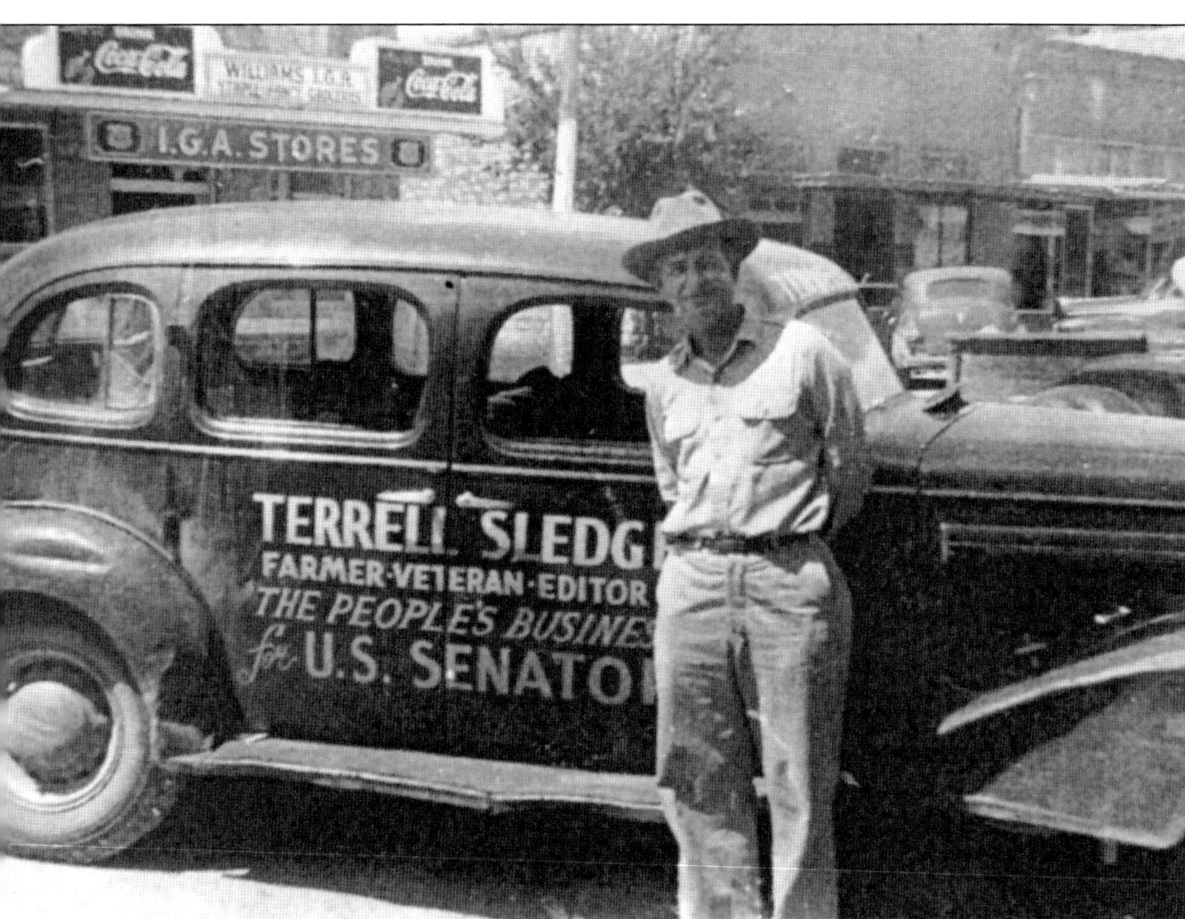

Following his military service, Sledge returned to Kyle and pursued politics and the newspaper business. He unsuccessfully ran for the US Senate, not expecting to win but advocating for the interests of small towns and small businesses. He also published a progressive newspaper during those years. In 1949, Sledge was hired to teach night school for returning veterans. Men in his class were instrumental in forming the GI Forum, which advocated for closing the separate school for Mexican children in Kyle. Sledge was also an accomplished musician, an interest he shared with his wife, Frances, who was a music teacher in Kyle when they met. Sledge died in 1955 at age 51. (Courtesy of the Sledge family.)

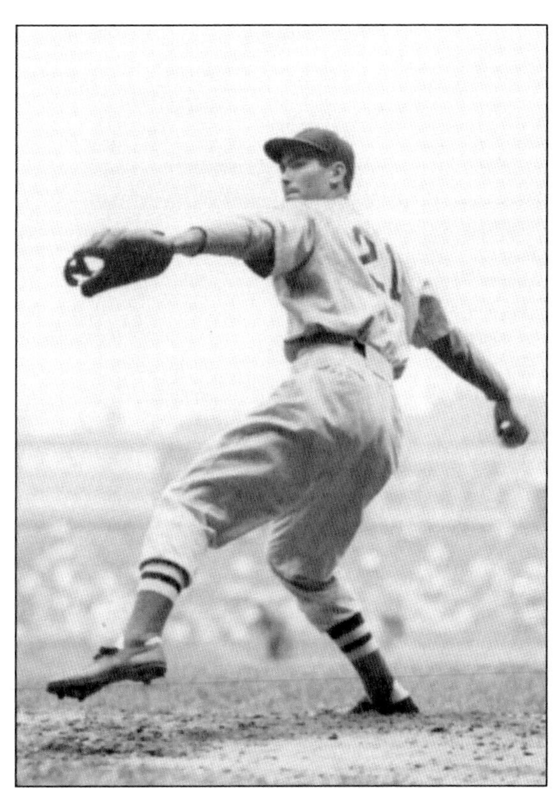

Cecil C. "Tex" Hughson was an outstanding athlete at Kyle High School. Following his graduation in 1933, after a brief stint working on the bridge between Kyle and San Marcos for 25¢ an hour, Tex enrolled in the University of Texas, where he played baseball for legendary coach William "Uncle Billy" Disch. He signed with the Boston Red Sox in 1937 and was soon a minor league star. He joined the major league team in 1941. Although his pitching career was cut short by arm problems and military service, Hughson had a 96-54 record in five full and three partial seasons. He was the winning pitcher in the 1944 All-Star game and pitched two games in the 1946 World Series against the St. Louis Cardinals. These photographs are from a 1942 game against the New York Yankees, a team he loved to beat, according to his daughter. (Both, courtesy of the Hughson family.)

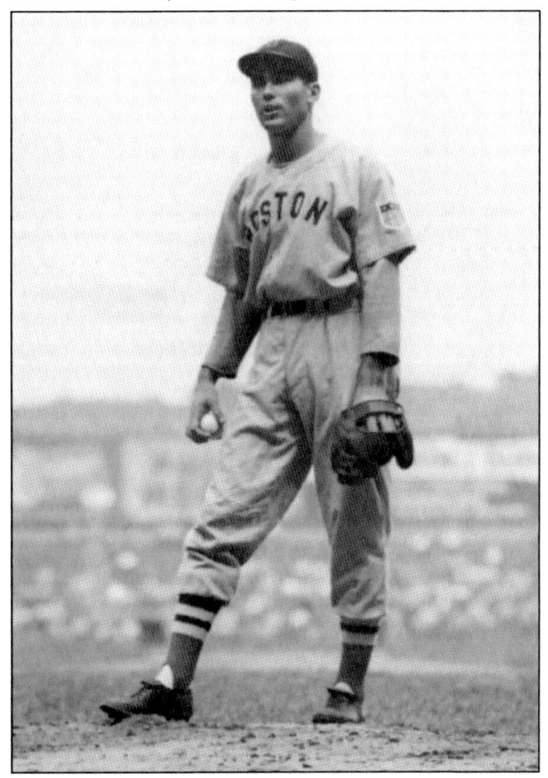

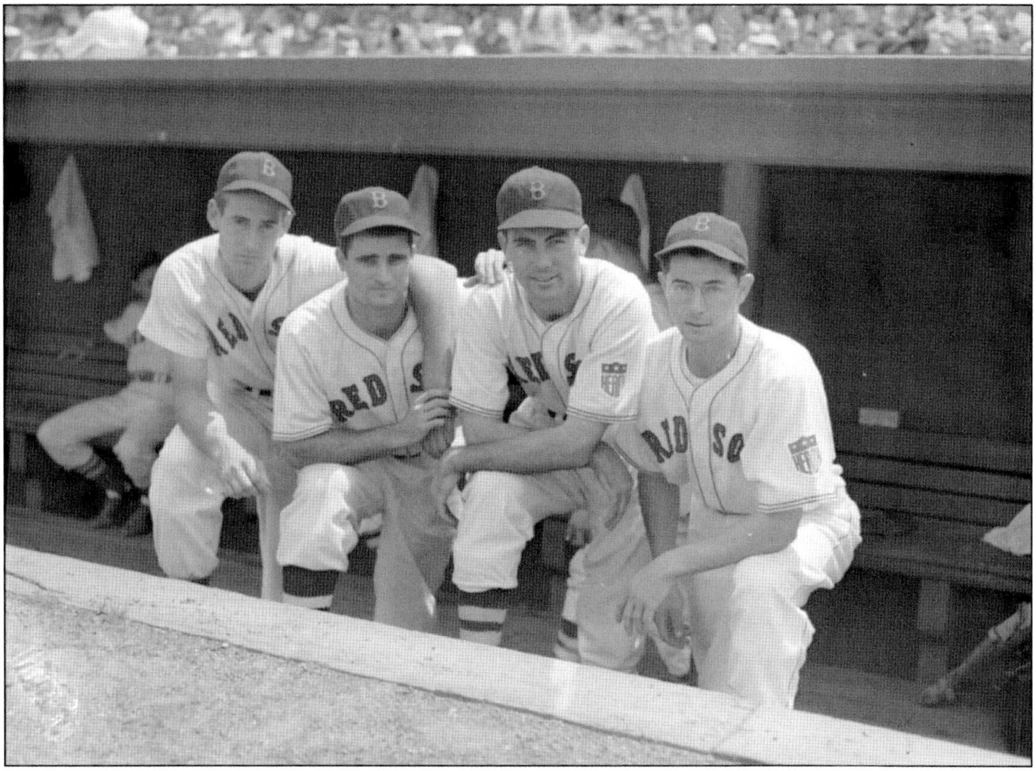

After Tex Hughson retired from baseball in 1949 because of arm problems, he returned to San Marcos and worked in his family's ranching and meatpacking businesses. He was also instrumental in forming the San Marcos Little League in 1952 and threw out the first pitch of the season wearing his Red Sox road uniform. He continued his association with the Red Sox organization throughout the rest of his life, often attending spring training and maintaining his friendship with Ted Williams. Hughson served on the San Marcos School Board in the 1950s and was instrumental in the district's decision to integrate schools. Hughson died in San Marcos in 1993. He is pictured above second from the right on the dugout steps of Fenway Park with teammates, from left to right, Ted Williams, Bobby Doerr, and Dom DiMaggio and warming up below. (Both, courtesy of the Boston Public Library Digital Commonwealth.)

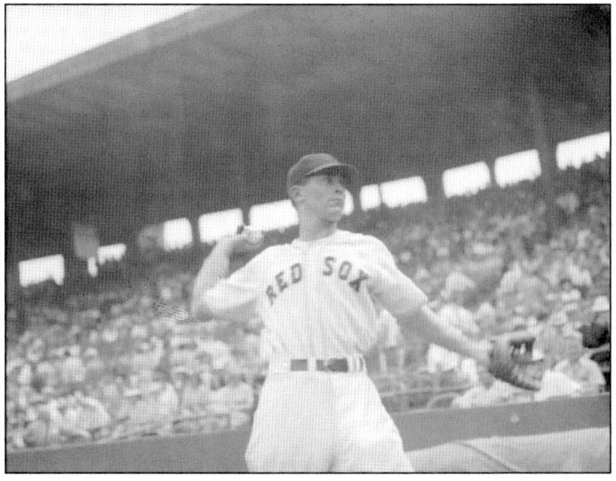

Five

Kyle during the Depression and World War II

The Great Depression was very hard for Kyle's 600 residents. With the closure of the bank, a department store, and the rail station, the future for Kyle looked as bleak as it did for the rest of the country. By 1932, "relief" work began, with unemployed men being hired to clean cemeteries, dig holes for trees, and paint the city hall. Adult schools for Mexican and African American residents were opened, and government-funded sewing rooms, a tannery, and a cannery employed people from the relief rolls. Schools in Hays County were not able to pay teachers until federal aid was available. In July 1936, the Plum Creek flood killed 17 people from Kyle, most of them on the E.C. Woods farm. The Works Project Administration (WPA) provided some employment with projects working on school buildings and creating the camp grounds at Camp Ben McCulloch in Driftwood. By 1940, Kyle had grown to 871 residents, the economy had improved, and people were preparing for the coming war. Selling defense stamps and bonds, practicing blackouts and air raids, and gathering aluminum and paper involved all residents in war preparation during 1941. Once the war began in late 1941, men not in the service drilled on the streets as the Home Guard, sometimes using bed slats for rifles. Troop trains passing through Kyle were greeted with waves from citizens at the tracks. Tutta Barton recalls that when VE Day came on May 8, 1945, residents gathered in the gym not to celebrate but to express humble gratitude for their survival. The celebration came later, when Japan surrendered in August.

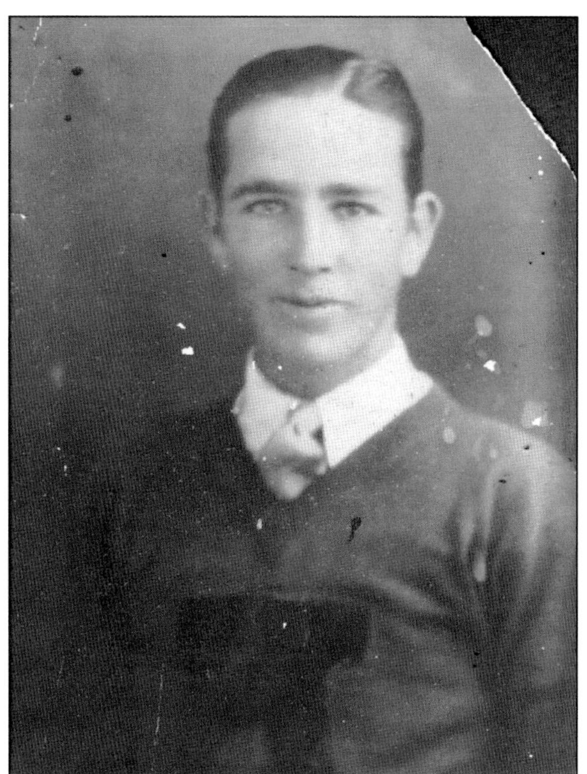

Cecil Bales grew up in Kyle during the Depression and, like many young people at the time, left school to work to help his family. He worked at the cotton gin and later as the school janitor. He joined the Civilian Conservation Corps with some other boys from Kyle and spent a year working in the Kit Carson National Forest in New Mexico and a year at Fort Bliss in El Paso. (Courtesy HFP.)

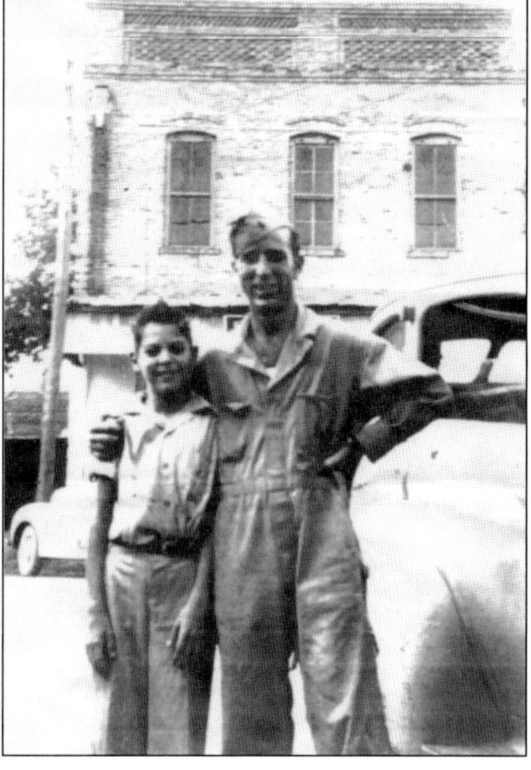

After serving in World War II with two of his brothers, Cecil Bales (right) returned to Kyle and worked for Lex Word at the Bon Ton, the store he would eventually purchase from Word in the 1960s. Bales is shown here with Lex Word Jr. (Courtesy of the Word family.)

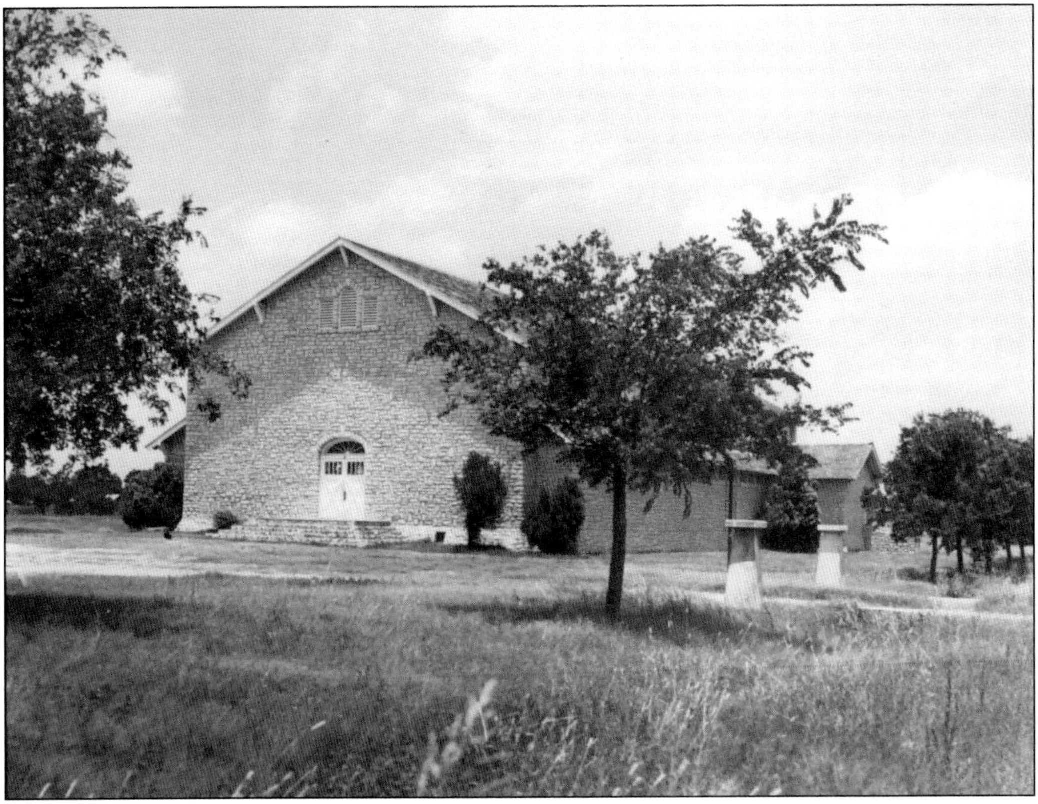

In an effort to create jobs for unemployed residents, Kyle citizens met in 1933 to consider how they might participate in WPA programs. They submitted an application to build a new school structure, and with local bond funds supplementing government support, construction on a new gymnasium-auditorium and home economics cottage began in 1936, employing 29 men. The buildings were completed in 1937 and are still in use today. The gym has served as the cafeteria for Kyle Elementary and is now identified as the Ernest Kimbro Multipurpose Building. (Courtesy of the Word family.)

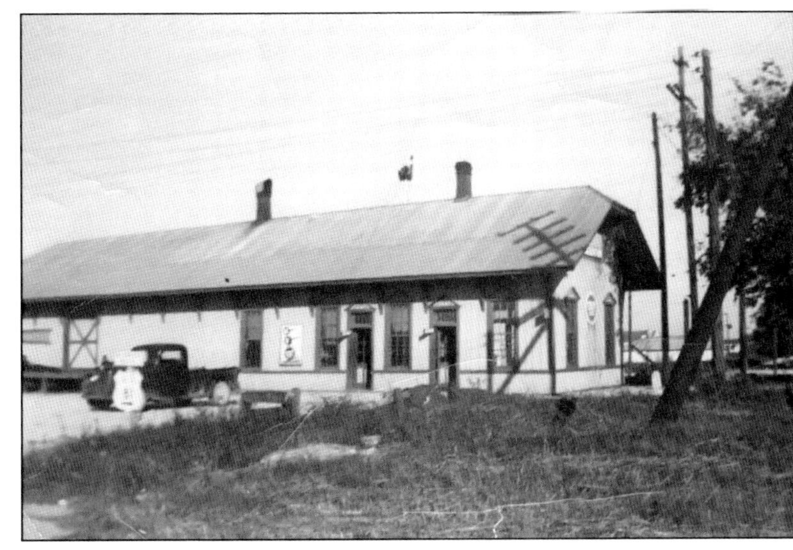

Even though rail business declined during the Depression, the depot remained an important place in Kyle during the 1930s. (Courtesy HFP.)

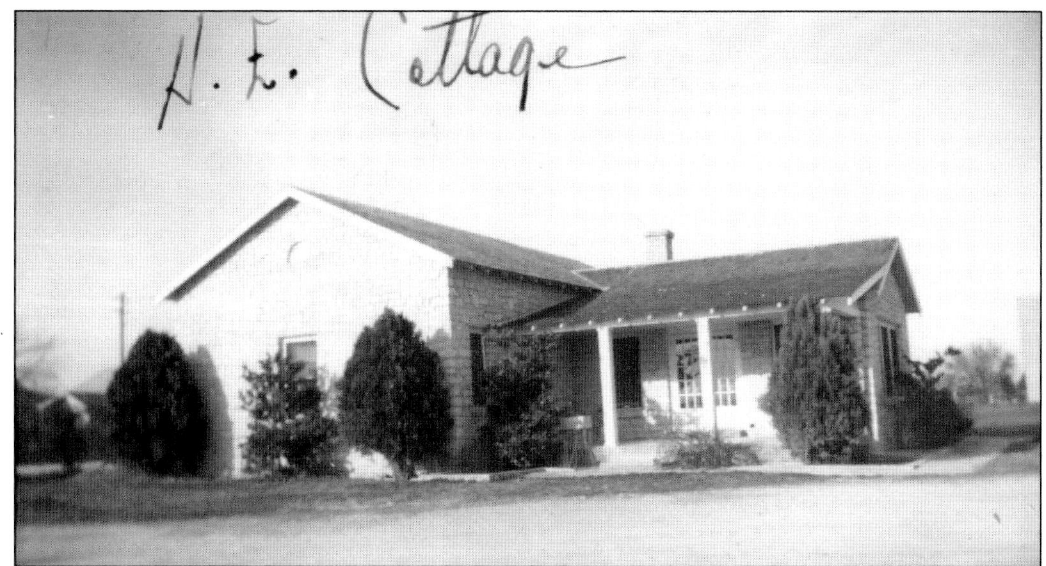

The home economics cottage has served a variety of purposes in addition to classroom space, including offices for the Hays Consolidated Independent School District (CISD). (Courtesy of the Miller family.)

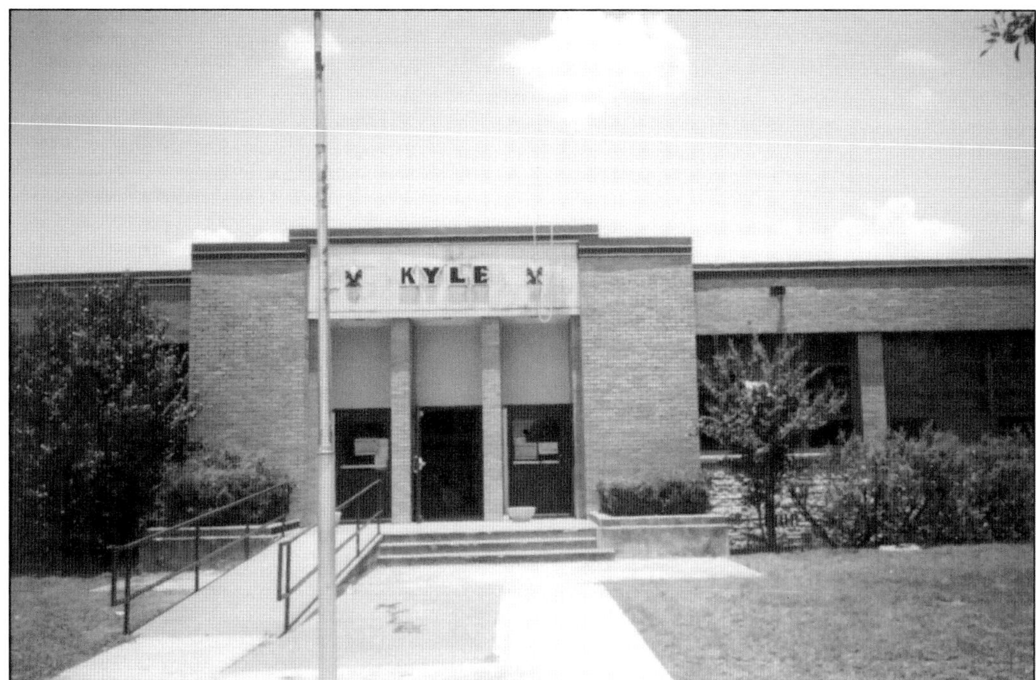

As soon as the gym and home economics cottage were completed, the Kyle School District again used bond funds to supplement WPA funds for a new classroom building to replace the 1911 two-story structure. Materials from the old structure were sold to help pay for the new building, so classes were scattered around town to the new gym and home economics cottage, homes, churches, the fire hall, and even the Groos garage. (Courtesy HFP.)

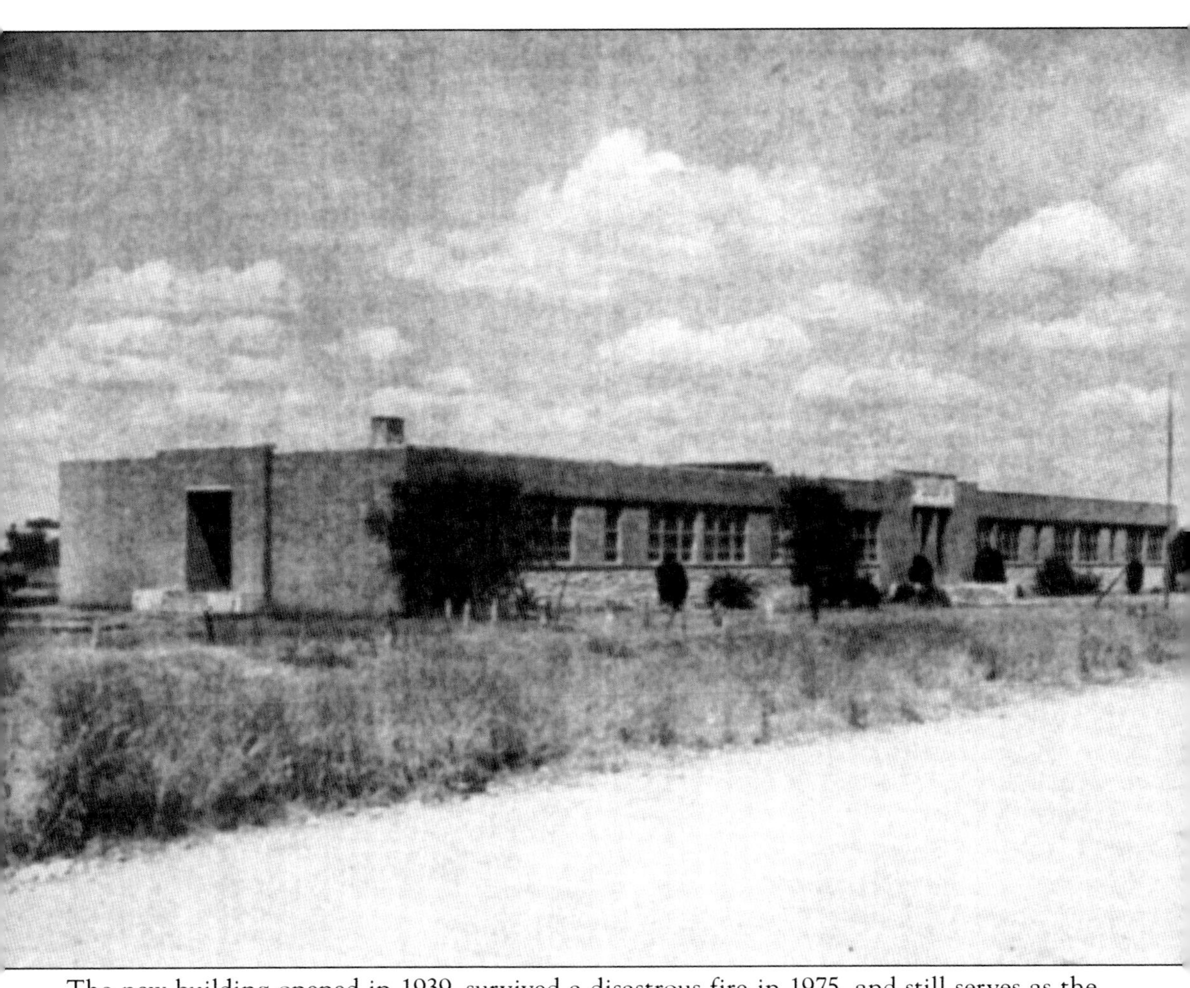

The new building opened in 1939, survived a disastrous fire in 1975, and still serves as the elementary school in Kyle. (Courtesy HFP.)

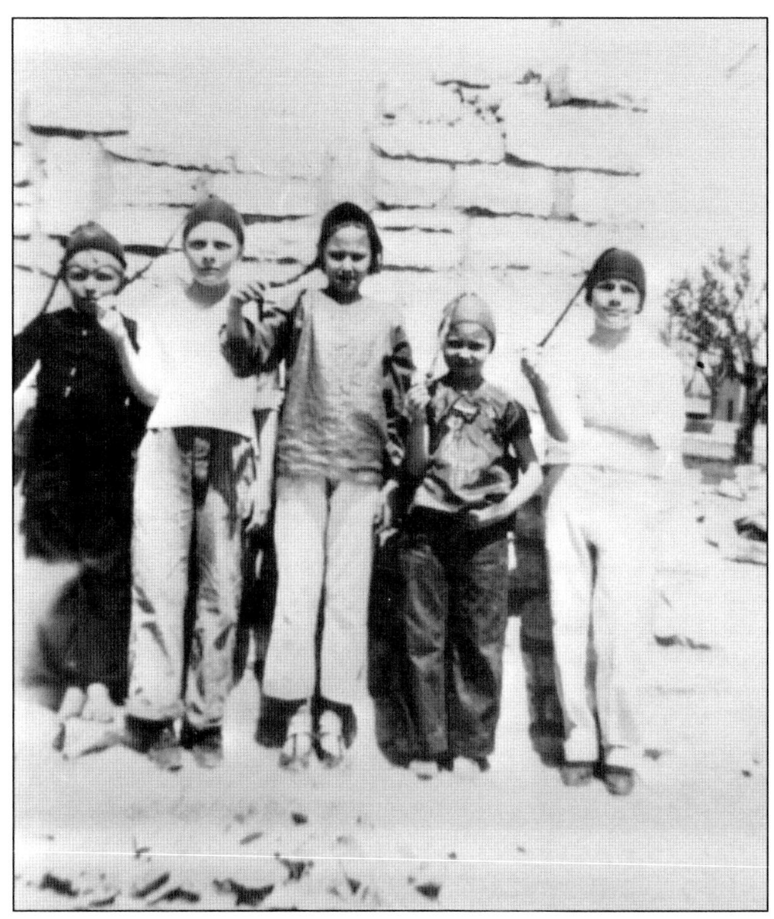

Riso Millhollon taught in the Kyle schools from 1929 to the 1960s. She also operated a kindergarten in her home when her own daughter was young. Pictured are students from her 1936 fourth grade class when they studied China. From left to right are Milton Dees, Florine Schmeltekopf, Alice Herzog, Louise Dupree, and Dorine Schmeltekopf. (Courtesy HCCM.)

TEACHER'S CONTRACT

THE STATE OF TEXAS, County of Hays

Contract with Mrs. Minnie Jo Schmeltekopf
Teacher of Elem. Grades School
Home P. O. Kyle Texas

This contract entered into this 1st. day of Sept. , 19 44, between the school trustees of Kyle Ind. School District of Hays County, and Mrs. Minnie Jo Schmeltekopf teacher, holding a valid certificate of Per. Elem. grade, witnesseth: That the said trustees have engaged the said Mrs. Minnie Jo Schmeltekopf as teacher of Elem. Grades elementary, high (erase one) school in said district for a term of 9 consecutive months of the school year 19 44 19 45, and for a term of ______ consecutive months of the school year 19___ 19___ (this latter term to be filled in only in case the teacher is employed for two years) said term to begin, unless otherwise agreed upon by teacher and trustees, on the 18 day of Sept. , 19 44, and on the ______ day of ______ 19___, at a salary of $ 1,089.00 for the school year 1944 1945, and at a salary of $______ for the school year 19___ 19___. Said salary is to be paid in 12 equal and consecutive monthly installments. (The entire salary should be paid in full within the fiscal year ending August 31st, This contract must show the classification given the school by county board of education in proper space above.)

It is agreed that the said teacher shall discharge under this contract the duties required in accordance with the school laws of Texas, and the regulations of the State Superintendent of Public Instruction and the county superintendent of public instruction of said county. It is further agreed that no verbal agreement entered into between the teacher and trustees not covered by this contract and no written agreement, aside from this contract, shall become a part of the contract or bind either of the parties to the same. It is further agreed that in no case shall any part of the salary promised under this contract be paid from the funds which may be apportioned to the said school district during any future year.

It is further agreed that $______ per school month shall be charged for pupils under scholastic age and $______ per school month for pupils over scholastic age (twenty-one or more years of age on September 1), and said amount, when collected, shall be paid to the school board herein named.

It is further agreed that the teacher herein employed shall make a full and complete term report and shall deliver his or her Teacher's Daily Register, properly filled out, to the county superintendent before receiving pay for his or her last month of service rendered said school.

This contract is consummated only upon its approval by the county superintendent, and it shall become operative from and after the date of said approval. If the school is classified as a high school by the county board of education, or if high school subjects must be taught, the teacher of such high school subjects must hold a certificate authorizing the teaching of high school subjects before this contract can be entered into by the board of trustees and the teacher and approved by the county superintendent.

Witness our signatures this the 1st. day of Sept. 1944, 19___.

Minnie Jo Schmeltekopf
Teacher

R. C. Parks
J. A. Scott
Trustees.

Approved ______, 19___ County Supt.

Filed in my office ______, 19___ County Supt.

TEACHER'S COPY

M179 J.1932-642-57,500.

This teacher's contract reveals the terms of teachers' work during this period. Minnie Jo Schmeltekopf was first hired to teach in Kyle in the middle of the school year, when another teacher left suddenly to teach in a school in an internment camp during World War II. Schmeltekopf is said to be the first "American" woman to marry into a German immigrant family when she married Walter Schmeltekopf in 1937. (Author's collection.)

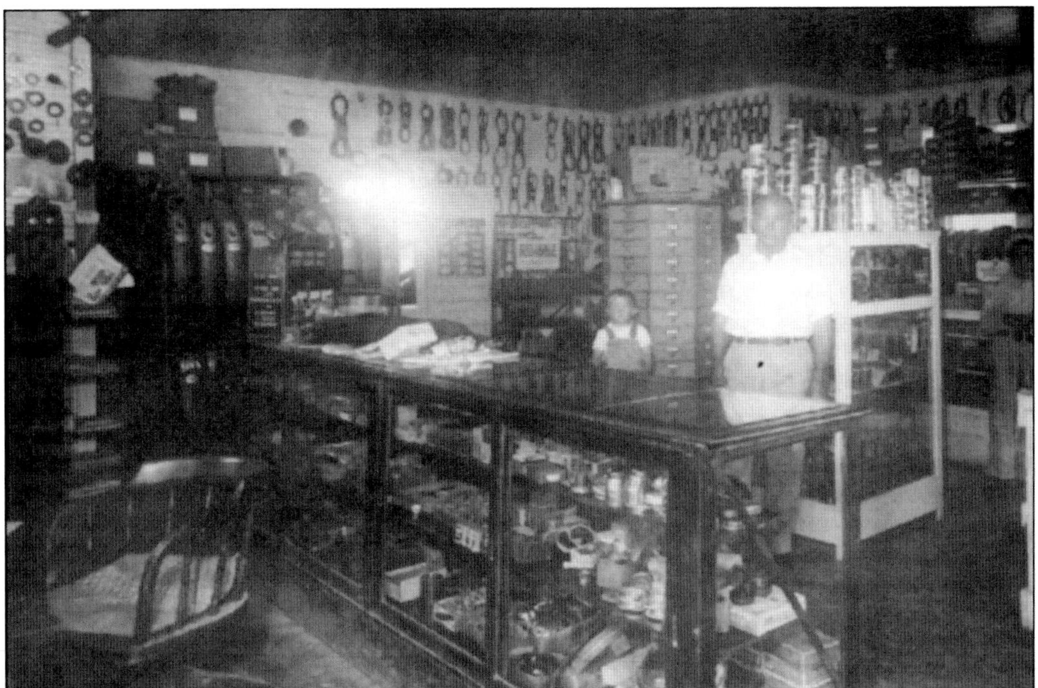

Built in 1936, the Groos Auto Shop was the first business built on Highway 81. Before the auto shop, the Groos family ran the Groos Patch Company in the 1920s, when all tires were made with cotton string. With few paved roads, flat tires were frequent problems. The Groos family made tire boots in Kyle, which covered and protected the inner tube. The Groos Patch Company employed 10 people and shipped tire boots into Mexico and across the nation. (Above, courtesy HFP; below, courtesy of Robert Frizzel.)

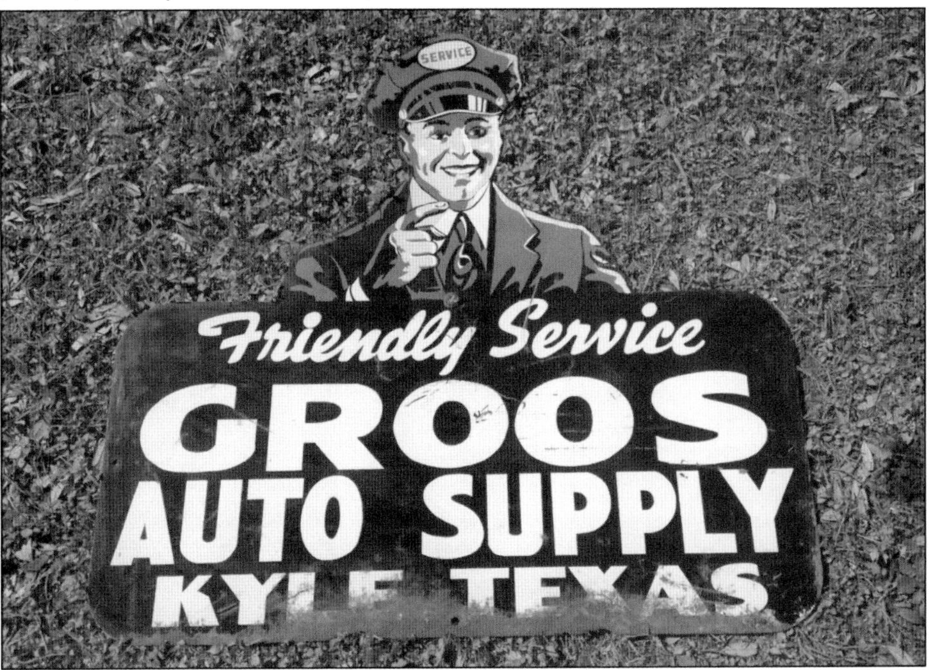

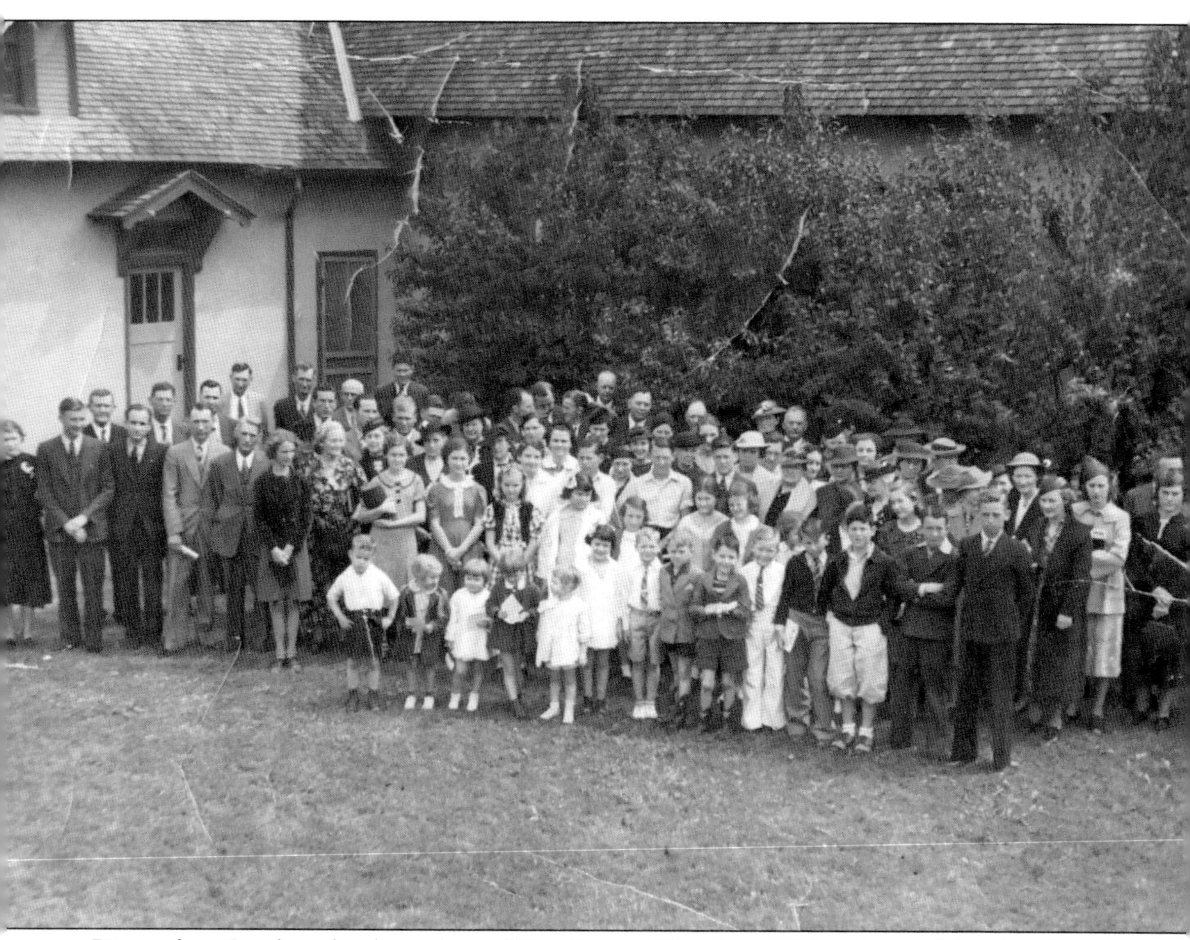

Pictured are Sunday school members of First Baptist Church in 1935, in front of the church built in 1882. This structure burned in 1940, and the church met at city hall until a new building was constructed in 1948. (Courtesy of the Word family.)

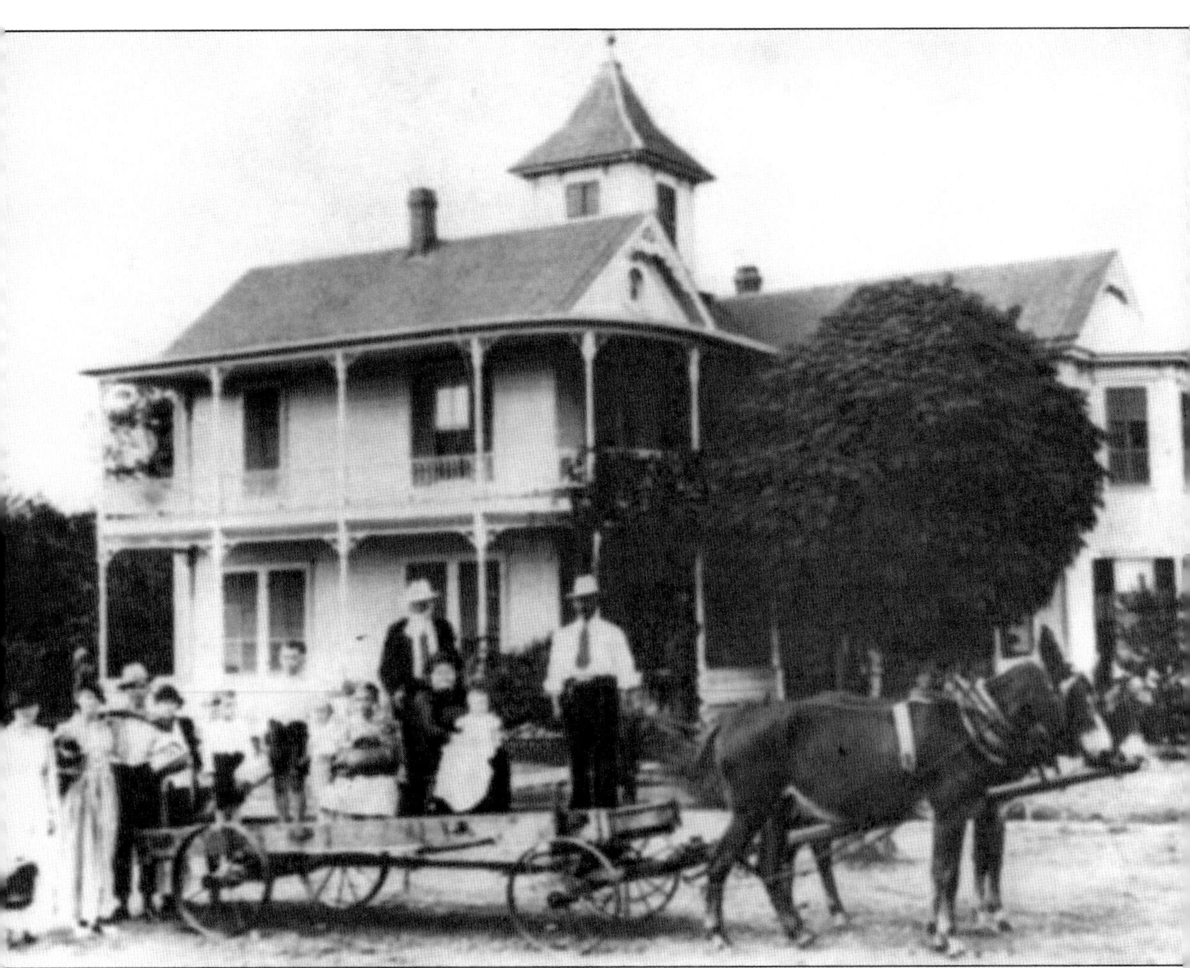

The community was still going strong 50 years after the first German immigrants settled in Kyle. The Heidenreich family held a celebration of the anniversary of their family's arrival in Kyle on August 20, 1935, at the John A. Heidenreich home. (Courtesy IBC.)

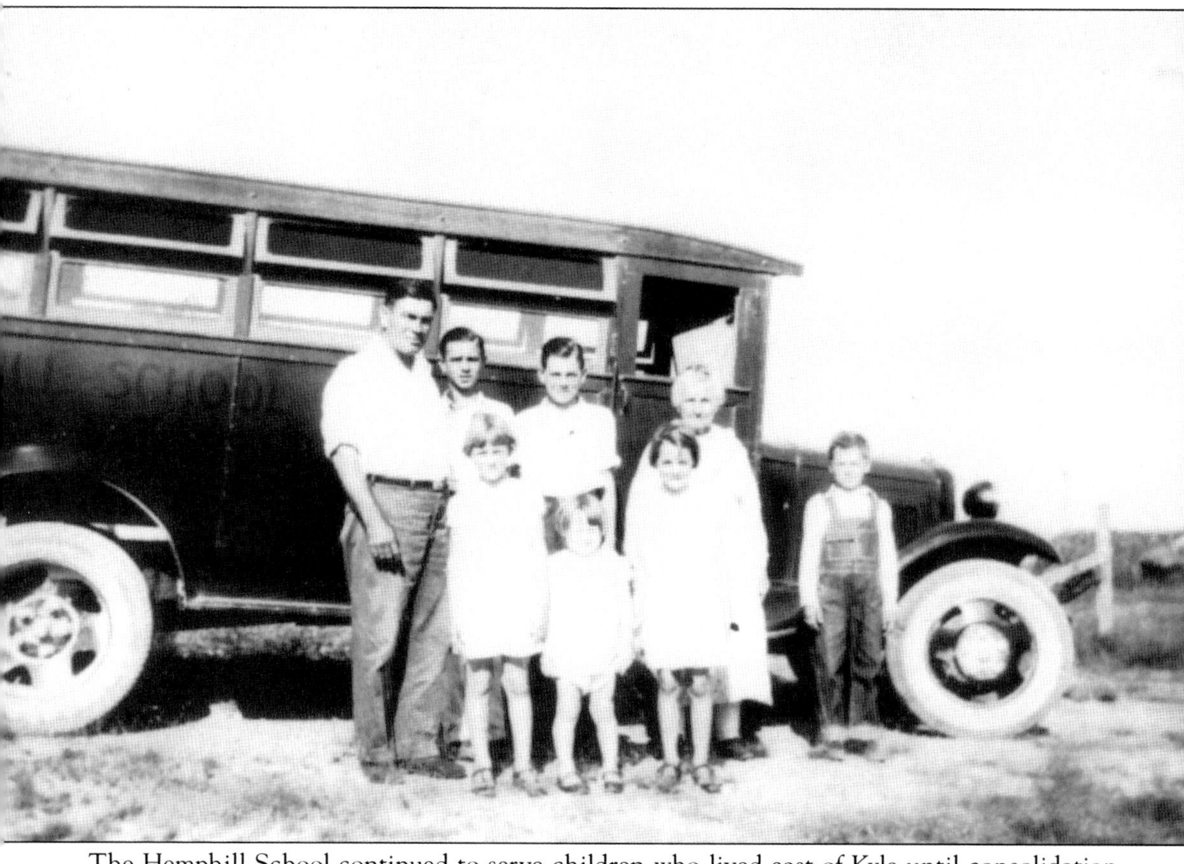

The Hemphill School continued to serve children who lived east of Kyle until consolidation in 1945; although, in later years, some children rode the bus into Kyle. The bus pictured was built in 1932 by Ed and Otto Hill. From left to right are (first row) Florine, Julianne, and Dorine Schmeltekopf; (second row) driver Henry Schmeltekopf, H.J. Heidenreich, Lawrence Schmeltekopf, Grandma Hill, and Calvin Schmeltekopf. (Courtesy HCCM.)

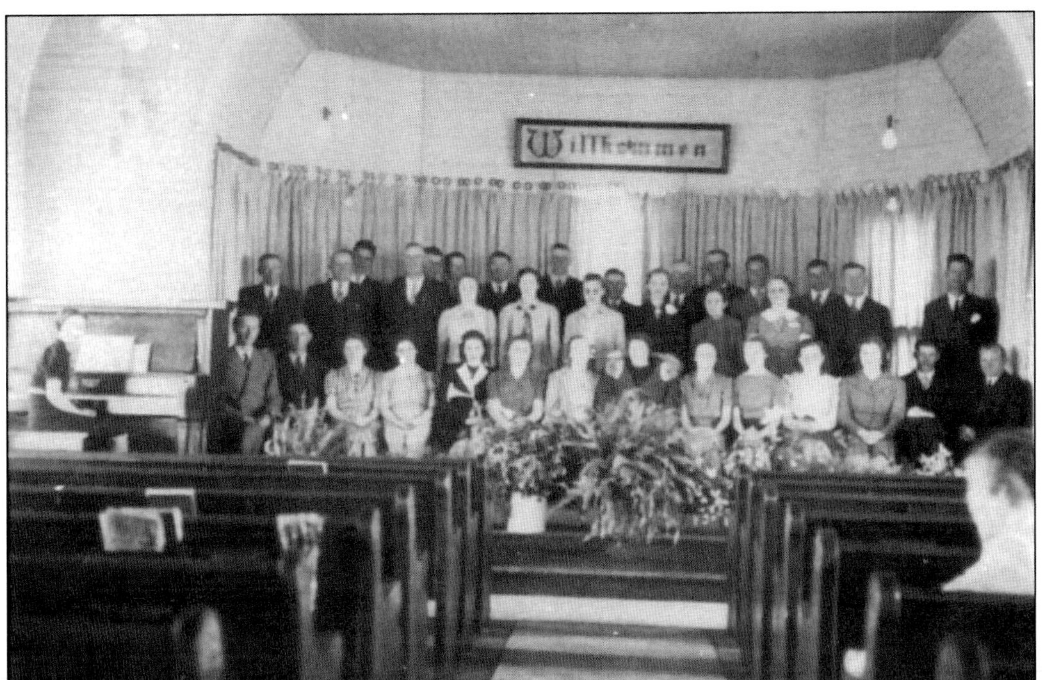

The Kyle German Baptist Church was a strong force in the success of the immigrant community. The above photograph shows the interior of its first building (1893), which was expanded in 1931 before it burned in 1939. Note that the welcome sign is written in German. The photograph below is of the new church, built on the same site in 1941. At that time, the name of the church was changed to Immanuel Baptist Church, possibly reflecting the anti-German sentiment of the country. This building is still used by the church today. (Both, courtesy IBC.)

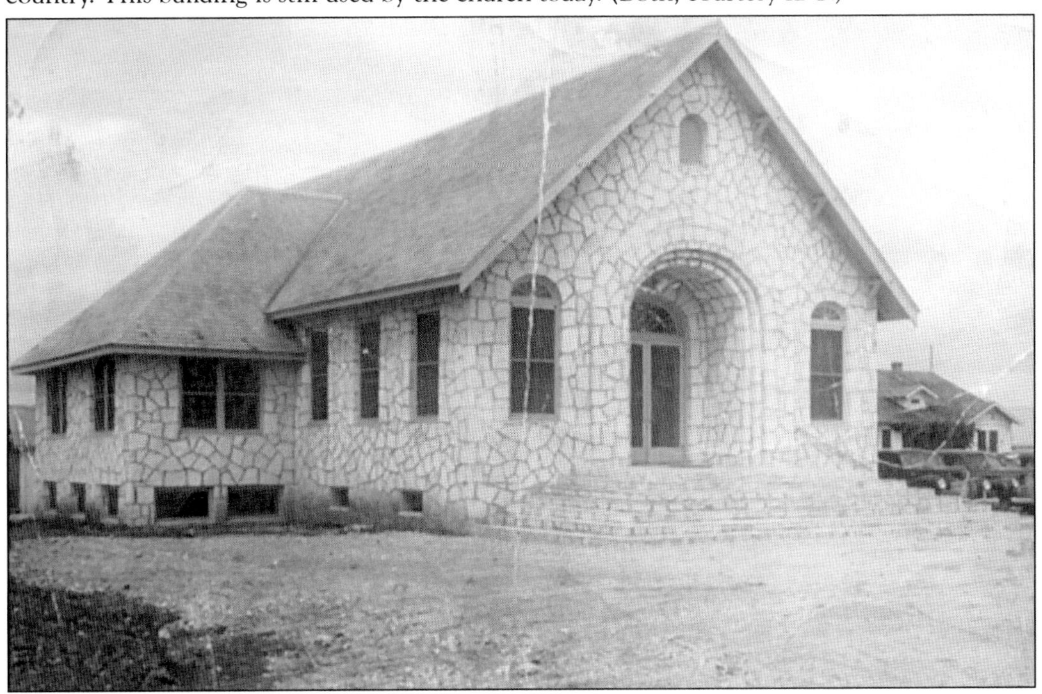

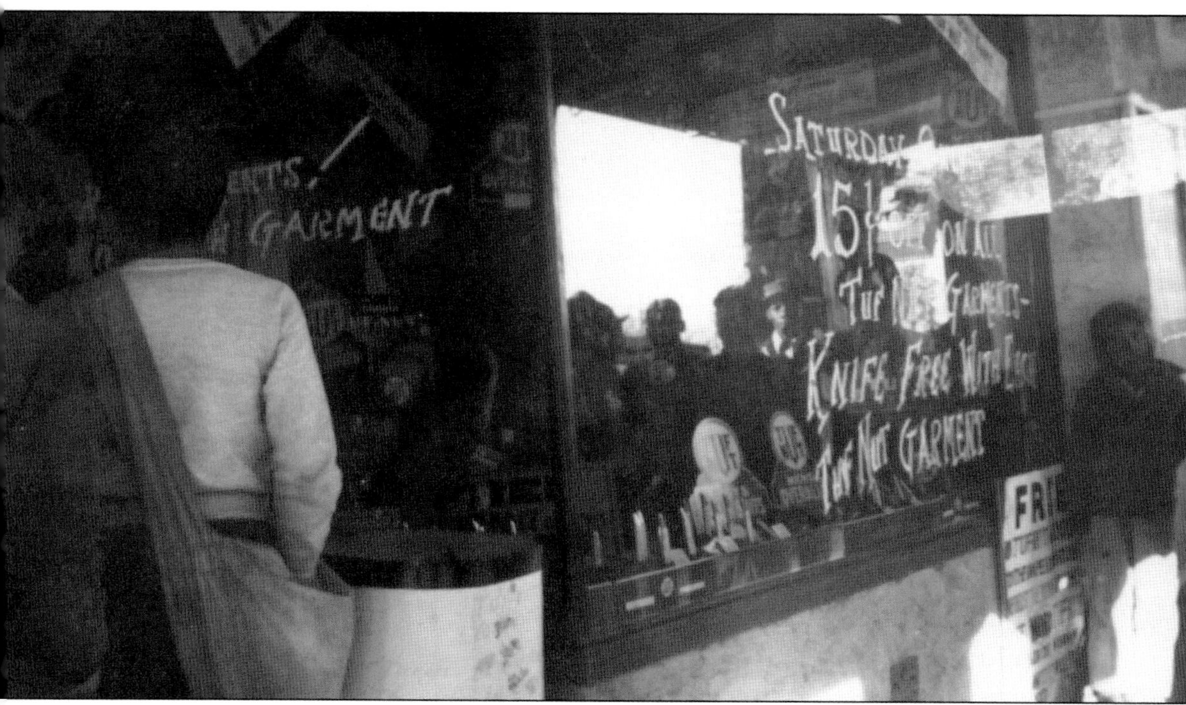

When many businesses failed during the drought of 1929 and the Depression that followed, the Bon Ton survived in spite of dropping sales and unpaid accounts. Fire struck the building in 1934, destroying much of the stock and killing the janitor. Merchandise that could be salvaged was moved to another location until the structure could be rebuilt. (Courtesy of the Word family.)

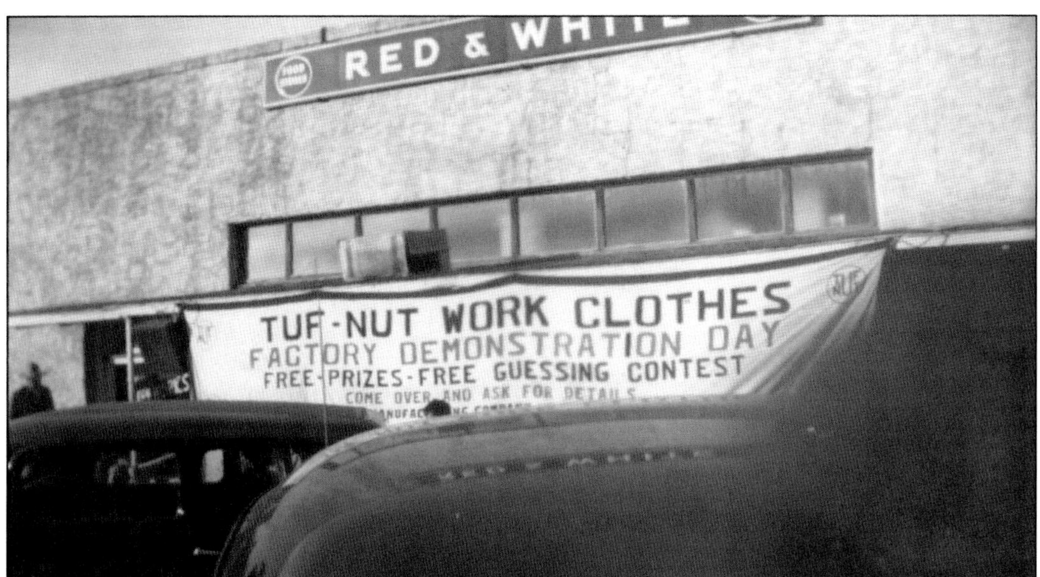

The Bon Ton not only sold groceries and work clothes, but served as a meeting place for the community for many years. (Both, courtesy of the Word family.)

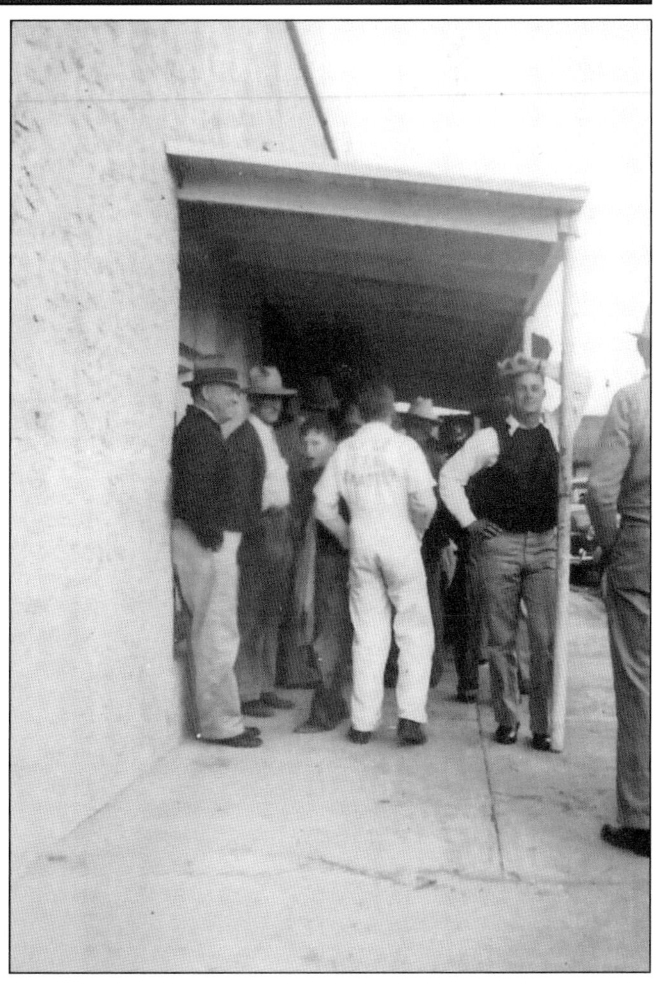

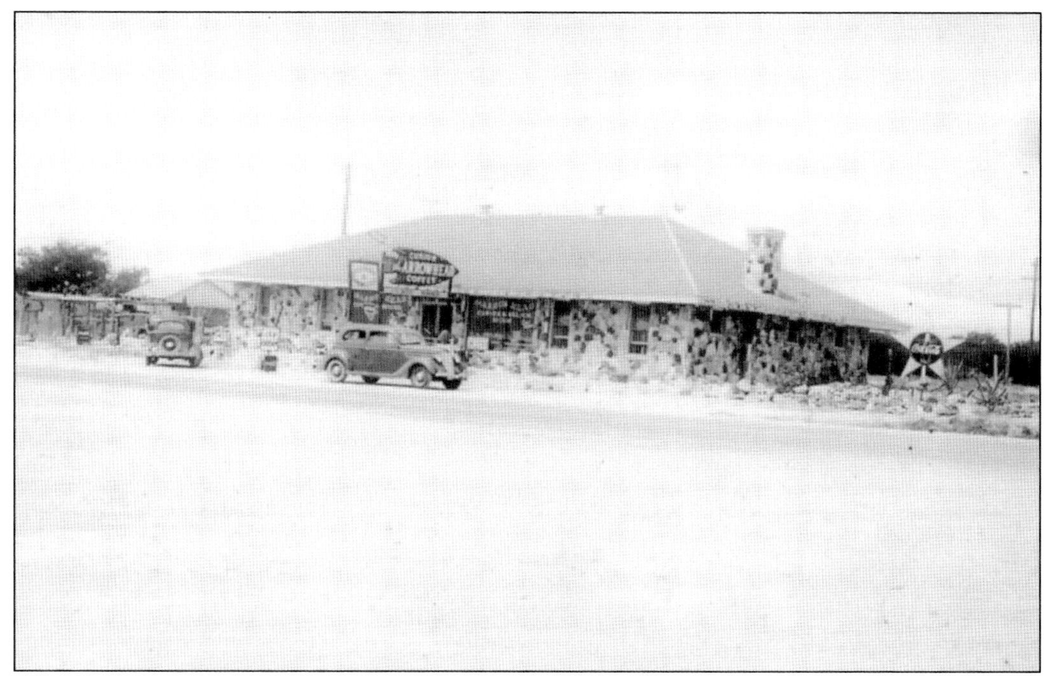

The rock structure pictured was built in the 1930s and served the rail travelers from the depot and later automobile travelers on Highway 81. Called the Arrowhead Trading Company, the building housed a souvenir ("curios and relics") store and later a café. The café had a jukebox and was a popular gathering place for young people in the 1950s. In the years since, the building has housed a variety of businesses. (Both, courtesy of the Miller family.)

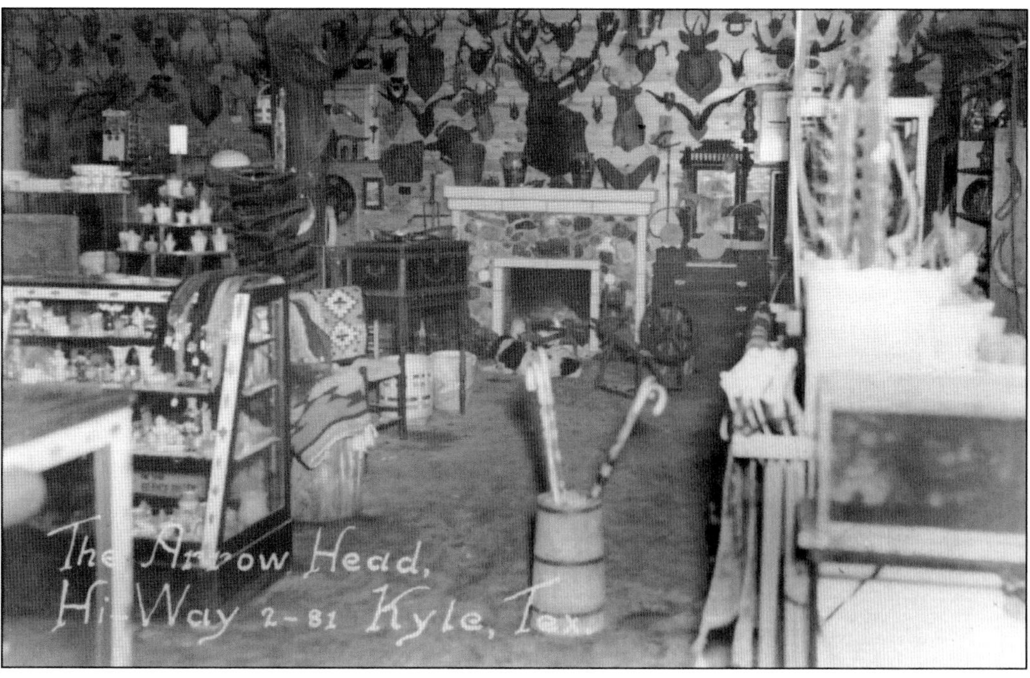

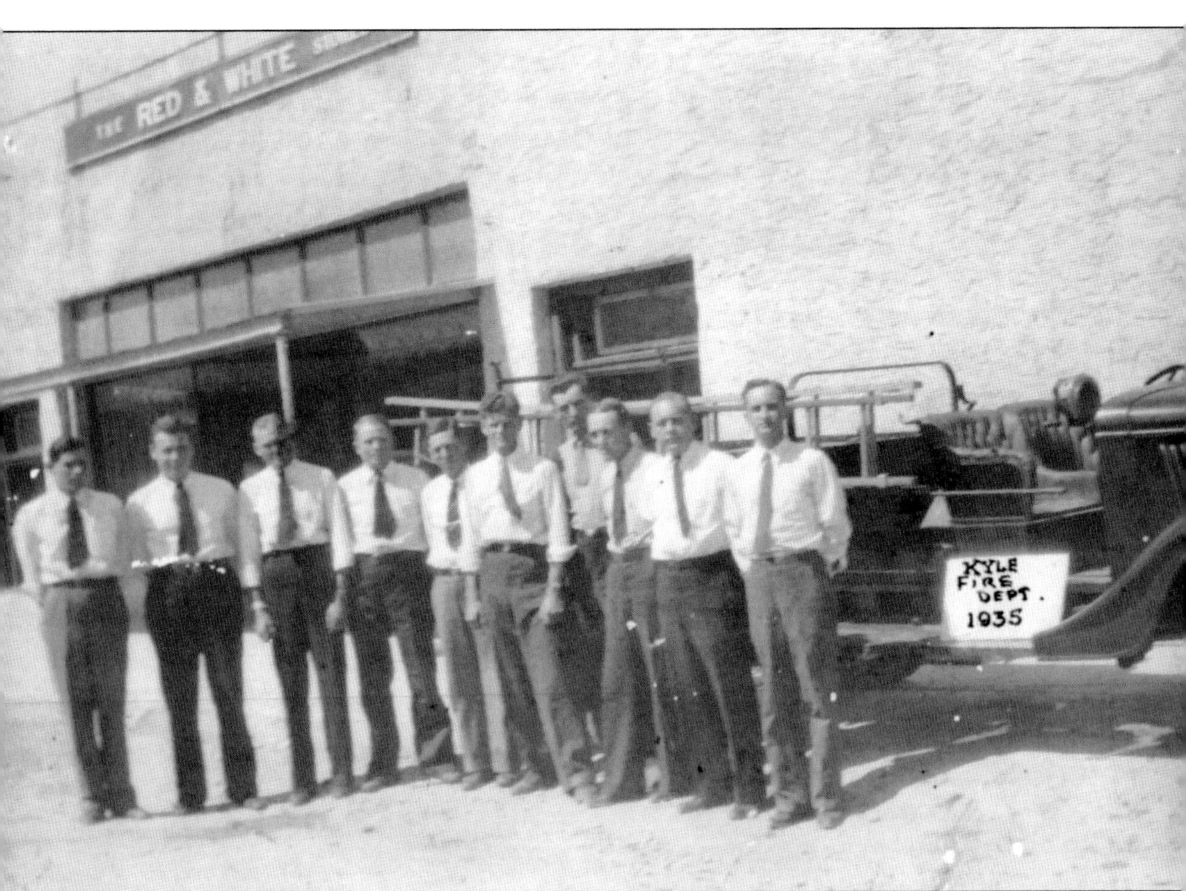

Fire was a constant threat in the first century of Kyle's existence. Wooden structures, open flame stoves for heating and cooking, and trash-burning often resulted in the tragic loss of lives and property. After the Bon Ton fire in 1934, the volunteer fire department was reorganized, membership was increased, and new equipment was purchased. The volunteer fire department, pictured in 1935, was an integral part of the community. From left to right are Chief Cecil Evans, Charles Young, R. Toalson, A. Schmeltekopf, J. Howard, F.W. Miller Jr., R. Homan, Lee Williams, Newt Millhollon, and Bob Kercheville. (Courtesy of the Schmeltekopf family.)

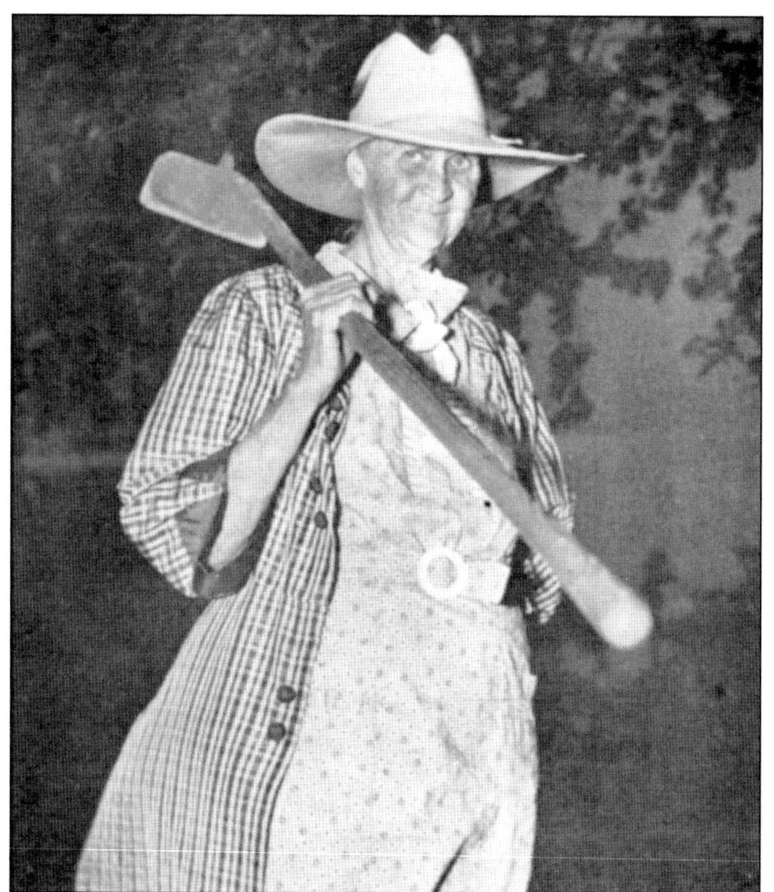

Kyle made national news when *Life* magazine ran a story of Mayor Mary Kyle Hartson and her all-woman government during the 1940s. Nominated as a write-in candidate by her friend Mamie Word, Hartson was elected mayor in 1937 and served until 1946. The photograph at left is from the *Life* article and shows Hartson with a hoe, noting that she "cleaned up" the town. In the 1942 photograph below are, from left to right, Mamie Word, Lula White Kercheville, Mary Kyle Hartson, and Jessie Kercheville Sledgein. (Left, courtesy of Jim Cullen; below, courtesy of the Word family.)

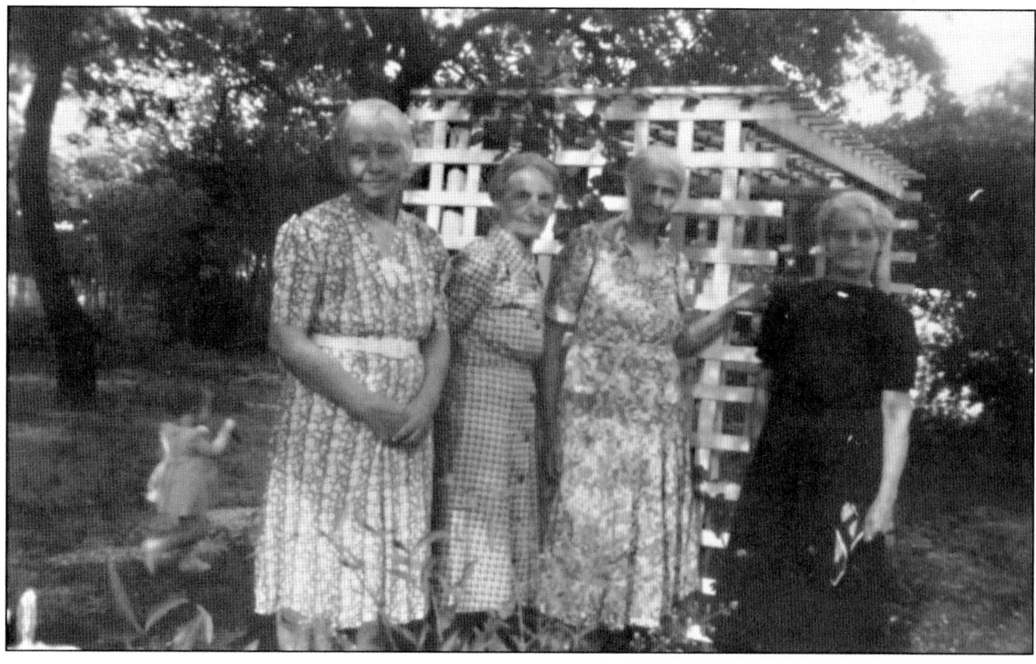

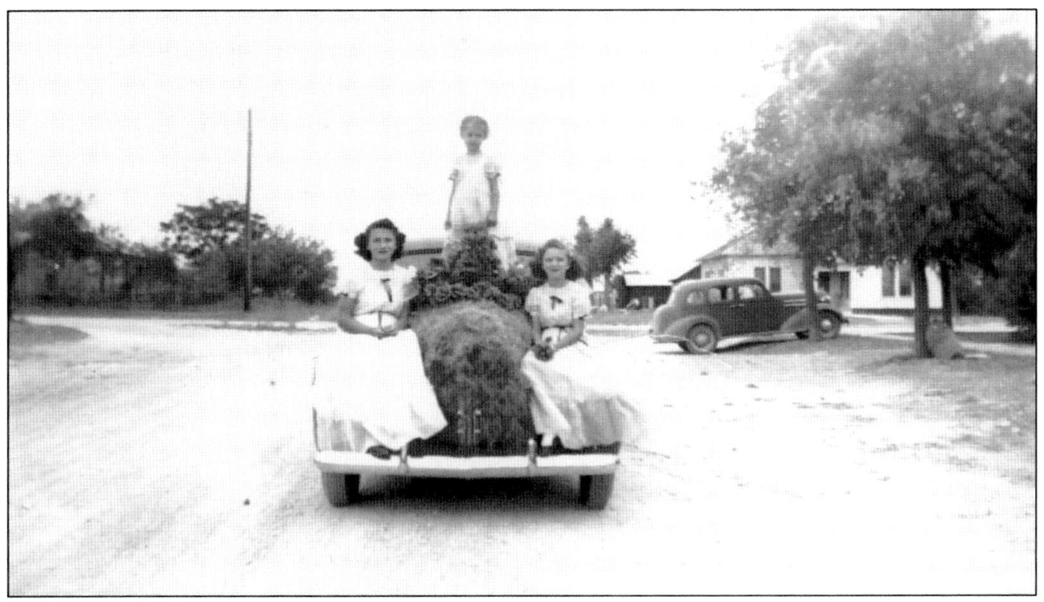

This 1940 parade included a decorated car carrying what appears to be "royalty" of the event being celebrated. From left to right are Virginia Guttery, Wynette Word (standing), and Nancy Kercheville. (Courtesy of the Word family.)

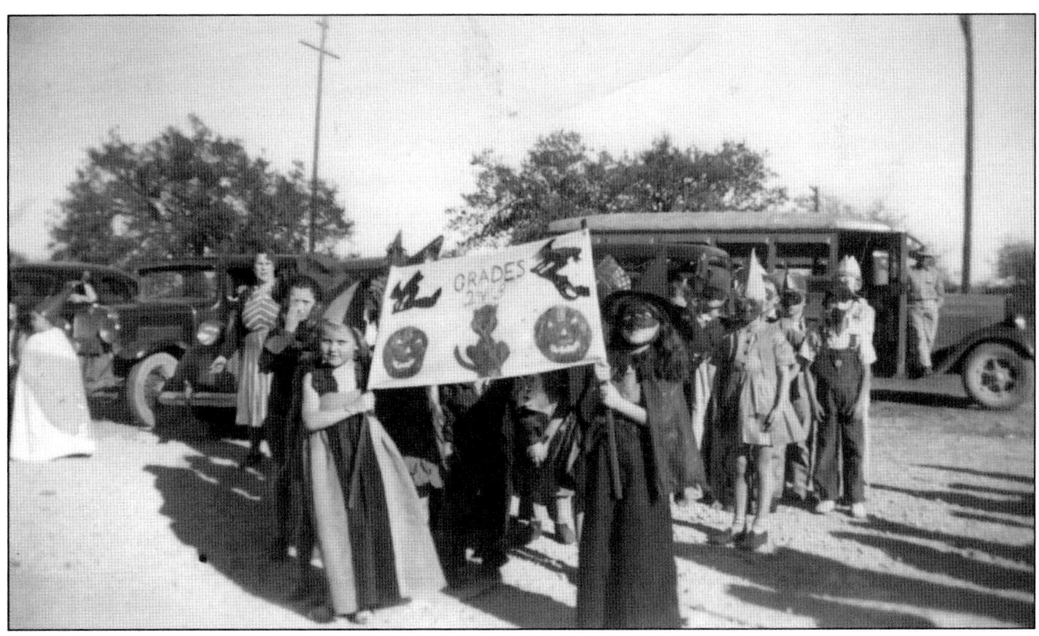

In spite of World War II, the children in Kyle still celebrated Halloween 1942 with a parade. Pictured are second and third grade students in their costumes. (Courtesy of the Word family.)

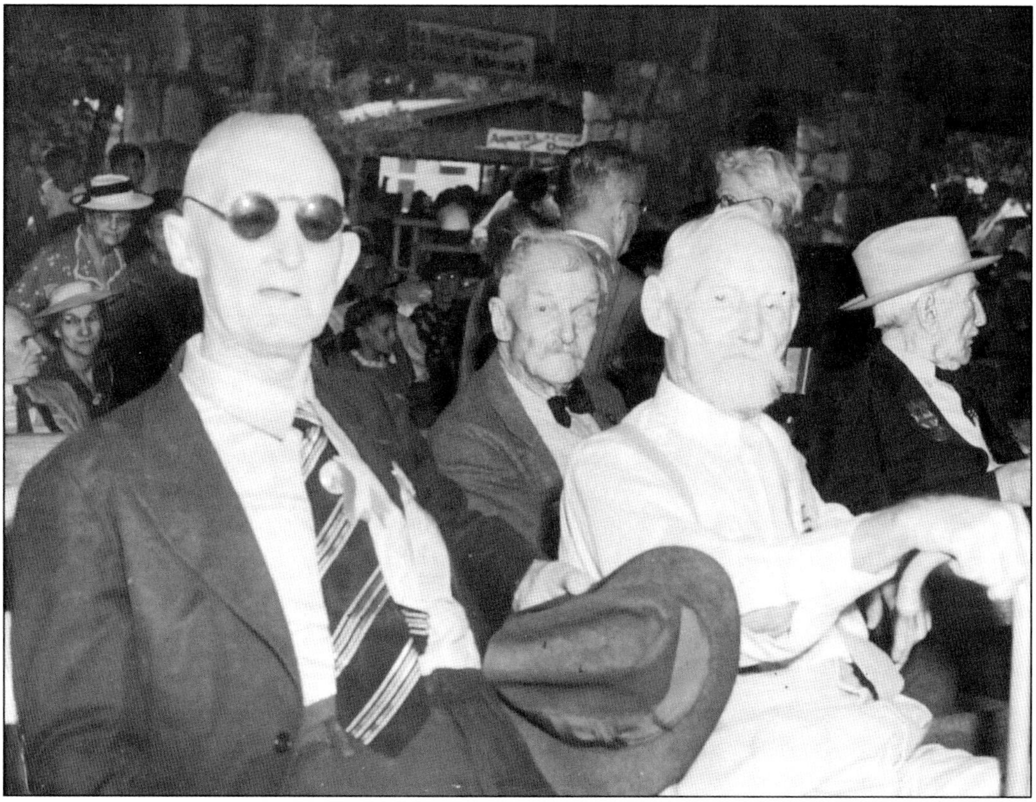

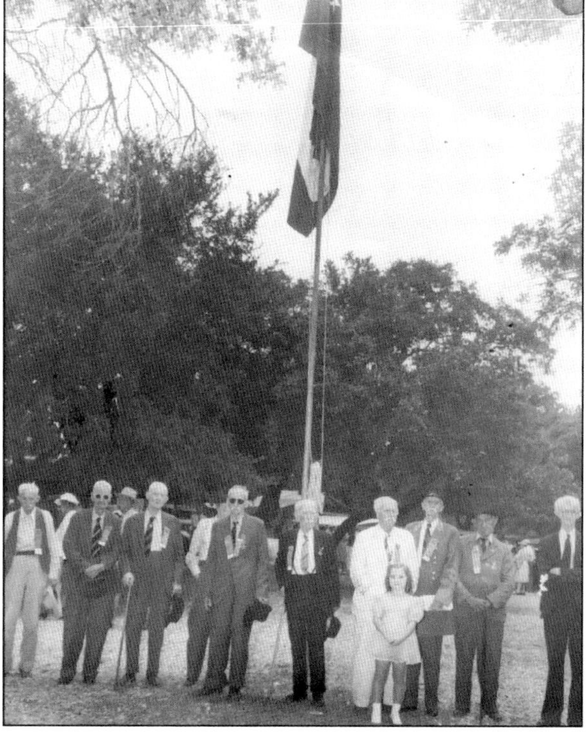

Held each year in Driftwood, the Camp Ben McCulloch Confederate Reunion was a popular summer event for many Kyle citizens. Other than 1918 (because of World War I), it has been held continuously since its inception in 1896. At the far right of the photograph at left is editor T.F. Harwell of the *Kyle News* at the 1941 reunion. (Both, courtesy of the Neal Douglass Collection, Austin History Center, Austin Public Library.)

Six

Mid-Century Changes

After two decades of worldwide turmoil came postwar prosperity. However, Kyle and its residents faced new challenges at the middle of the 20th century. While the town's population did not grow significantly, the school population was larger than ever, putting a strain on the facilities that had been built in the 1930s. Because of the baby boom and the increased number of students staying in school to graduate, more classrooms and teachers were needed. Kyle, like other small towns, began to add extracurricular activities at school, which became important to the entire community. Few new businesses came to Kyle, as people were able to travel to neighboring larger towns more easily. However, social changes came to Kyle, as well as pressures to move beyond the segregated school system that had been utilized since the Kyle schools were founded. Discussions begun in the 1930s about consolidating with surrounding districts resurfaced periodically, with a failing referendum election held in 1963. A successful election was held in 1967, resulting in the consolidation of Kyle, Buda, and Wimberley into the Hays Consolidated Independent School District. No one was happier about the consolidation vote than Robert C. Barton Sr., a Buda teacher, administrator, and board member who had advocated such a plan for more than 40 years. Barton Middle School is named for him. These years marked endings and beginnings.

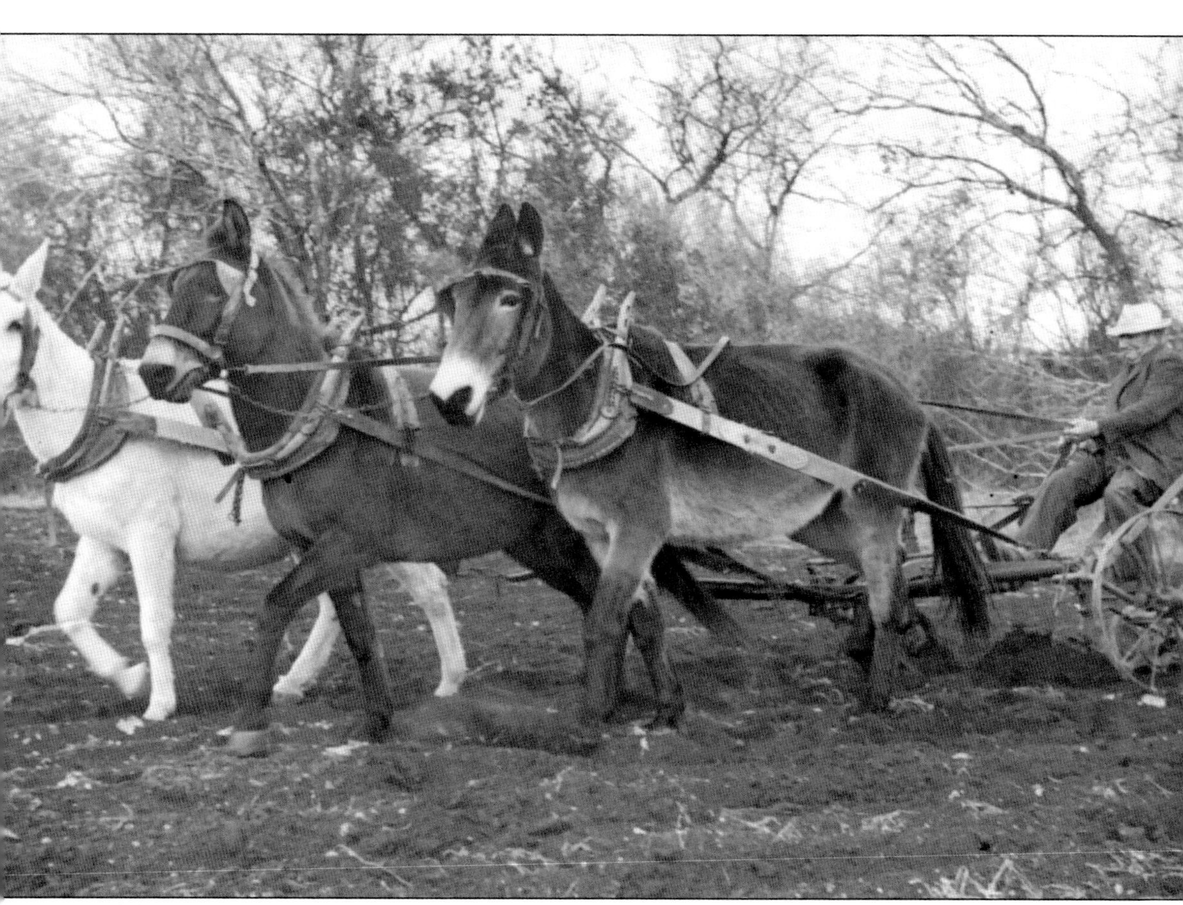

While many things changed in and around Kyle, some locals held onto old traditions. Pictured above, Gus Hessler still used mules to plow, as his ancestors had for years before. (Courtesy of the Word family.)

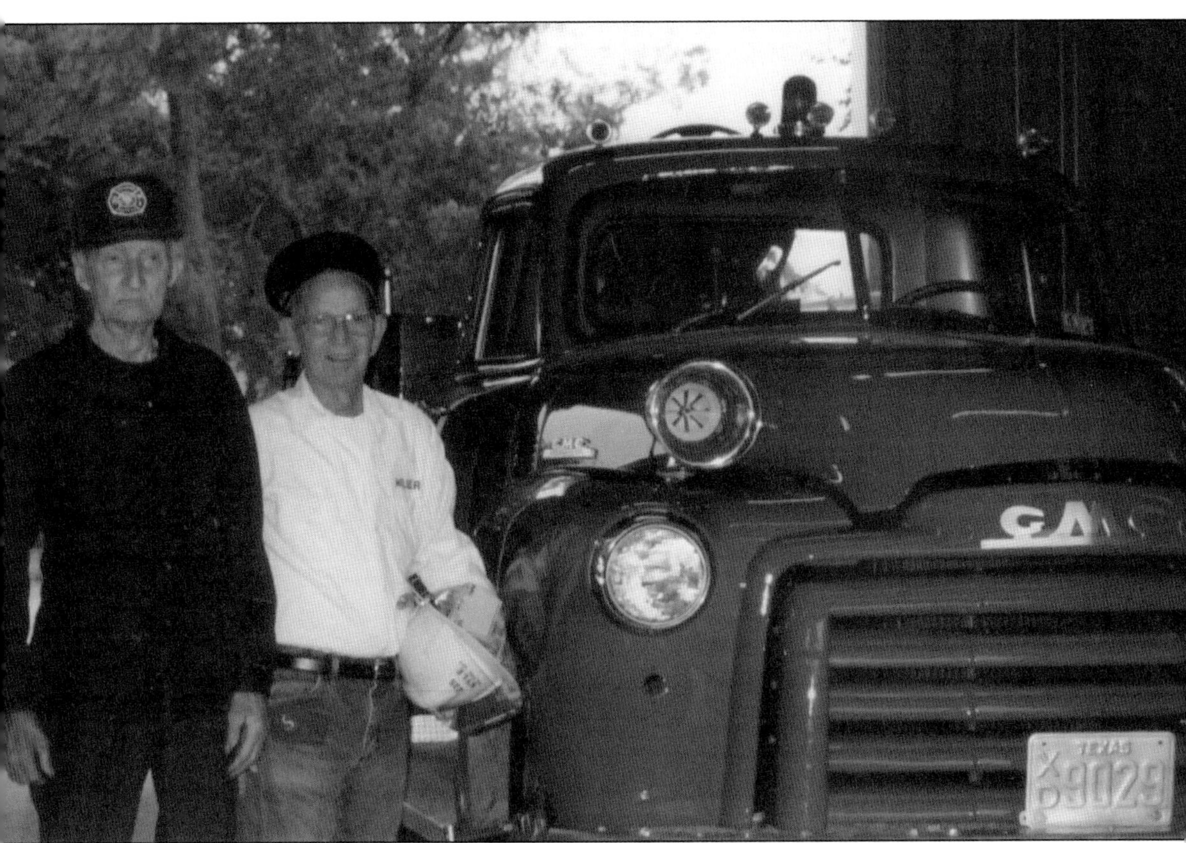

A review of Kyle history reveals how devastating fires could be to a community. Pictured in 1959 are two men who served as fire chief during the 20th century in Kyle, George Whitaker (left) and James Miller (right). The new fire station in Kyle is named after these two men. (Courtesy of the Miller family.)

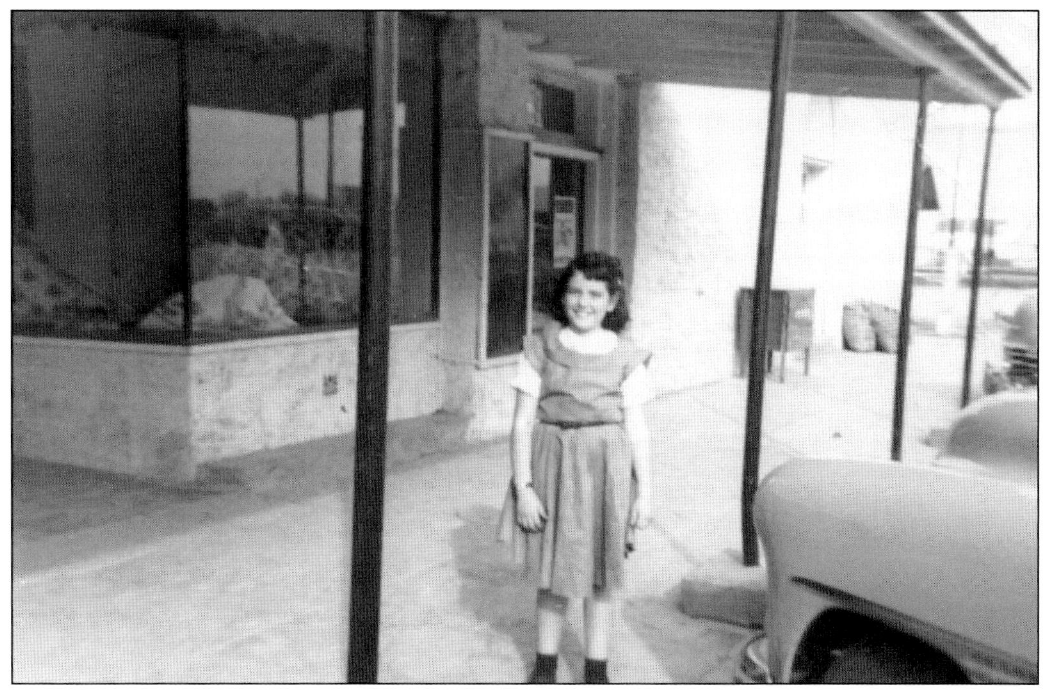

The Bon Ton continued to be the hub of activity in Kyle, as it had been for the last three decades. Lex Word sold his interest in the store to former employee Cecil Bales in 1963. The store continued in operation under other owners until it burned in 2002. In the above photograph is Nancy Word Osgood; below, a parade passes by the Bon Ton. (Both, courtesy of the Word family.)

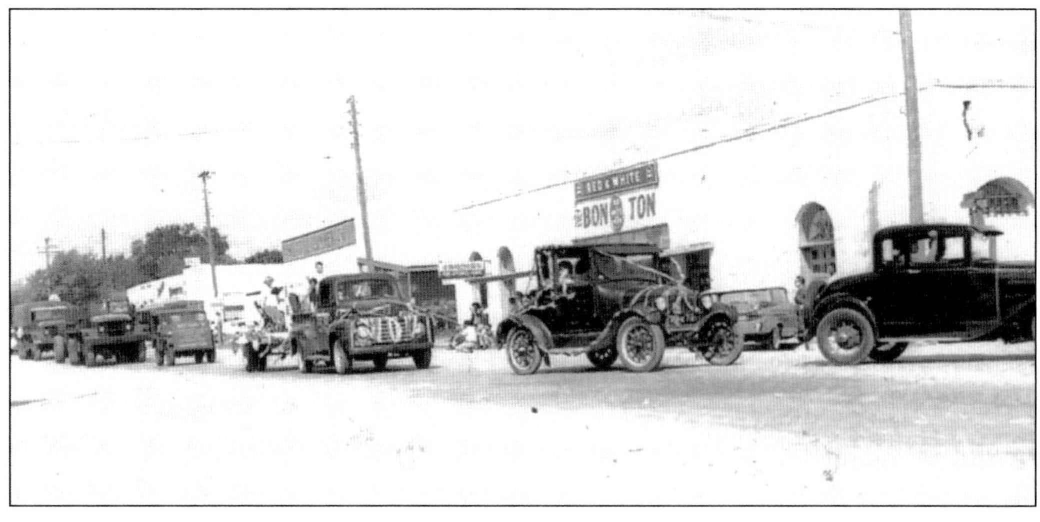

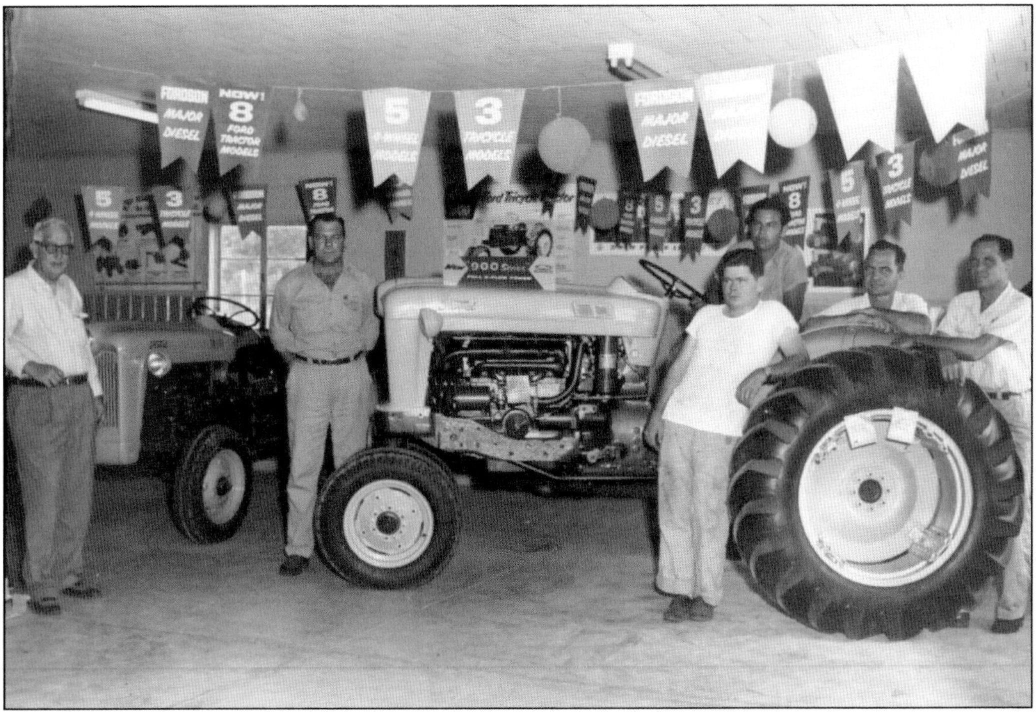

The Hays County Implement Company, next door to the Bon Ton, was opened in 1936. It prospered during the Depression and was sold in the 1960s. Pictured above are, from left to right, Lex Word, Lawrence Schmeltekopf, Jesse Sawyer, Panteleon Tenorio (on the tractor), Joe Wiegand, and Johnny Gruenbein. Pictured below are, from left to right, Sawyer, Wiegand, Word, Schmeltekopf, Gruenbein, and Tenorio. (Both, courtesy of the Word family.)

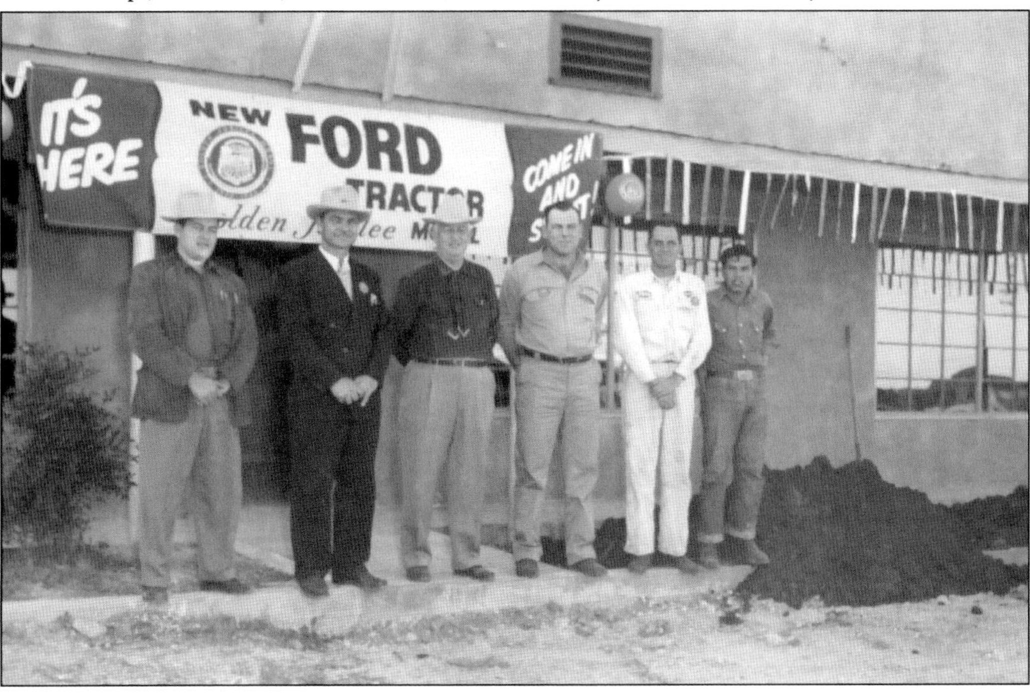

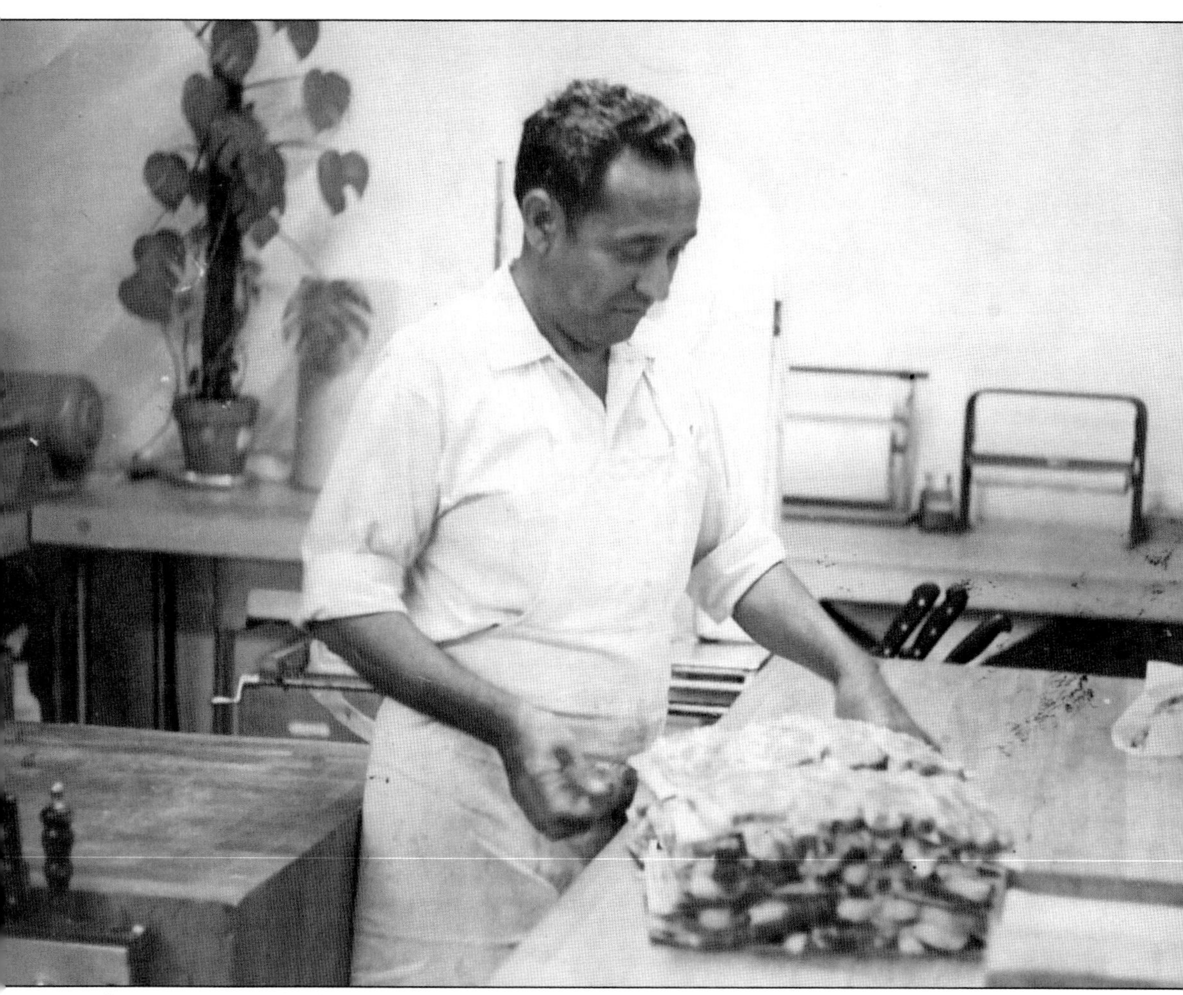

Blas Tenorio is a third-generation citizen of Kyle; his grandfather worked at the Nance Mill. He joined the Army in 1943, returning to Kyle in 1945 to work at Millhollon Grocery and attend night school for veterans. He and his brother Sam purchased their own store in 1953 and later moved it across the street. Tenorio was the first Hispanic elected to the Kyle City Council and has been active in the community in many ways. (Courtesy HFP.)

One of the most unusual enterprises in Kyle was P.J. Allen's float-making business. The son of a former Hays County sheriff and Texas Ranger, Allen attended college at Southwest Texas State (now Texas State University) in San Marcos and went to New York, where he worked as a dancer and commercial display designer. He moved back to San Antonio in 1946 and then to Kyle in 1958. His business covered several barns and smaller buildings near his home. Starting with plans and sometimes scale models, Allen designed floats for parades throughout the state. After his death, his family held auctions to share the warehouse of float parts with others. (Right, courtesy HFP; below, courtesy of the Allen family.)

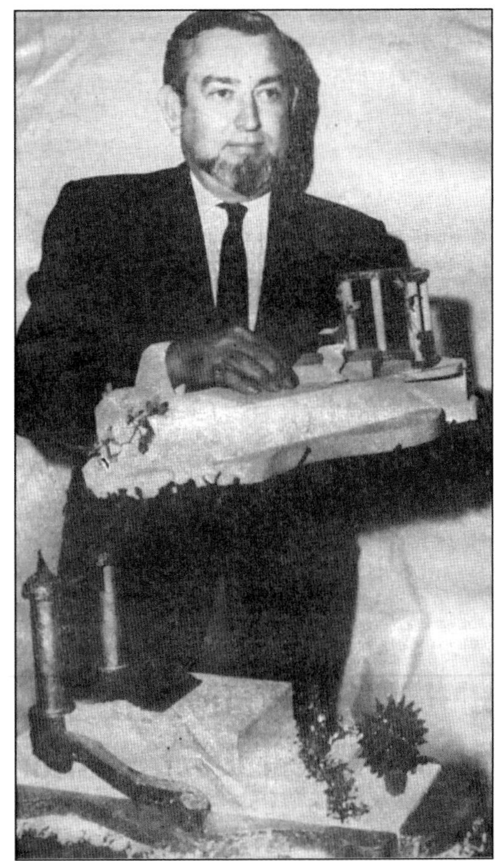

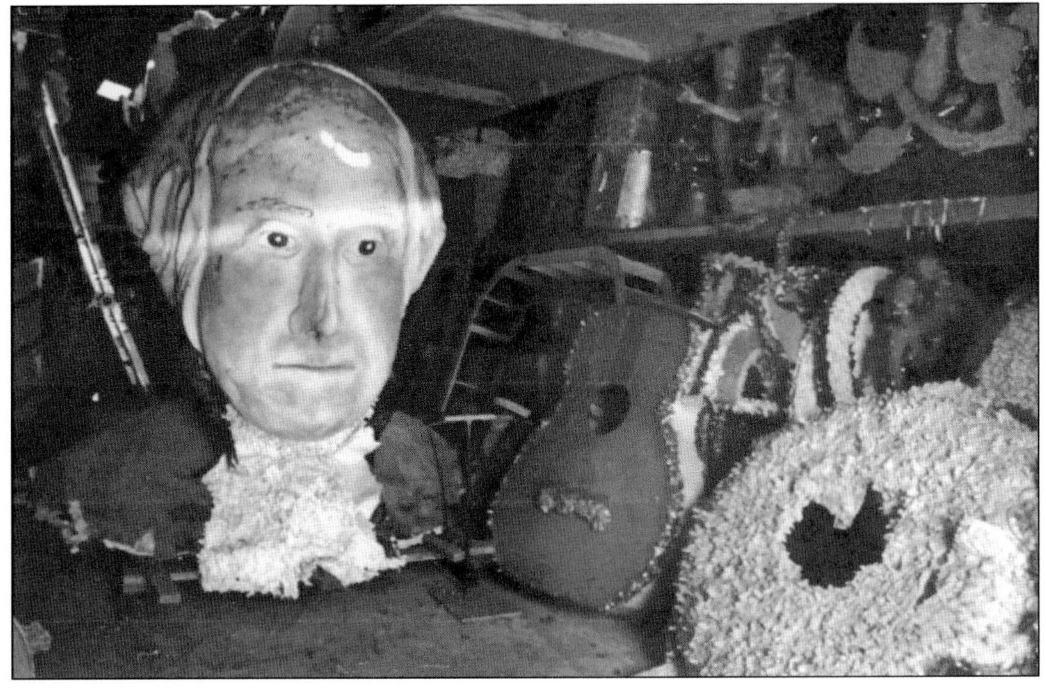

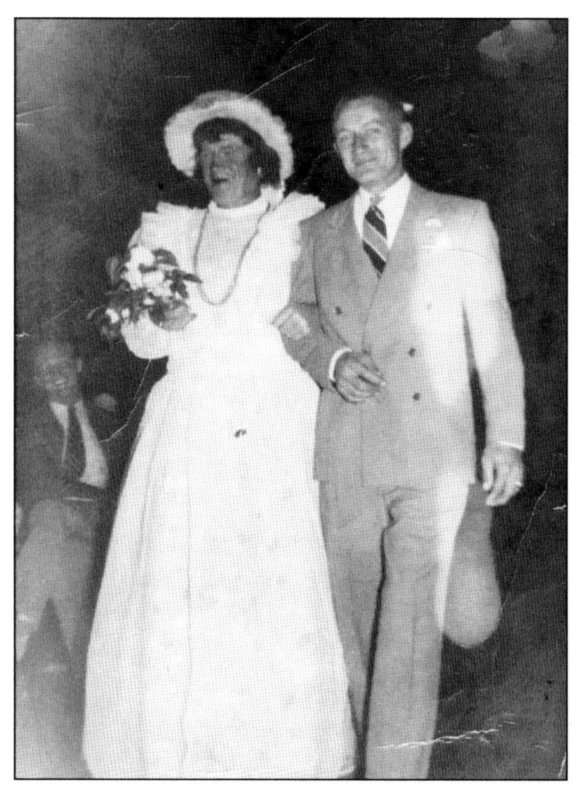

Civic organizations were formed and flourished during the postwar years in Kyle. The Lions Club was formed in 1948 and quickly grew in membership. In the photograph at left, Lions Club members Adolph Hill (left) and Jesse Hauptrief (right) are the stars of a "womanless wedding" held as a club fundraiser. The Home Demonstration Club for rural homemakers was formed in 1936. After a few years of inactivity during war years, the club was reestablished in the 1950s. A club meeting is shown below. (Courtesy of the Schmeltekopf family.)

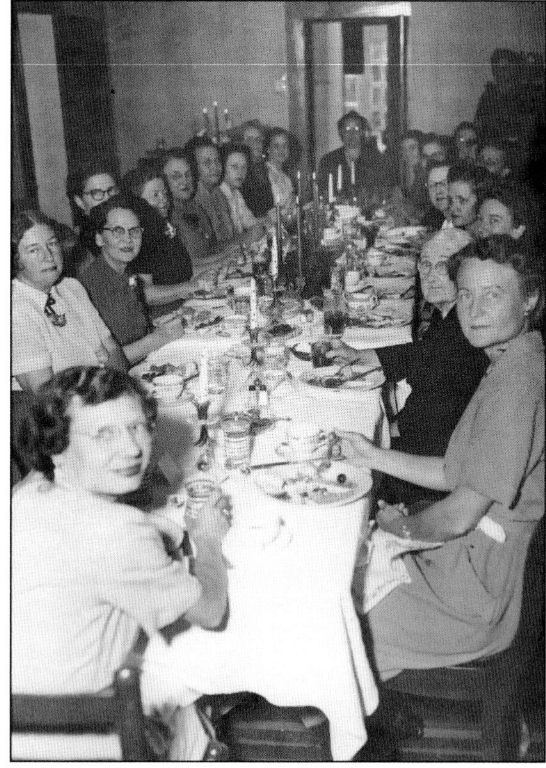

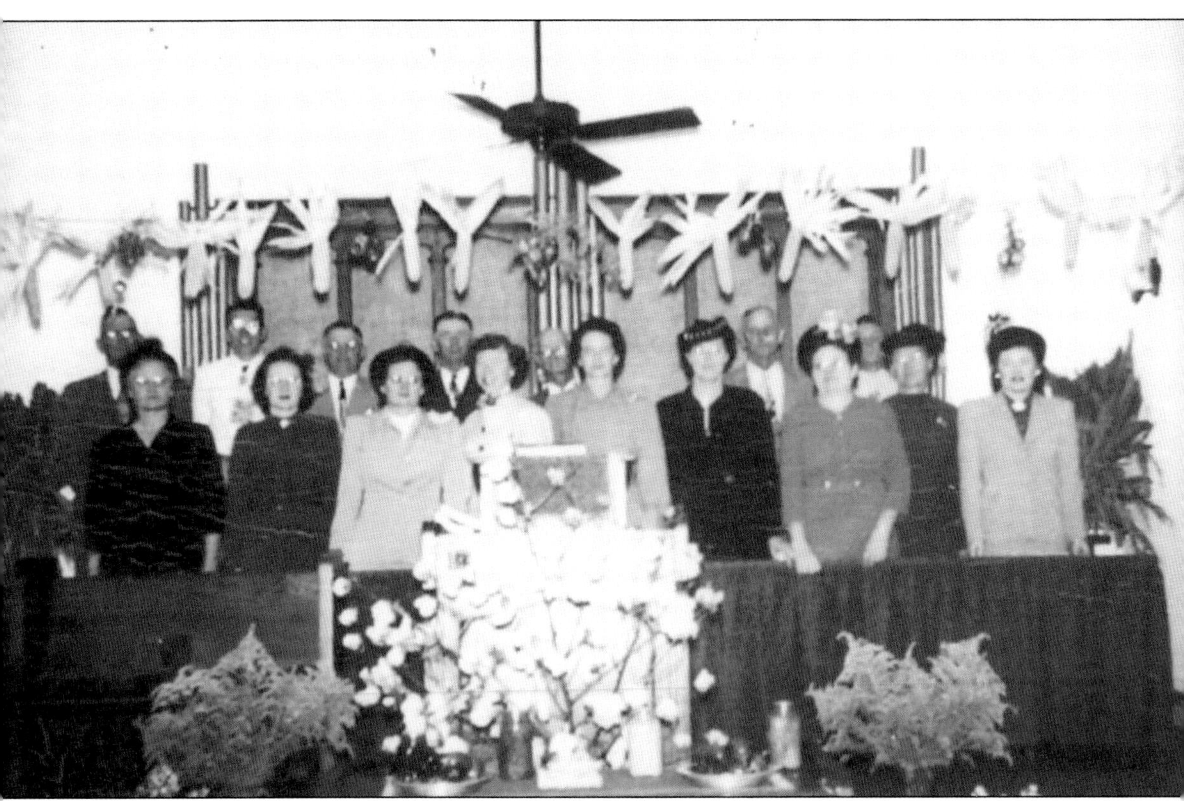

Immanuel Baptist Church, originally formed as Kyle German Baptist Church by German immigrant families in late 19th century, continued to be active in postwar years. The fall Harvest Mission Festival celebrated the agricultural heritage and lifestyle of the congregation. This photograph shows the church in October 1949, decorated with corn, cotton, produce, and preserved food. (Courtesy IBC.)

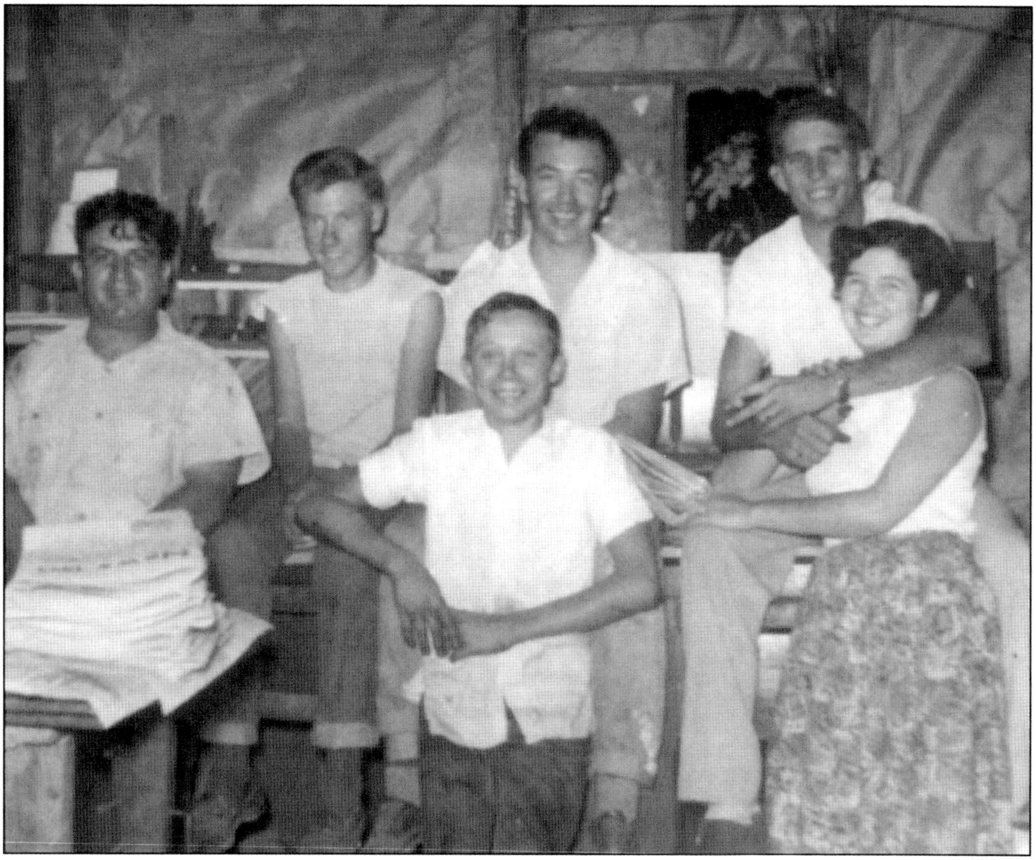

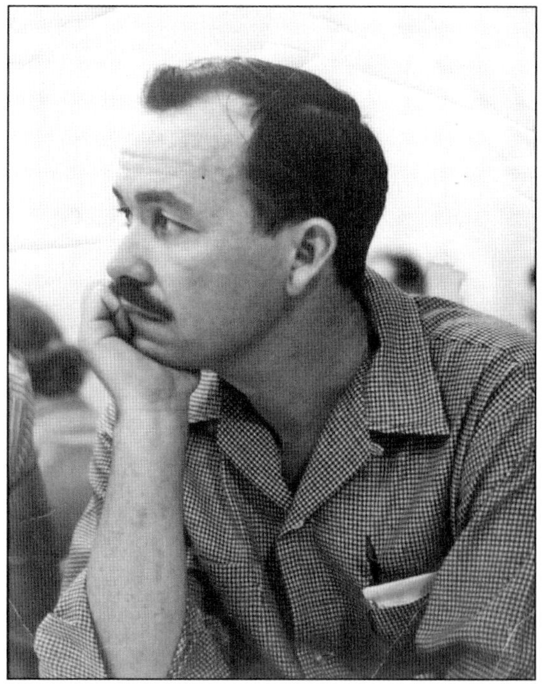

In 1953, the *Kyle News* was purchased and operated by two young men with no prior newspaper experience. Shown above are new owners Bob Barton (second row, second from right) and Moe Johnson (second row, far right, with wife Gene). Before long, Johnson left journalism for teaching and coaching. Barton was involved in the newspaper business and politics for the rest of his life. (Both, courtesy HFP.)

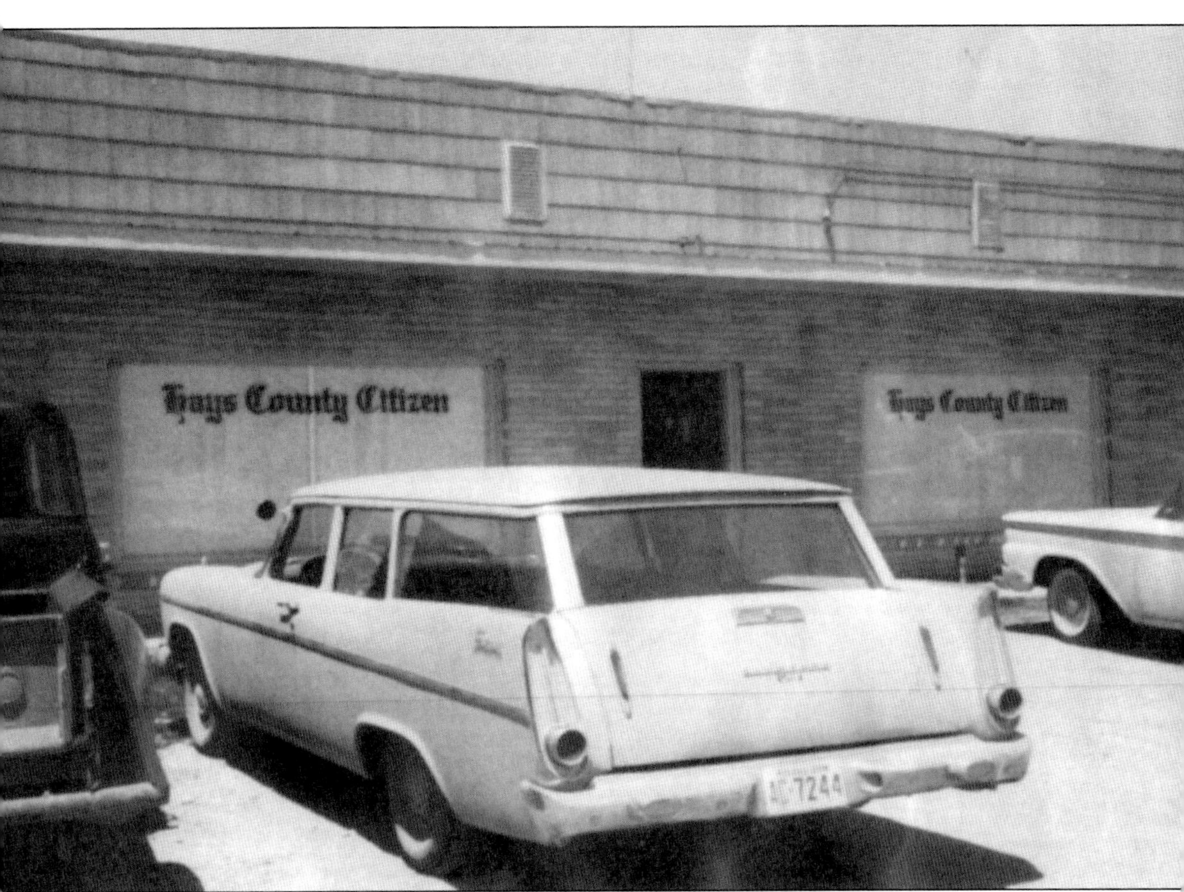

Barton changed the name of the *Kyle News* to the *Hays County Citizen* and operated it until 1978, when it was sold. He later founded the *Hays Free Press*, which is still published by the Barton family today. (Courtesy HFP.)

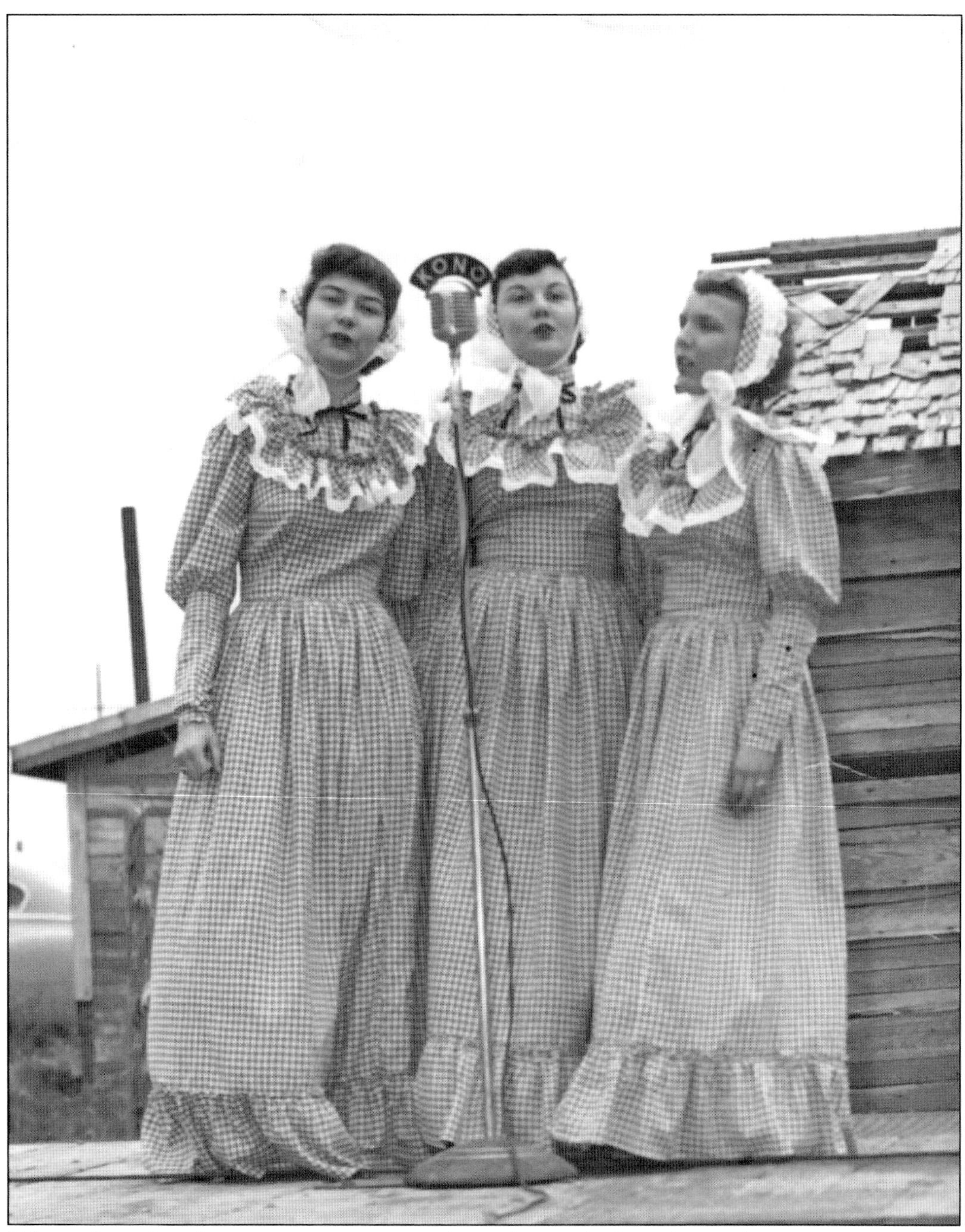

Kyle residents found many ways to entertain themselves and others during the postwar years. This trio of Kyle High School girls sang for many events in the community and throughout the area. The group included, from left to right, Wynette (Tutta) Word, Joan Strawn, and Mary Margaret Teasley. (Courtesy of the Word family.)

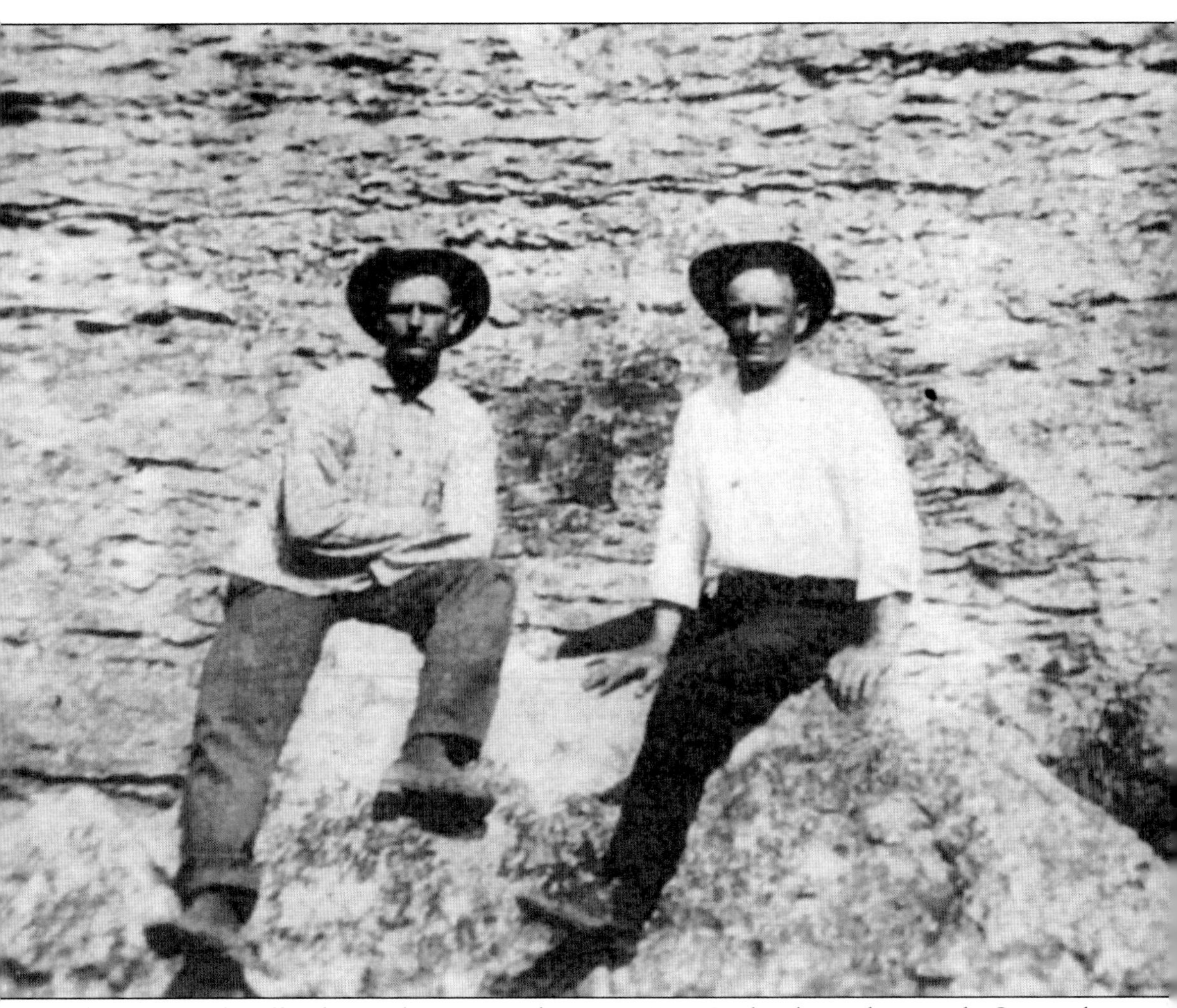

The river nearby offered several recreational opportunities. In the above photograph, Otto and Ernest Hill climb the rocks near the river. (Courtesy of the Schmeltekopf family.)

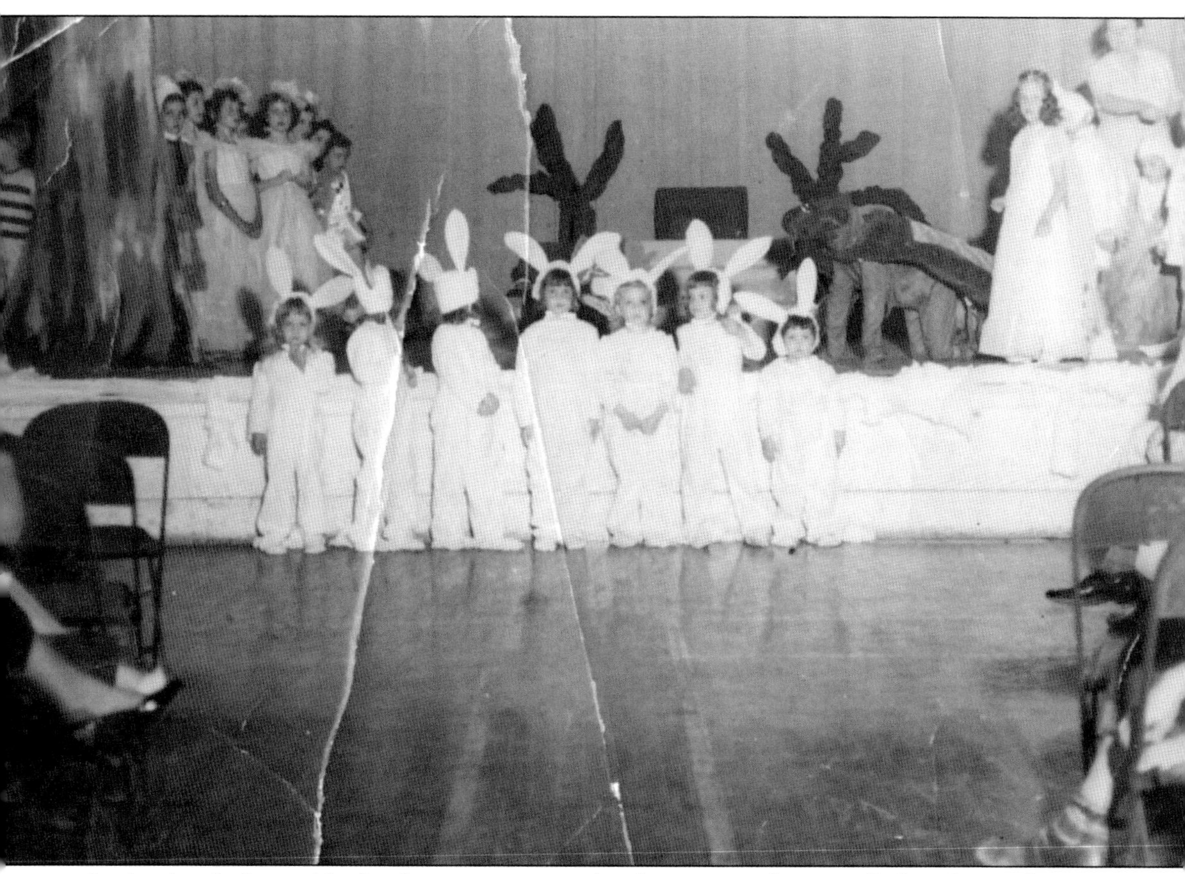

In the days before public kindergarten, private kindergartens often enrolled students of various ages. This photograph shows Riso Millhollon's kindergarten students performing with the older school students in the gym. (Courtesy of the Schmeltekopf family.)

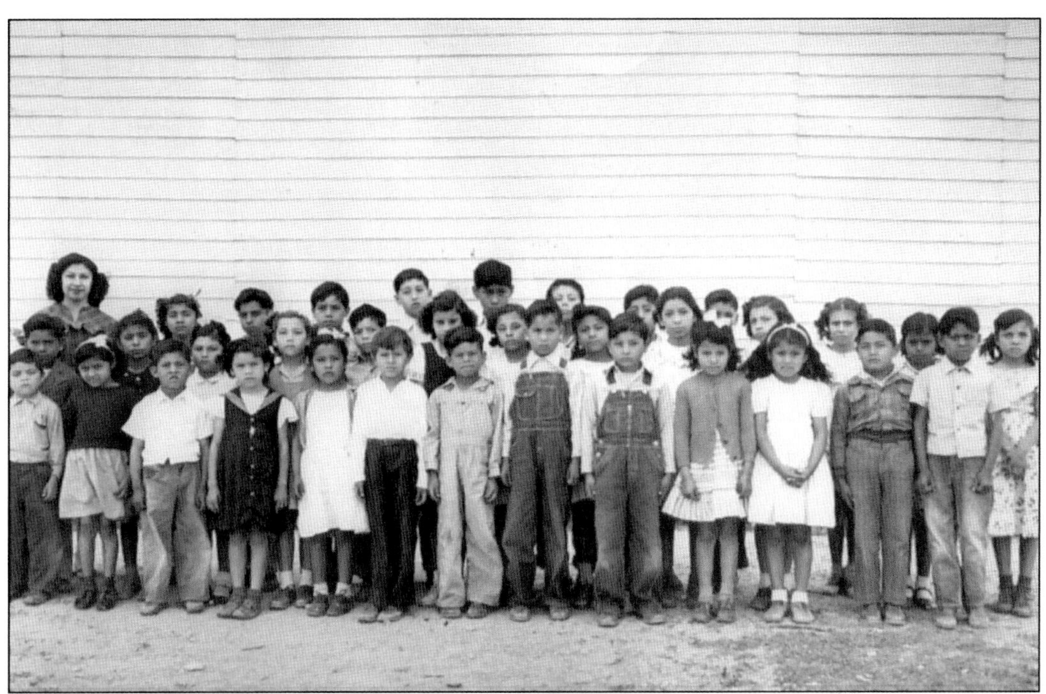

Kyle, like many towns in Texas, operated separate schools for Mexican American children, contending that the language issue justified the practice. Some Mexican American children "crossed over" and attended the "Anglo" schools so they could graduate from high school. Pictured above is Sarah Ortunio Gomez (third row, far left) with her class in 1947. In 1941, Gomez became the first Mexican American to graduate from Kyle High School. She later became a teacher in the district and taught at the Mexican school until it was combined with the "town" school. (Courtesy of Sarah Ortunio Gomez.)

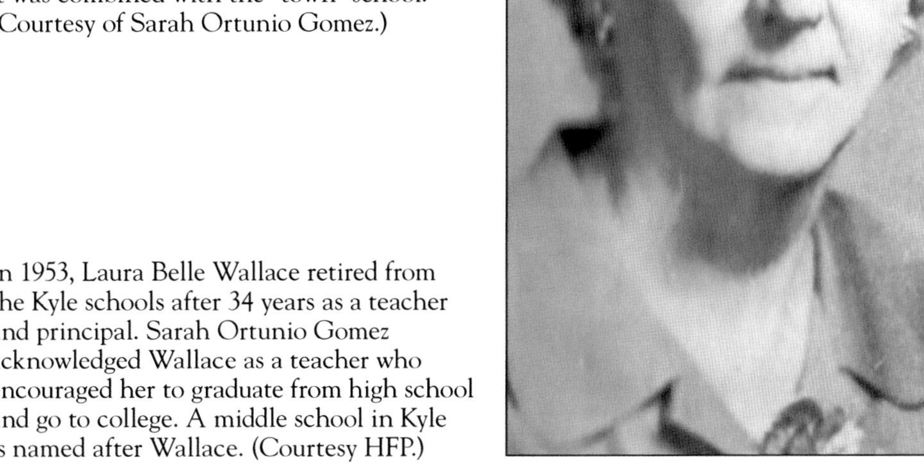

In 1953, Laura Belle Wallace retired from the Kyle schools after 34 years as a teacher and principal. Sarah Ortunio Gomez acknowledged Wallace as a teacher who encouraged her to graduate from high school and go to college. A middle school in Kyle is named after Wallace. (Courtesy HFP.)

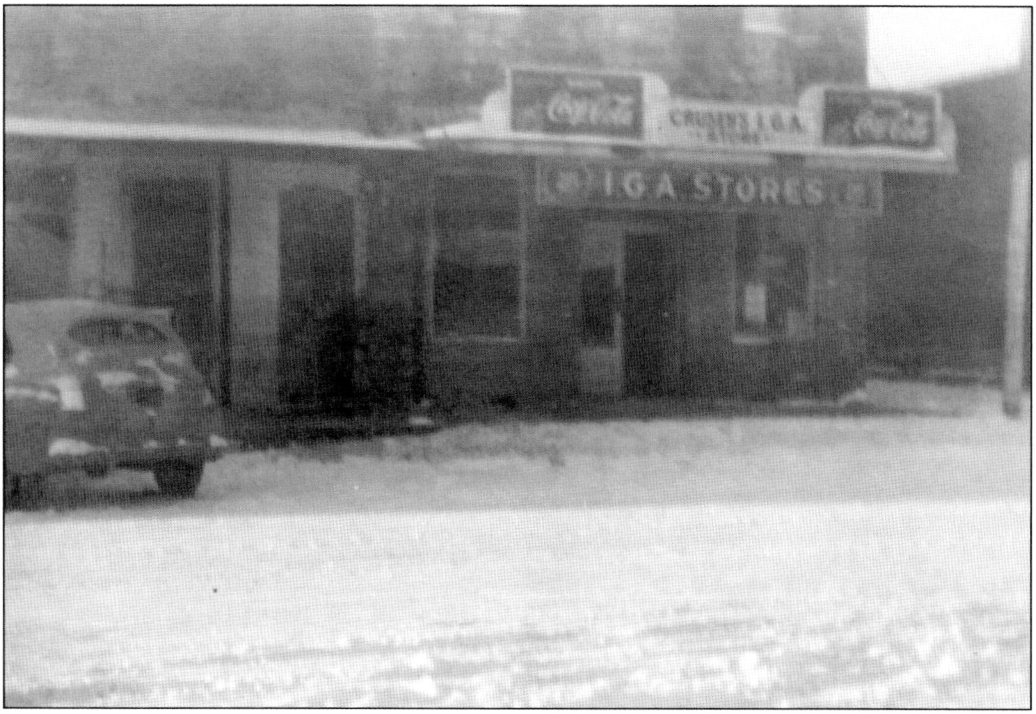

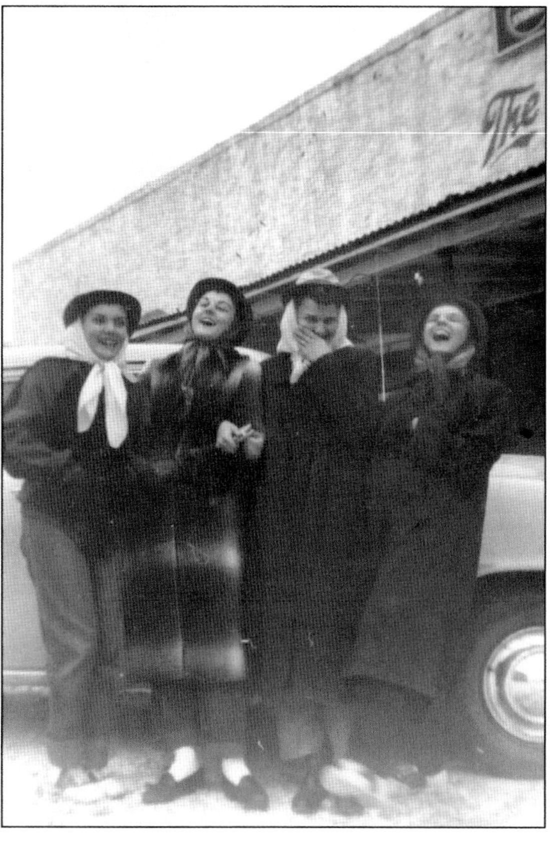

Snow is an unusual occurrence in central Texas, so a big snowfall in Kyle was a rare photo opportunity in 1950. The above photograph shows Causey's store on Center Street. In the photograph at left are, from left to right, Lora Lee Sampson, Joan Strawn, Ann Miller, and Margaret Teasley, bundled up in front of the Bon Ton. (Above, courtesy of the Miller family; left, courtesy of the Word family.)

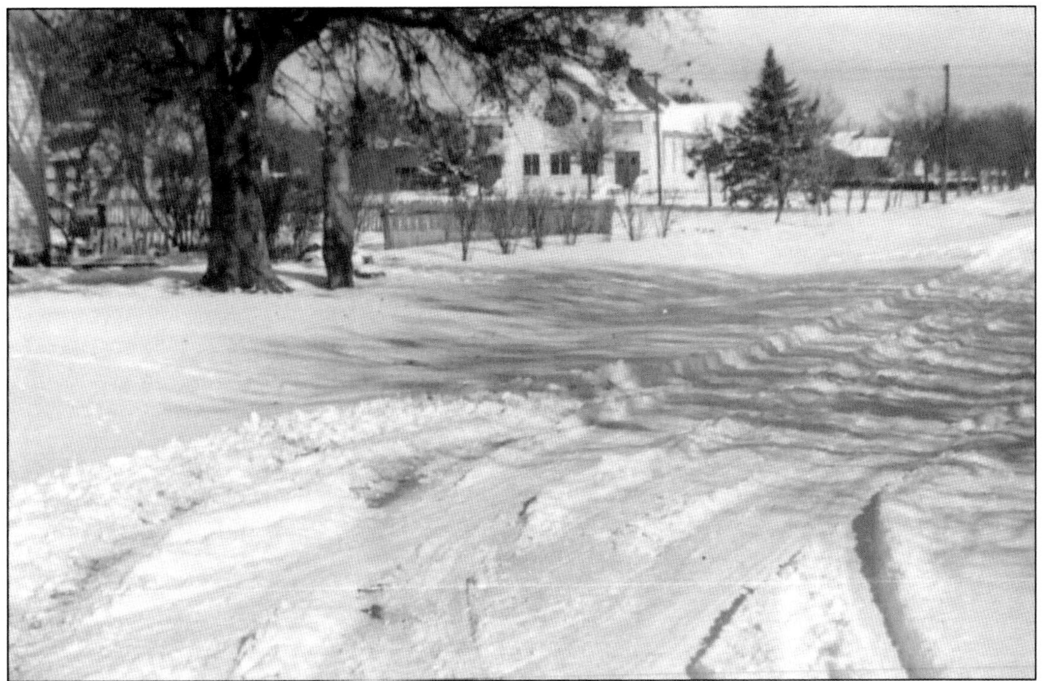

These snow-day photographs show the new First Baptist Church, constructed in 1948 after several years of the church not having a building. The structure was built of Oak Hill–quarried stone, with an oak floor and acoustical tile ceiling. The building cost was $30,000, and the church was free of debt when it was finished. The auditorium seated 235 people. (Both, courtesy of the Miller family.)

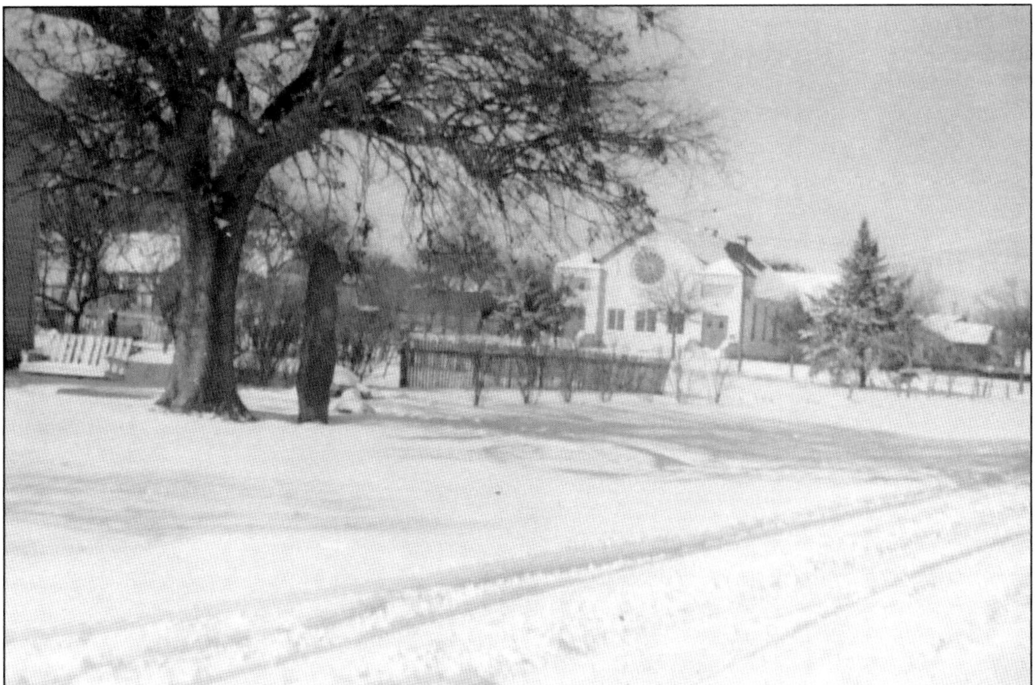

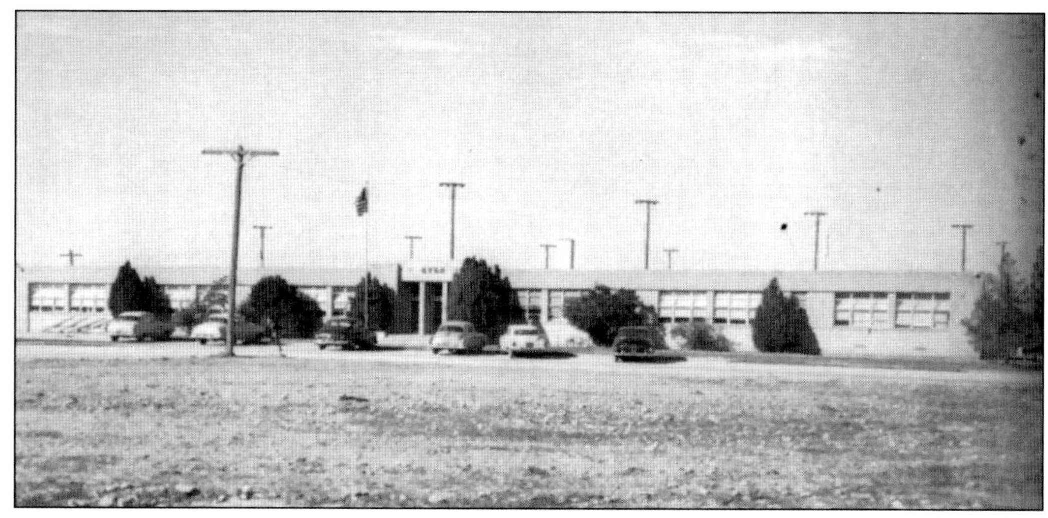

As the school population continued to grow, there was a need to expand the 1930s school building. Several additions were made to the structure over the years. The above photograph shows it in 1957, and the photograph below shows an additional building constructed that same year. (Both, courtesy HFP.)

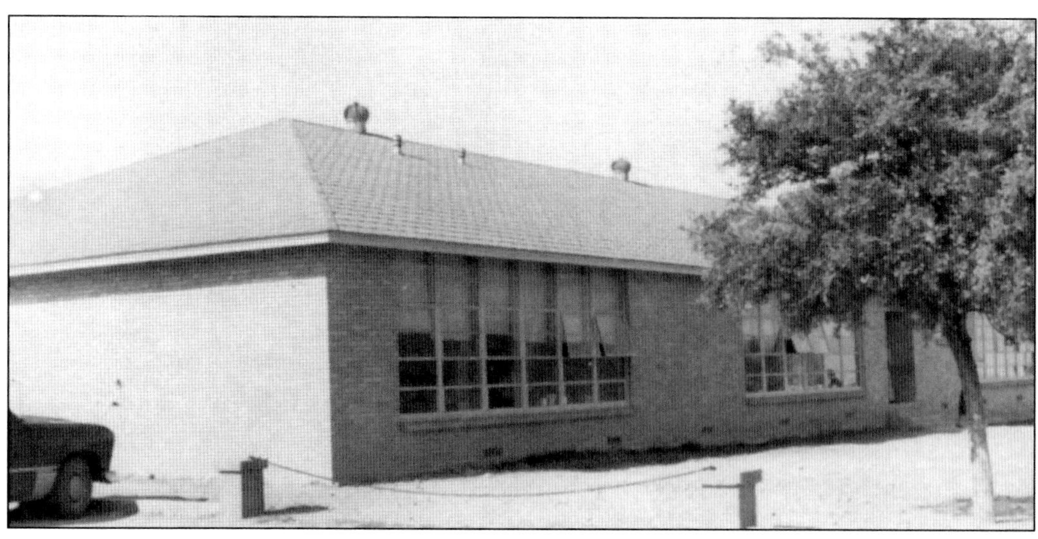

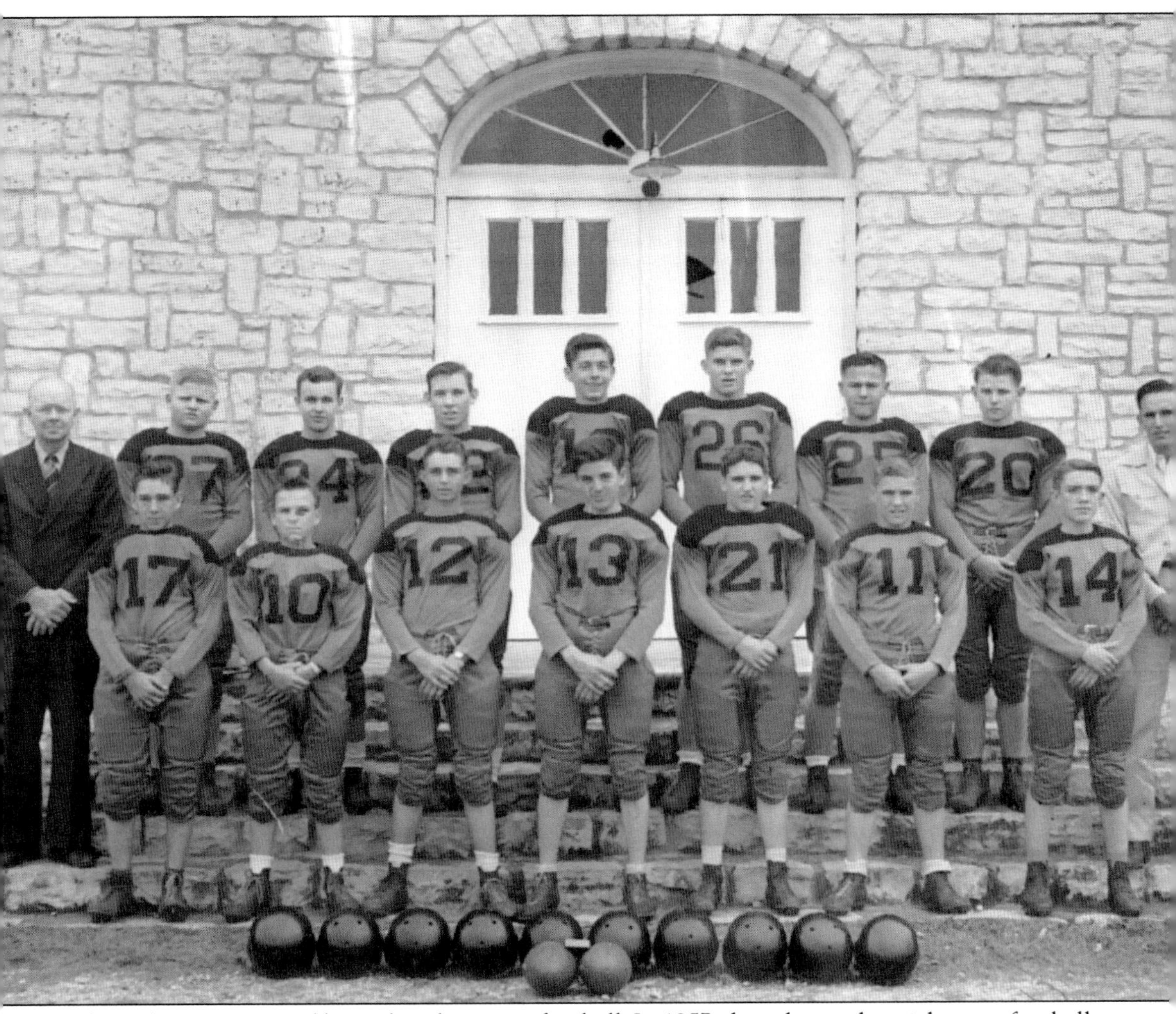

The Kyle team pictured here played six-man football. In 1957, they changed to eight-man football as part of an experiment by the University Interscholastic League. By 1960, Kyle had enough students to play traditional 11-man football. (Courtesy of the Schmeltekopf family.)

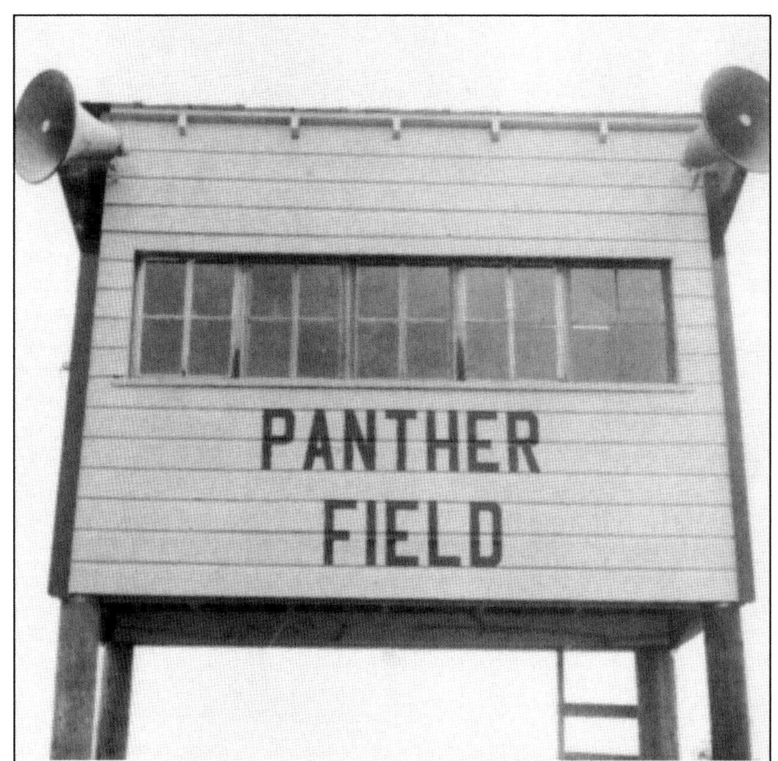

Panther Field, behind the current Kyle Elementary School site, was the home football field. These photographs show the press box and scoreboard in 1957. (Both, courtesy of the Schmeltekopf family.)

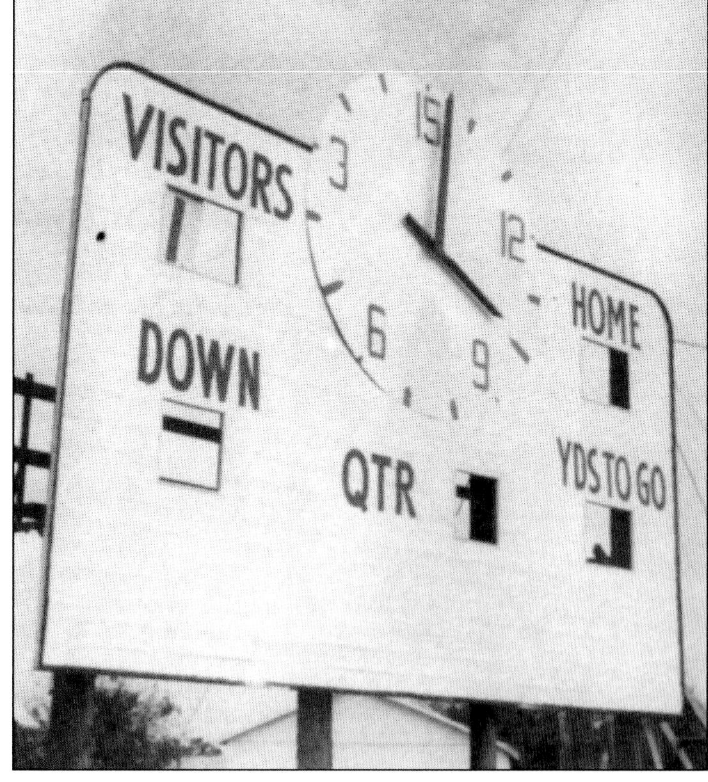

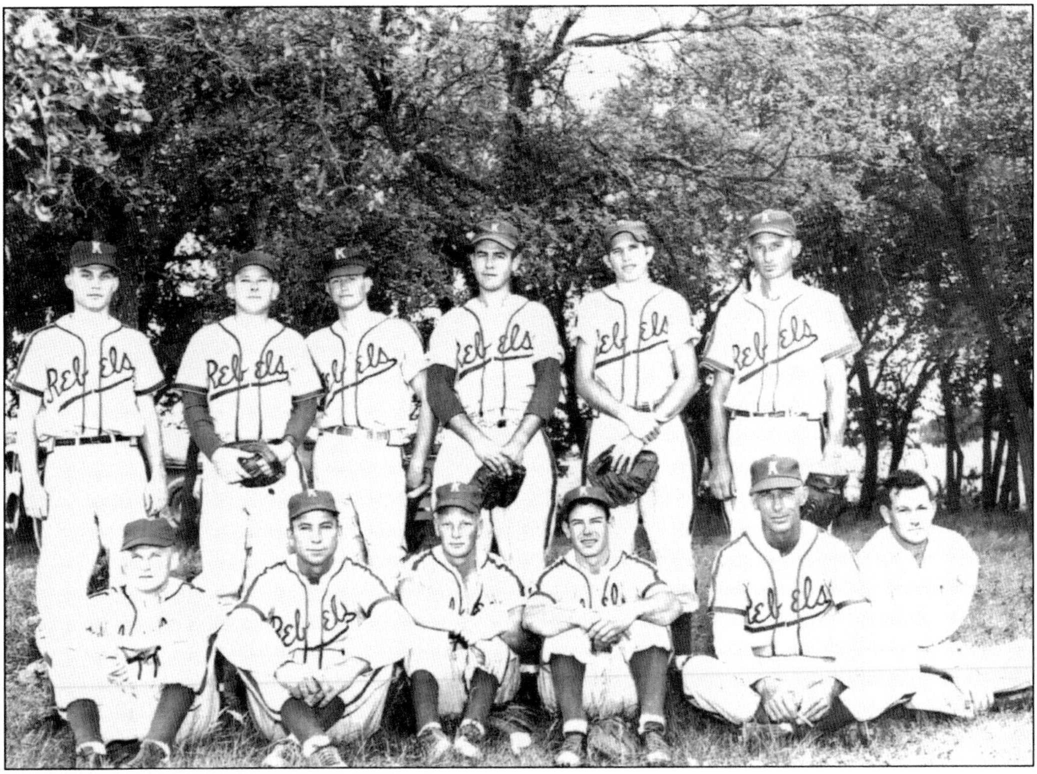

For many years during the postwar era, the town of Kyle had a popular baseball team called the Rebels. Later, when the high school had a team but no uniforms, they wore the town team uniforms with "Rebels" on the front. The photograph below shows girls from the volleyball team in front of the gym in 1953. (Above, courtesy HFP; below, courtesy of the Word family.)

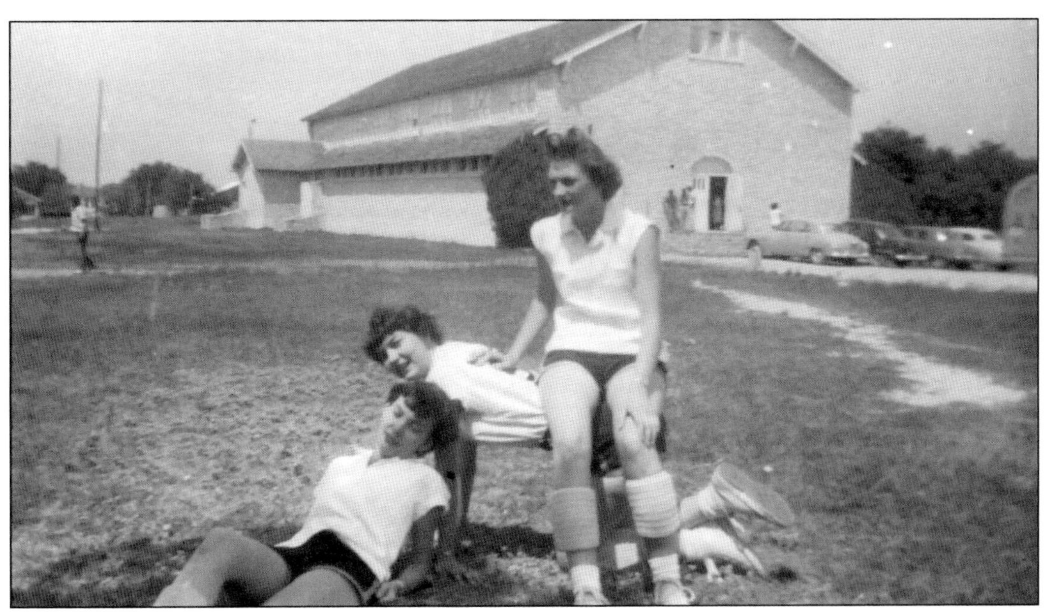

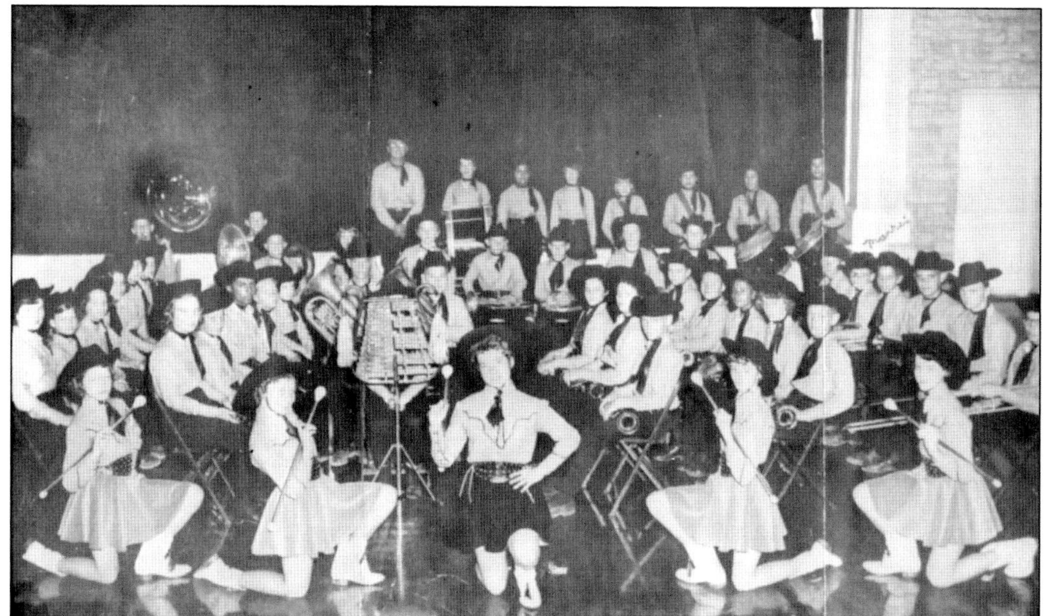

Although early Kyle schools had a band, the first "modern" school band in Kyle was formed in 1953, with some financial support from the Lions Club. The above photograph shows the first Kyle band in their Western-style uniforms. (Courtesy of the Schmeltekopf family.)

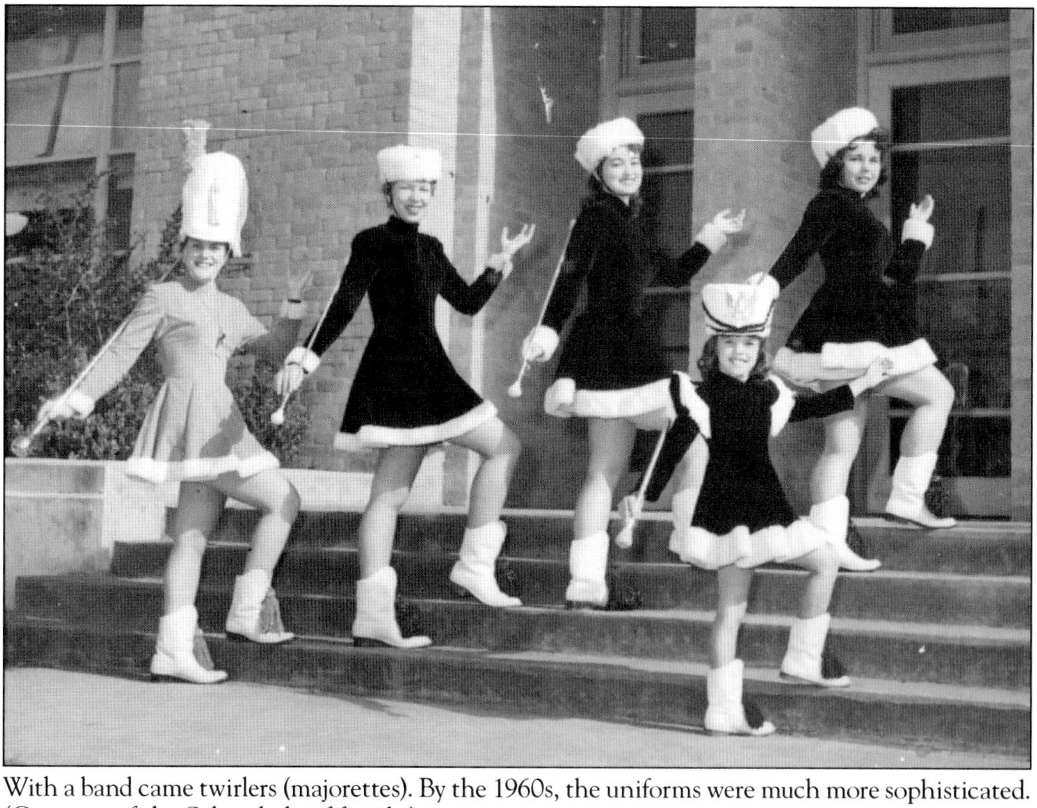

With a band came twirlers (majorettes). By the 1960s, the uniforms were much more sophisticated. (Courtesy of the Schmeltekopf family.)

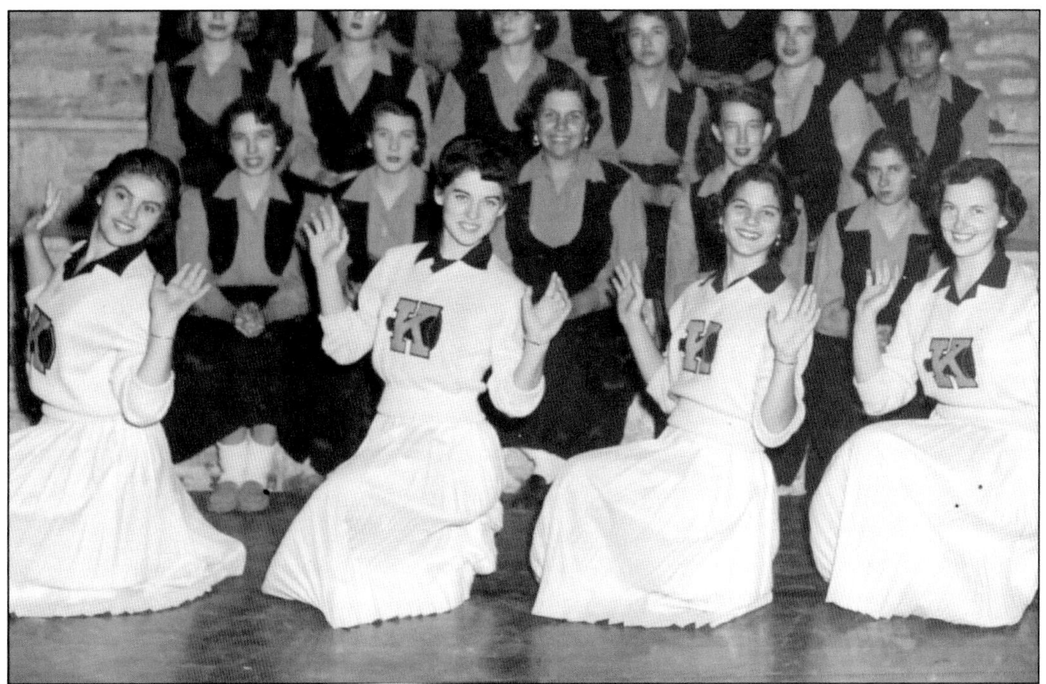

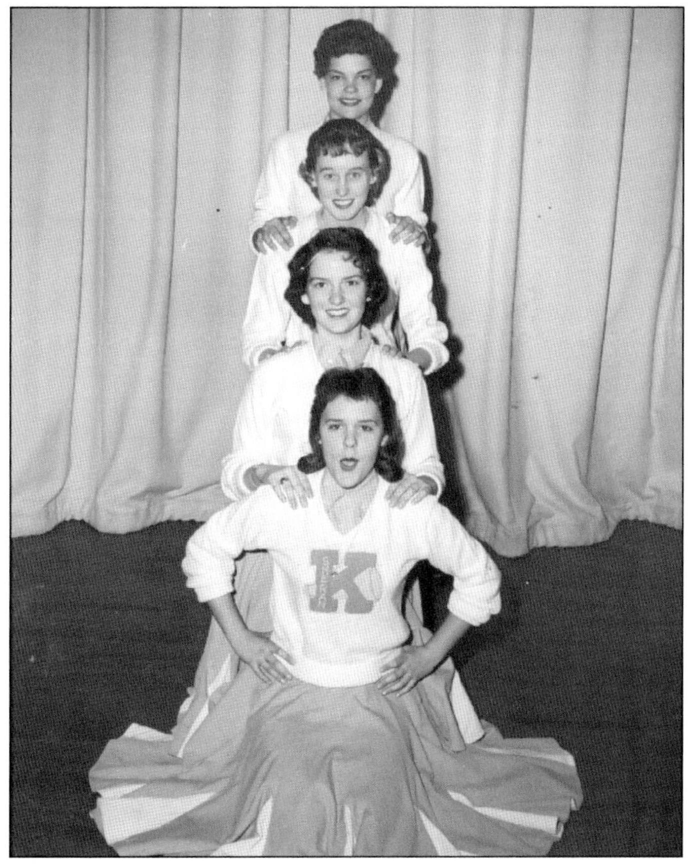

Cheerleaders were also important to extracurricular activities at Kyle High School. At the time of these photographs, cheerleaders were elected by popular vote, unlike twirlers, who had to try out for judges. (Both, courtesy of the Schmeltekopf family.)

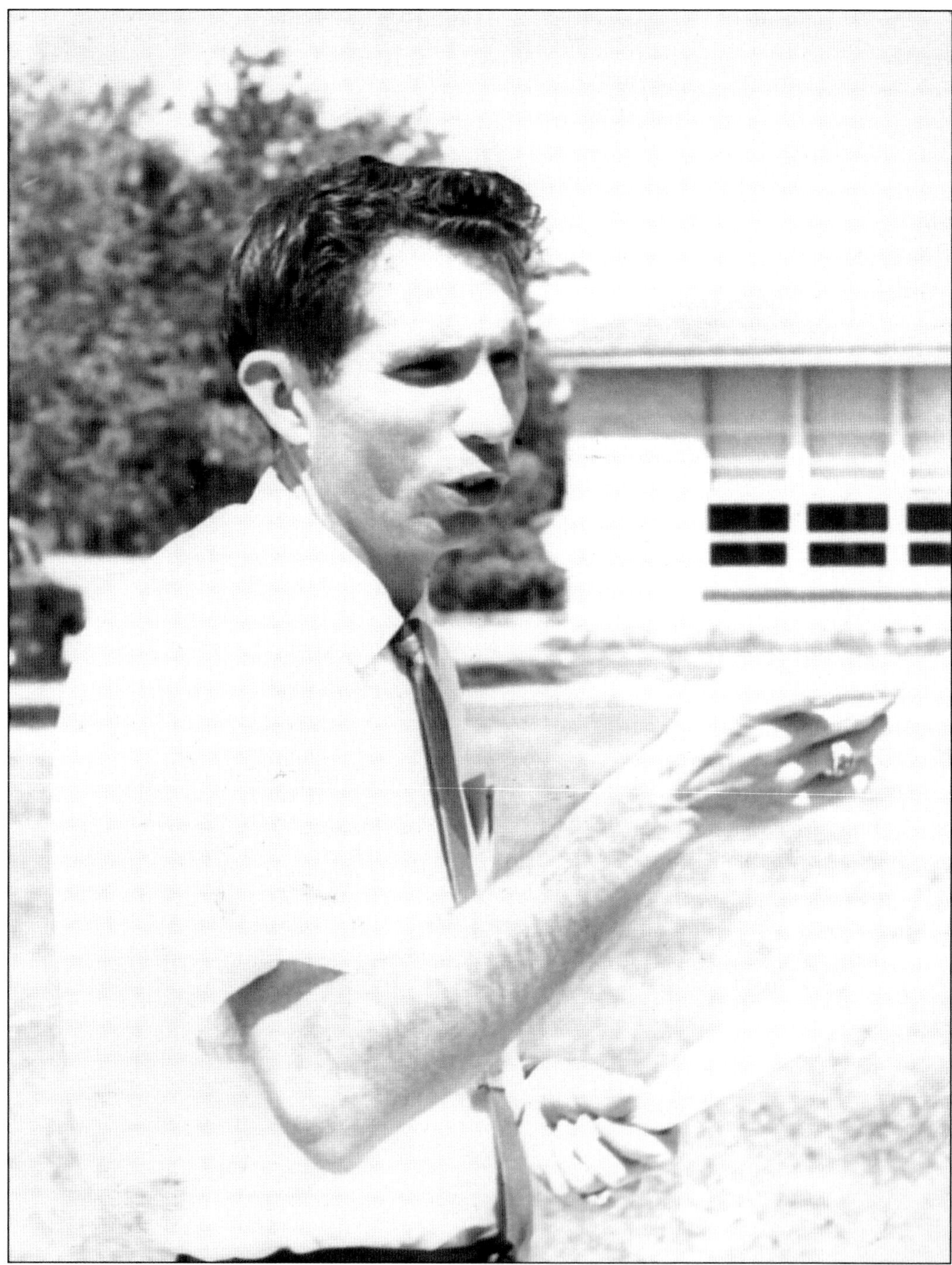

In 1954, William M. "Moe" Johnson, a young man from rival Buda, was hired as a coach in Kyle. After a successful stint in coaching, Johnson accepted the superintendent's job in 1960. During his first year as superintendent (six years after *Brown v. Board of Education*), the Kyle schools passed a referendum requiring integration of the schools. Johnson later became the superintendent of the newly formed Hays Consolidated Independent School District when Kyle joined Buda and Wimberley to create a new district in 1967. (Courtesy HFP.)

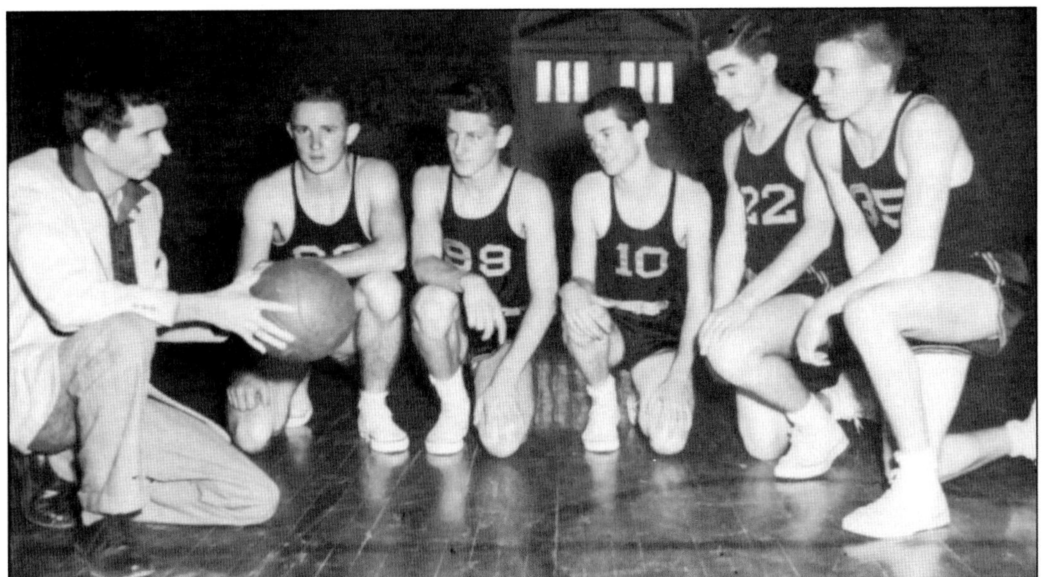

Coach "Moe" Johnson (far left) was 24 years old and had not finished his degree when he was hired to coach in Kyle. Although he coached all sports, his basketball teams posted an impressive 172-34 record, winning district every year and going to the state tournament multiple times. During his time as coach, the Kyle Panthers lost only one home game. (Courtesy HFP.)

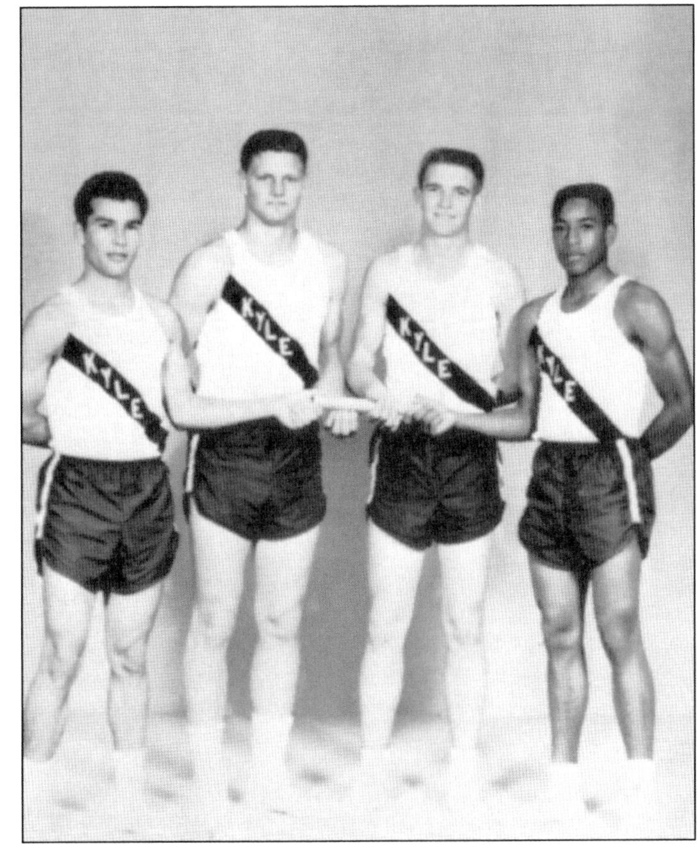

In the fall of 1961, African American students attended desegregated Kyle schools for the first time. One of those students was Clarence "Poochie" Green, pictured here with the sprint relay team that won second in state. Green was the first African American student to earn a varsity letter at Kyle High School. From left to right, the other members of the team are Joe Castillo, Alan Miller, and Bill McGee. (Courtesy Word family.)

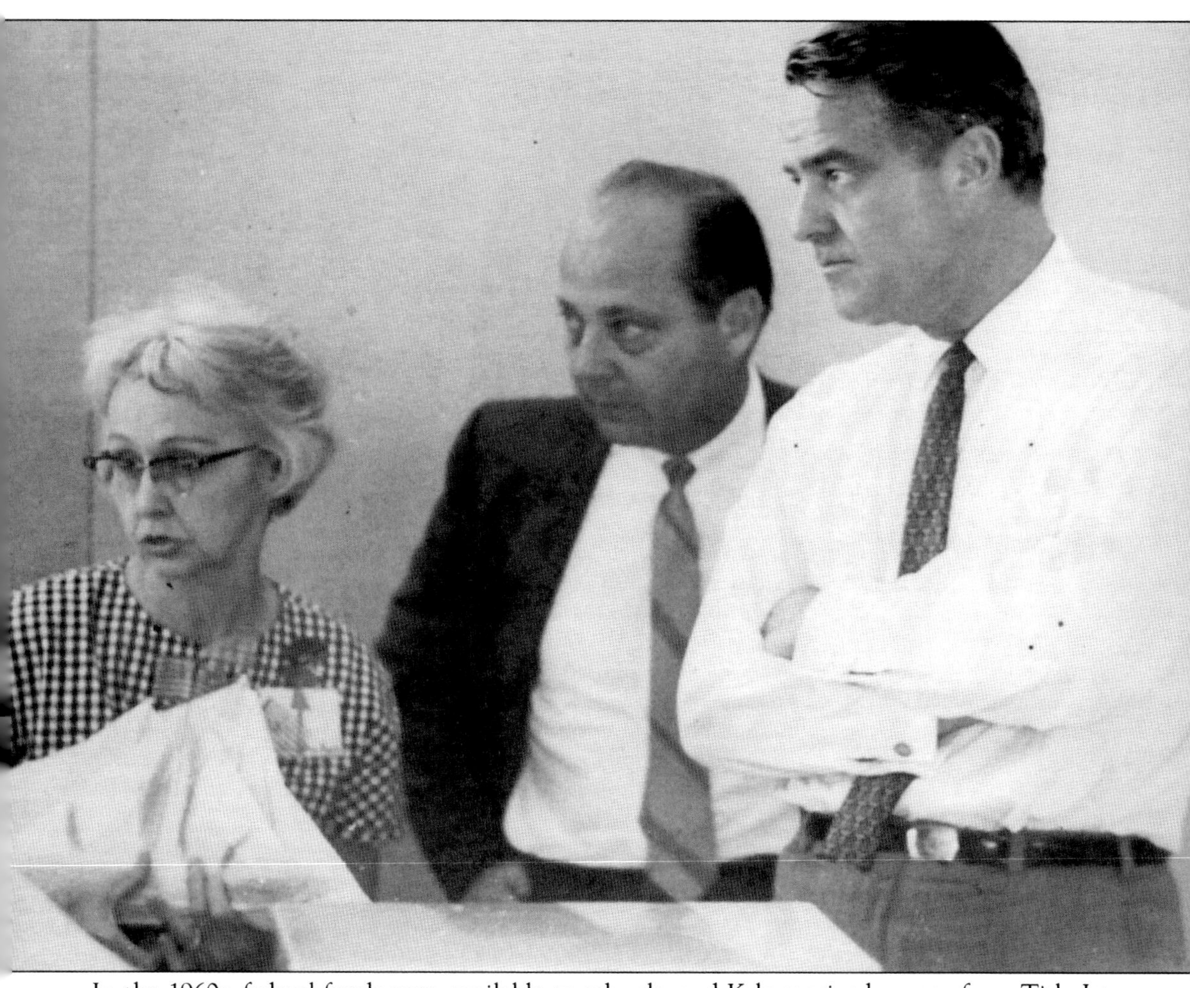

In the 1960s, federal funds were available to schools, and Kyle received money from Title I to help low-income students. A Head Start summer program was hosted, beginning in 1965. The program had important visitors that summer, although the rumor that President Johnson would visit was incorrect. This photograph shows teacher Riso Millhollon with US ambassador Bill Crook (center), who opened the regional Office of Economic Opportunity (OEO), and Sargent Shriver (right), OEO director. (Courtesy HFP.)

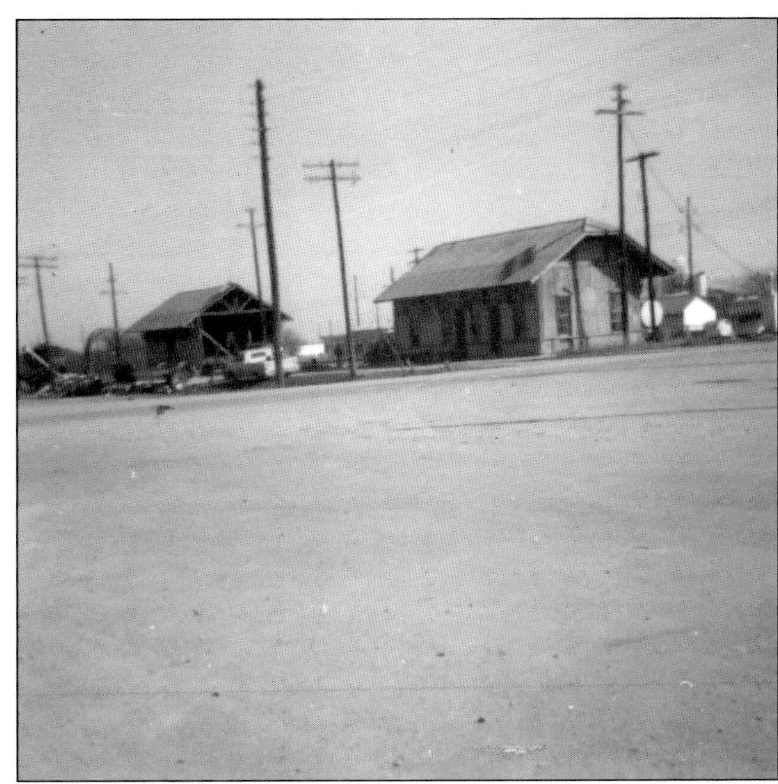

In 1967, Austin automobile dealer Charles Nash purchased the depot from Kyle and moved it to his Three Seasons Farm east of Kyle. The Nash family remodeled the depot into a vacation home. The depot was cut in two and reassembled after the move. The town was without a depot until it was returned to Kyle in 2003. (Both, courtesy of the Miller family.)

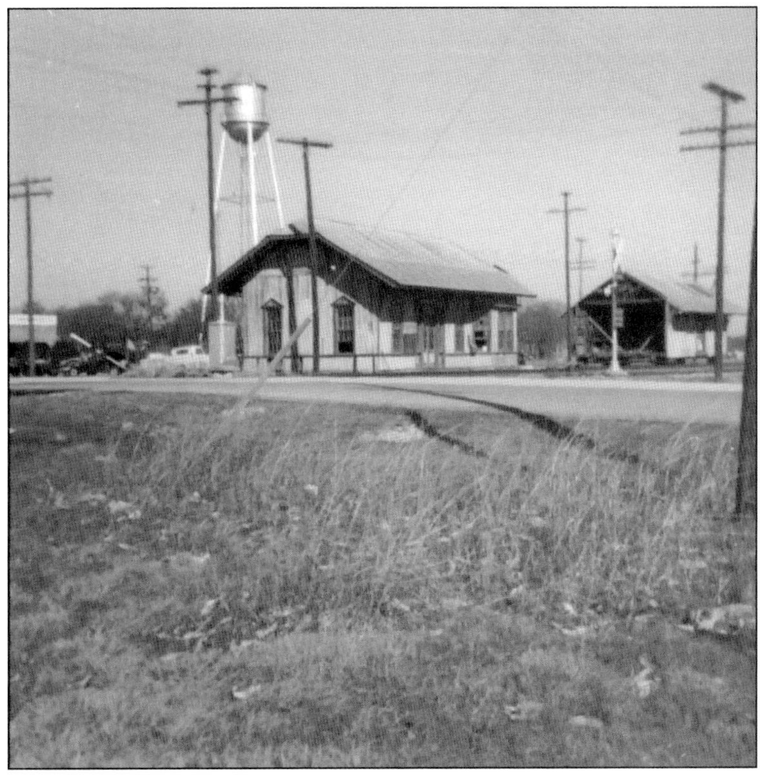

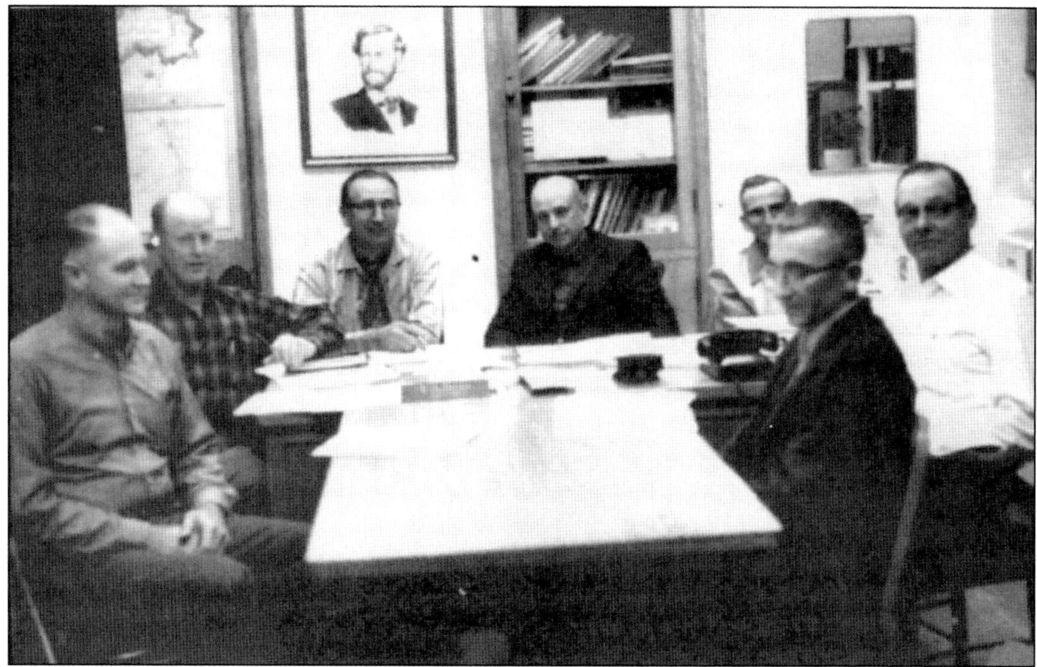

Following the passing of the referendum election to create the Hays Consolidated Independent School District (CISD) in 1967, a new board was formed with representatives from each of the districts: Kyle, Buda, and Wimberley. The law provided that the board of the largest district would follow consolidation, but a "gentlemen's agreement" before the election was that all but three members would resign to allow representatives of the other districts to be appointed. Pictured here is the first Hays CISD School Board. From left to right are Ted Lehman, Tim Harris, Raymond Czichos, D.J. "Red" Simon, Robert Schneider, Lloyd Hennig, and Ralph Pfluger. (Courtesy HFP.)

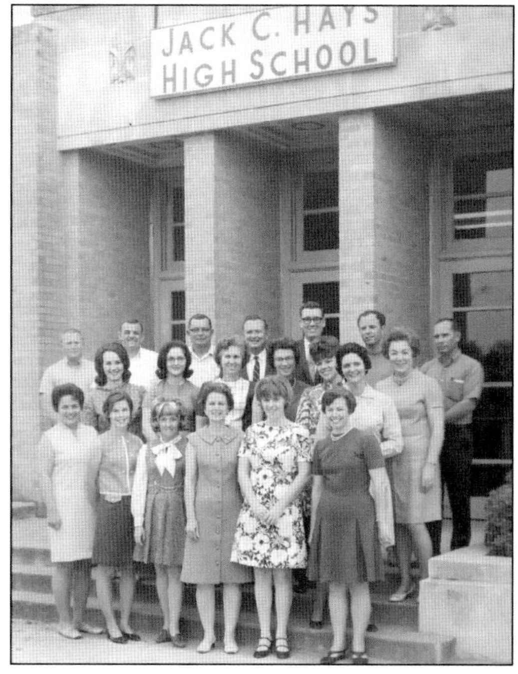

Since the May election came too late to open the consolidated high school in the fall, the first Jack C. Hays High School (housed at Kyle High School) opened in the fall of 1968. The first faculty is pictured. (Courtesy of the Schmeltekopf family.)

ABOUT THE ORGANIZATION

The Hays County Historical Commission is a group of volunteers appointed by the Hays County Commissioners Court for a two-year term to preserve the history and cultural resources of Hays County. In addition to implementing the State Historical Marker program of the Texas Historical Commission on a local level, the Hays County Historical Commission is active in the preservation of area cemeteries and historical sites. The commission's purpose is to provide to the public information and educational resources on the significance of Hays County heritage.

Since its establishment in 1953, the Hays County Historical Commission has erected markers at important sites across the county, inventoried every cemetery in the county, and conducted a survey of historic locations. The commission is active in nominating properties to the National Register of Historic Places and also publishes books and brochures pertaining to the history of the county and produces documentary films on historic topics.

Consistent with our mission to preserve history on a local level, this book was printed in South Carolina on American-made paper and manufactured entirely in the United States. Products carrying the accredited Forest Stewardship Council (FSC) label are printed on 100 percent FSC-certified paper.

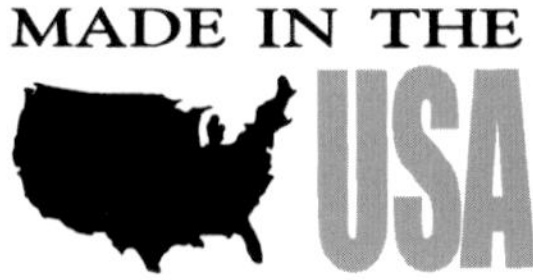